Blockbusting
in Baltimore

Blockbusting in Baltimore

THE EDMONDSON VILLAGE STORY

W. EDWARD ORSER

THE UNIVERSITY PRESS OF KENTUCKY

Publication of this book was made possible by a grant
from the National Endowment for the Humanities

Copyright © 1994 by The University Press of Kentucky

Scholarly publisher for the Commonwealth,
serving Bellarmine University, Berea College,
Centre College of Kentucky, Eastern Kentucky University,
The Filson Historical Society, Georgetown College,
Kentucky Historical Society, Kentucky State University,
Morehead State University, Murray State University,
Northern Kentucky University, Transylvania University,
University of Kentucky, University of Louisville,
and Western Kentucky University.

Editorial and Sales Offices: The University Press of Kentucky
663 South Limestone Street, Lexington, Kentucky 40508-4008

07 06 05 04 03   6 5 4 3 2

Library of Congress Cataloging-in-Publication Data

Orser, W. Edward
    Blockbusting in Baltimore : the Edmondson Village story /
W. Edward Orser
        p.   cm.
    Includes bibliographical references and index.
    ISBN 0-8131-0935-3 (pbk.)
    1. Edmondson Village (Baltimore, Md.)—Race relations.
2. Baltimore (Md.)—Race relations. 3. Demographic transition—
Maryland—Baltimore. 4. Afro-Americans—Housing—Maryland—
Baltimore. 5. Afro-Americans—Maryland—Baltimore—Segregation.
6. Edmondson Village (Baltimore, Md.)—Population. 7. Baltimore
(Md.)—Population. I. Title
F189.B16E266   1994
305.896'07307526—dc20   94-8631

This book is printed on acid-free recycled paper meeting
the requirements of the American National Standard for
Permanence of Paper for Printed Library Materials.

Manufactured in the United States of America

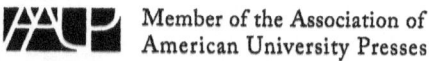   Member of the Association of
          American University Presses

Contents

List of Maps and Figures   vii
Preface   ix
1 The Trauma of Racial Change   1
2 The Making of a Rowhouse Neighborhood   21
3 Continuity and Undercurrents of Change   48
4 A White Community Responds to Change   84
5 African American Pioneers   131
6 The Legacy of Blockbusting   160
Appendix A: Suggested Reading   182
Appendix B: Home Ownership on Selected Blocks, 1955-1973   186
Notes   190
Bibliography   226
Index   234

Maps and Figures

Maps

1 Racial composition and population for Baltimore City, 1930-1970 / 2
2 Racial composition of the Edmondson Village neighborhood, 1940-1970 / 3
3 Development of the Edmondson area, 1921-1941 / 24
4 Post-World War II development of the Edmondson area / 58

Figures

1 The Edmondson area: rowhouse suburbs, 1938 / 16
2 View up the Edmondson Avenue hill, 1954 / 17
3 Rowhouse styles / 26
4 "Areaway" houses, Edmondson Avenue / 28
5 James Keelty Company's daylight rowhouses / 29
6 Row of daylight houses, Normandy Avenue / 31
7 Rowhouse, Normandy Avenue / 32
8 Section of Sanborn Map, the Edmondson area, 1928 / 34
9 Early Keelty "English type" daylight rowhouses, Wildwood / 36
10 Architectural variety in Wildwood rowhouses / 37
11 St. Bernardine's Roman Catholic Church, c. 1929 / 39
12 Handwritten receipt for a Keelty house, 1922 / 40
13 Edmondson Village Shopping Center, 1952 / 50
14 Newly opened Edmondson Village Shopping Center, c. 1947 / 51
15 Hecht Company Department Store opening, 1956 / 53
16 Christmas lights at the shopping center, 1958 / 56
17 Group homes development plan by Keelty Company, 1950 / 61
18 St. Bernardine's Roman Catholic Church memorial, 1948 / 79
19 Pickets at the Morris Goldseker Company office, 1969 / 134
20 Edmondson Village Shopping Center, 1979 / 155
21 Young Edmondson Village residents today / 158

Preface

Each semester in my course on community in American culture, I suddenly pose this question to the students: "Imagine an American community of twenty thousand people; then imagine that ten years later its population is still twenty thousand, but *virtually none* of the residents are the same; how do you account for that?" After looks of initial puzzlement, hands shoot up: "A flood or other natural disaster?"; "A nuclear accident?"; "Economic dislocation—they all worked for the same employer, and the plant moved?" The hypotheses go on, but each eventually is dismissed by the group as relatively implausible. To be sure, some of these ecological or economic crises might produce massive dislocation, but how to account for an equal amount of resettlement? Then someone eventually asks: "Racial change?" And, invariably, throughout the room there is a collective "oh—yes, sure!"; then class members settle back as if nothing more need be said, because we all, presumably, "understand." Each time this happens I find myself reflecting again on what this exercise says about American culture and ourselves as participants in it: that collective behavior based upon dynamics so powerful that they could hardly be accounted for even by catastrophic degrees of environmental or economic impact can be triggered by race, and that such social dynamite is nevertheless so much a part of our cultural surround that we simply accept it as a given, as something that we presume we understand—whether consciously or at some other level of our psyche, and whether we really do or not.

The hypothetical, of course, is not hypothetical at all. It corresponds to the real case of the west Baltimore area called Edmondson Village, where roughly forty thousand people did indeed change places—some twenty thousand leaving, twenty thousand arriving—over a period of approximately ten years, between 1955 and 1965, in an especially acute instance of blockbusting that triggered white flight and racial change on a dramatic scale. As a teacher of American Studies at the University of Maryland Baltimore County, a campus located on the west side of the

Baltimore metropolitan region, I continued to encounter references to this particular episode in student family history assignments. Typically they cropped up in interviews with parents or grandparents—whether whites whose families had fled the neighborhood or African Americans whose families had moved in behind them. The range of feelings was wide: among whites they ranged from anger and bitterness to bewilderment and a sense of loss; among African Americans there often were measures of satisfaction with new opportunities but also feelings of disappointment and frustration. The interpretations differed, particularly for those on the two sides of the racially dividing experience, as did assignments of responsibility and blame. But common to all was a sense of social dynamics that seemed beyond individual control and a sense of disjunction, as if their lives had been marked at this one key point by a dramatic experience that still seemed unresolved and a legacy that was uncertain. I came to interpret these references as expressions of, and testimony to, the trauma of rapid racial change, and I set out to try to trace its dimensions.

If the legacy of that trauma is still somewhat unresolved for Edmondson Village residents, past and present, the fact of the matter is that it still is unresolved in many ways for American culture as a whole, because the phenomenon was by no means unique to Edmondson Village. It happened in other Baltimore neighborhoods, in sections of numerous cities, large and small, and in many regions of the United States. In some places they called it "panic peddling"—but, by whatever name, it was a process that dramatically changed the shape of America's urban areas in the postwar decades and laid the groundwork for persistent patterns of race and residency. Despite what we like to feel have been significant changes since that era in legislation, in institutional procedures, and in public attitudes, mechanisms that sometimes may have been more subtle and processes that may have been more gradual nevertheless have continued to produce similar results, if on a less dramatic scale. Therefore, I found it compelling to try to understand the Edmondson Village case for what light it might shed on these larger patterns of race in our national culture, past and present.

Blockbusting, of course, was a logical extension of the pervasive system of residential segregation that American society had crafted—by law and by custom—to create and preserve a dual housing market in American cities, severely circumscribing housing opportunities for African Americans. In the changing social climate of post-World War II urban America a silent conspiracy that had seemed so unshakable suddenly proved exceedingly vulnerable, even fragile. Ironically, it was not amelio-

Preface

rating racial attitudes or institutional reform that produced the transformation as much as it was entrepreneurs out to exploit the crevices in the system for financial gain, profiting at the expense of both populations. One result of such cataclysmic change was rapidly resegregated communities. Whites paid dearly for their decisions to flee; African Americans gained sorely needed residential options, but the toll for them was high as well.

This is the story I set out to explore, but it soon became apparent to me that the focus needed to be broader than the episode of blockbusting. In order to try to understand the character of a white community that panicked in this way, it was necessary to look back to the circumstances of community formation and to examine the social and cultural patterns that gave Edmondson Village its particular identity. But it also was essential to look at the African American community that replaced the white one in similar terms, examining the character of those who were pioneer settlers in the period of racial change and tracing their experience over time to the recent past. I realized that I needed to provide these twin perspectives in order to feel that I could adequately interpret this moment of social trauma. This book is primarily a history of racial change triggered by blockbusting, but it also is an exploration of the kind of community that developed in this rowhouse suburb of Baltimore, an attempt to answer how and why that community responded to the challenge of racial change in the way it did, and a study of the experience of the succession African American community in the aftermath of such traumatic dynamics. Its chronological parameters are 1910, the eve of rowhouse development on this predominantly rural western edge of the city, and 1980, twenty-five years after the first African Americans took up residence in what had been an all-white residential environment.

My early encounters with the Edmondson Village story came through family history interviews, and oral history seemed like a fruitful avenue to explore it further. The moment of racial change is still recent enough to be vivid in the memories of those who observed it firsthand, and the constructions that individuals place upon their own experience can be immensely helpful in trying to understand the complex dynamics underlying an episode where attitudes and feelings represent such relevant data. This study is based in part upon some thirty in-depth oral history interviews conducted over a period of ten years with individuals positioned to offer a variety of perspectives on the community's past, including whites who lived in Edmondson Village prior to the period of racial change and African Americans who came after them. I asked interviewees to share their views on the entire community experience, not just on the episode of racial change. While traditional historians often have been reluctant to depend very heavily on oral history sources, I found it essential to do so in order to gain insight into how community residents interpreted their own experience.

At the same time, however, it became clear to me that other evidence was necessary to place their views in perspective, especially when they varied in their interpretations of the racial change process. Therefore, I turned to sources of quantitative data, including the tract records afforded by the U.S. Census, which provide aggregate figures on the community as a baseline for comparison, and my own survey of ten sample blocks, which traces individual households over time. The result, I hope, is a community history that combines both qualitative and quantitative sources to develop a comprehensive portrait of continuity and change.

My special thanks begin with those connected with the community's experience who agreed to participate in the interview process. They shared their stories with openness, patiently reflected on my questions—whether about everyday patterns of life or about social attitudes and behavior—and thoughtfully sought to place the dynamics of racial change in perspective. Since certain aspects of these interviews might prove too personal or controversial, I decided to employ the convention of assigning pseudonyms in most instances. I did so with some regret, because the story of Edmondson Village is the story not only of a social process but of individuals—little different from any of us—wrestling with the complexities of trying to build a satisfying and meaningful life and coming to terms—for better or worse—with social and cultural patterns that have been pervasive in American life.

My second debt is to my students in American Studies classes at UMBC, who have shared their own family experiences and wrestled with their own attitudes and perspectives as we have tried together to puzzle out the meaning of the Edmondson Village experience. As a teacher, I find it particularly satisfying that the research involved in the enterprise from its inception has contributed to classroom learning and, in turn, has been enriched by that process. Several students conducted related research projects, which they have permitted me to draw upon, and their contributions deserve thanks by name: April Lunn, Monica Murray, Kelly O'Shea, Doug Stanton, and Nancy Swartz.

My colleagues in American Studies at UMBC share the kinds of concerns about social and cultural process that I bring to this project and provide the supportive atmosphere for teaching and research that makes such endeavors rewarding. For their contributions, both direct and indi-

Preface

rect, let me express my appreciation to Warren Belasco, Carole McCann, Patrice McDermott, and Leslie Prosterman. At various points Kathy Peiss, Linda Shopes, and Joseph Arnold read portions of the manuscript, extended encouragement, and offered constructive suggestions, for which I am also grateful. Throughout the many drafts of the project Carolyn Ferrigno has provided vital technical assistance, and she has prepared the manuscript in its final version; there must be a special category of thanks for the exceptional combination of skill and care she has exhibited in the process.

Nearby history has the benefit of convenient access, but it still depends heavily upon the quality of local resources for research. I benefited greatly from the collection in the Maryland Department of Baltimore's Enoch Pratt Free Library, especially the clipping files where articles have been painstakingly culled from local newspapers over the years. I found the staff members always efficient, helpful, and courteous, even in an era of woeful civic underfunding for such vital services as public libraries.

A project like this makes extraordinary demands upon one's family. For me this book would have been inconceivable without the patience, understanding, and support Jo, Stephen, and Sharon have extended through the many stages of research. In an era of debate about family values, I must also acknowledge my debt to my parents, George and Eloise Orser, who shaped my sensitivity to social issues, exhibited a genuine concern for people, and always emphasized the importance of human values. To my father, now deceased, and my mother, I dedicate this book.

1
The Trauma of Racial Change

The recent reflections of two women illustrate the poignancy and complexity of their experience in the west Baltimore neighborhood of Edmondson Village when racial change began to occur on a massive scale in the late 1950s, early 1960s. In an interview I conducted with a white former resident, Marilyn Simkins sought an explanation for the response of whites who panicked and fled the neighborhood: "They saw a very secure world changing very drastically," she said, "and they couldn't accept it. This was distasteful, and in some respects it was forced down their throats, and they felt they had no other choice, I guess."[1] In a separate interview session, Margaret Johnson, a pioneer from the era of initial African American settlement in the same neighborhood, described her own feeling about the flight of her white neighbors: "They were friendly, but they were prejudiced. They didn't want to live where colored people did.... They don't have to say it.... They didn't tell you [why they moved]; they just moved!"[2] Embedded in both statements—though not necessarily voiced in the careful choice of words and in the sense of dignity that each displayed—are shadings that range from anger and pain to wistfulness and bewilderment. Both testify eloquently to the trauma of rapid racial change on two different sides of the neighborhood succession experience, a trauma whose legacy continues to be felt in their lives and in the lives of countless other former and present residents of outer urban neighborhoods such as Edmondson Village. In fact, it is a collective trauma whose significance for recent American social and cultural history is still insufficiently appreciated and understood.[3]

The Role of Blockbusting

Edmondson Village, an extensive rowhouse neighborhood on Baltimore's west side, had been developed from the 1920s onward as a suburban en-

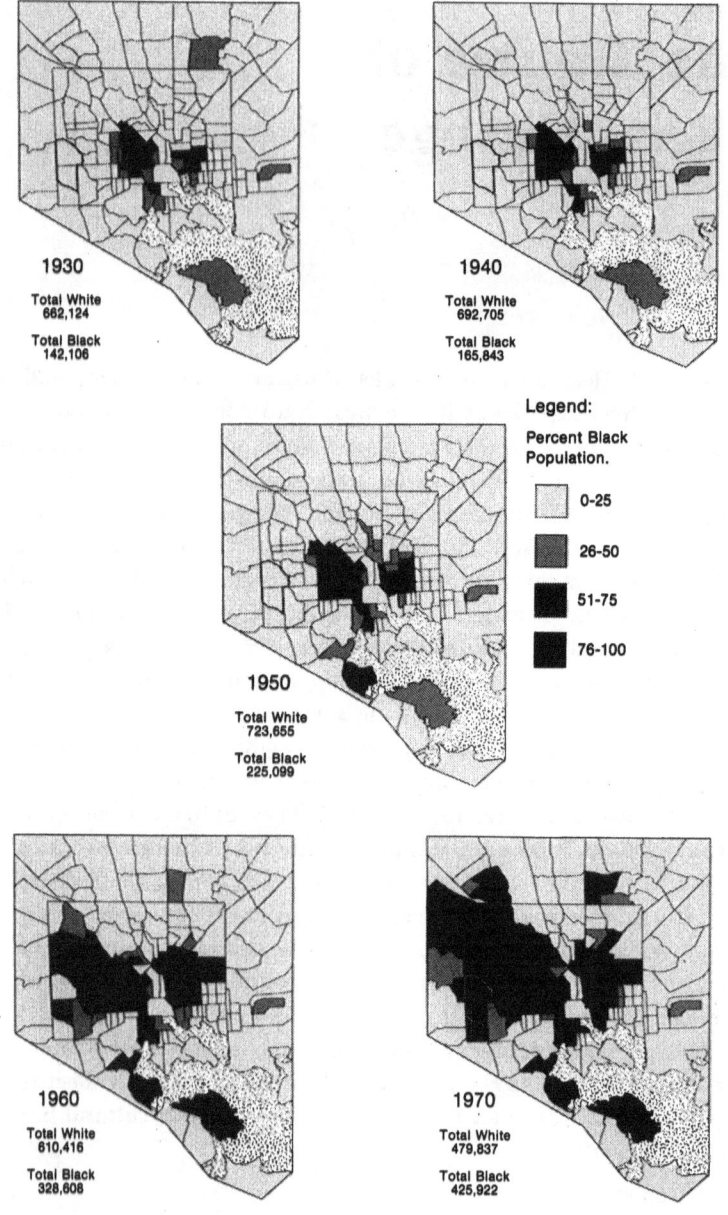

Map 1. Racial composition and population for Baltimore City, 1930-1970. Edmondson Village neighborhood boundaries are in bold outline on the city's west side. (Compiled by the author from U.S. Census tract data; map by UMBC Cartographic Services)

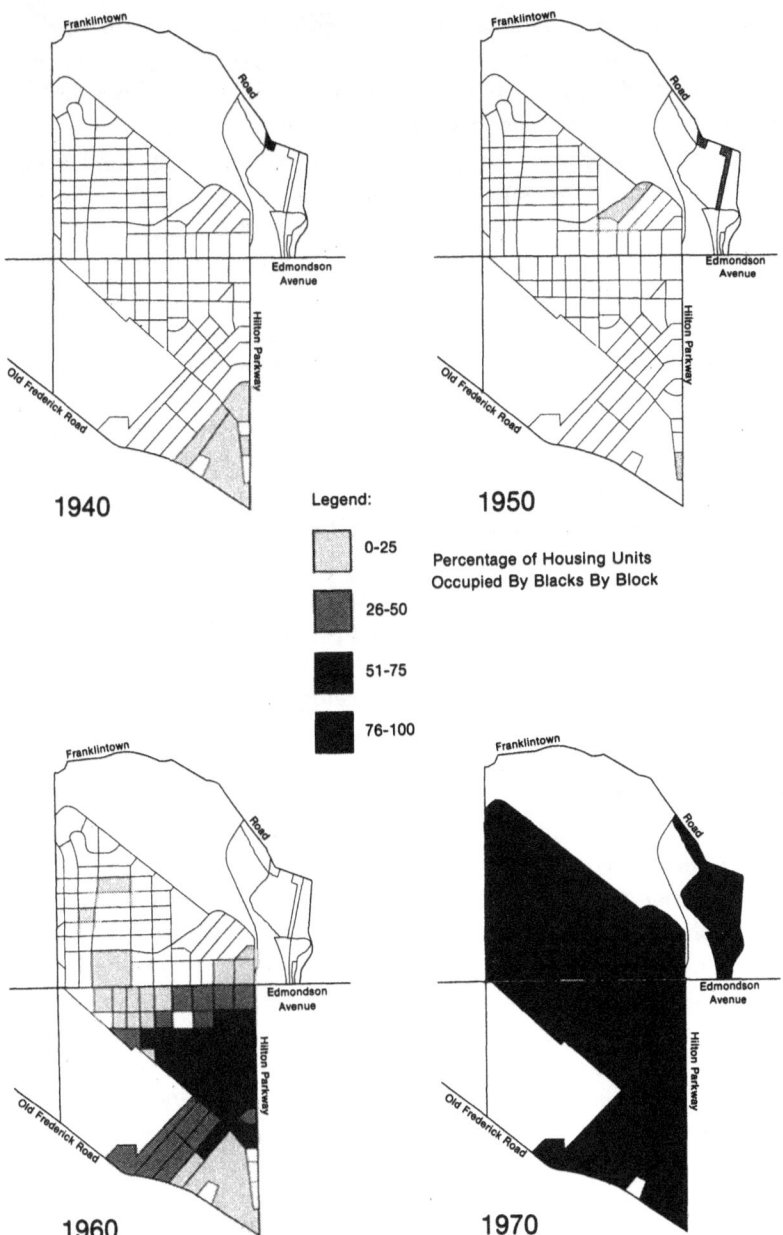

Map 2. Racial composition of the Edmondson Village neighborhood, 1940-1970. (Compiled by the author from U.S. Census tract data by block; map by UMBC Cartographic Services)

clave for Baltimore's burgeoning white middle class. During the single decade from approximately 1955 to 1965, however, virtually its entire population of twenty thousand was replaced in rapid fashion by a new population of equal size. Few explanations—whether natural, social, or economic—would be adequate to account for such massive displacement and resettlement. Yet, in the urban equation of mid-twentieth-century America a single factor represented sufficient causation: race. (See maps 1 and 2.)

That the experience of racial change is common enough in recent history for this statement to seem unremarkable is telling in itself. But in the Edmondson Village case, rapid racial change was triggered by a particularly intensive and systematic application of blockbusting. As contemporaries came to define it, blockbusting was the intentional action of a real estate operative to settle an African American household in an all-white neighborhood for the purpose of provoking white flight in order to make excessive profits by buying low from those who fled and selling high to those who sought access to new housing opportunities.

Blockbusters lit the match, but, as the definition implies, they were only one ingredient in a complex set of circumstances. Indeed, blockbusting exploited the crevices of an otherwise pervasive and systematic system that governed race and residence. In mid-twentieth-century urban America, a silent conspiracy sought to assure and preserve the segregated dual housing market. At the institutional level, the refusal of the real estate, financial, and governmental establishment to underwrite housing choices that challenged dominant patterns of residential segregation represented one pillar of a remarkably durable conspiracy. However, the dual housing market constituted an unwritten agreement in the restraint of trade, as legal historian Garrett Power has argued in his work on Baltimore, and the problem of enforcement was the temptation to "cheat," especially if there was an advantage to be gained by doing so. In these terms, blockbusters functioned as cheaters, operating outside the pale of mainstream institutions. While these operatives risked censure in withdrawing from the general conspiracy, their activities also permitted establishment institutions to maintain the illusion of upholding the racial status quo. In the early stages of post-World War II blockbusting, such agents were active on the margins of ghetto areas, engaging in transactions shunned by conventional real estate and lending institutions; in the later stages, they sometimes took advantage of more open mortgage policies that channeled funds into particular sections of cities deemed to be "changing." The financial pay-off for such activities often was immense.[4]

At the individual level, the refusal of white residents to consider the possibility of residential integration made their own racism the second pillar upholding the edifice of the dual housing market. Social and racial homogeneity frequently were the unwritten promises of residential community, especially in suburbanizing outer city neighborhoods, whether the provinces of the white elite or of whites with more modest income levels. It often was assumed that economic constraints made racial integration unlikely, though the assumption was much more credible for exclusive enclaves than for ordinary neighborhoods. But such reasoning betokened an unquestioned faith in the mechanisms of residental segregation, which led most white residents to take for granted the preservation of the racial status quo in housing. Ironically, this absolute position—which categorically ruled out heterogeneity and made their social world seem so secure—also heightened their vulnerability to the tactics of blockbusters, who could play on their presumptions of racial exclusivity to trigger their fears. Therefore, in particular historic moments when circumstances converged to threaten the conspiracy controlling the dual housing market, as in the instances of blockbusting in the post-World War II period, resistance or flight were the characteristic responses. When whites cried foul, blockbusters and their defenders could point out that they had only themselves to blame if they lost out in the process.

Finally, of course, the set of requisite circumstances depended upon pent-up demand for housing opportunity by African Americans, long restricted in terms of residential options but eager, even desperate, for improved housing and neighborhood amenities. Since they were denied entry to the real estate market beyond the perimeters of residential segregation, finding mainstream real estate and financing doors closed to them, their only access to home purchases came through the offices of blockbusters or speculators. Given these constraints, many African Americans nevertheless were ready to seize the opportunity for new housing on such terms, even if the costs were exploitative and the financial arrangements shaky. Indeed, when blockbusters were challenged on the ethics of their operations, they defended their practices as providing a necessary service others refused and therefore requiring greater risks, which justified higher profits.

The tactics used by blockbusters to manipulate the system to their advantage were not entirely new in the 1950s and 1960s. Gilbert Osofsky found that similar practices were employed at the turn of the century in Harlem, when New York's African American population swelled as a result of migration from the South, and speculators, dubbed "white blackmailers," channeled African American tenants into the temporarily depressed tenement market uptown.[5] From time to time in twentieth-century American cities, areas of African American concentration expanded in similar fashion in response to population pressures and changes in housing stock at the neighborhood and metropolitan level, especially as inner city housing aged and new housing became available on the suburban periphery. Typically, this kind of enlargement was incremental, occurring on the margins of the African American ghetto, and often it represented acquisition of residence in neighborhoods where physical deterioration or depressed housing prices had begun to occur. Sherry Olson has noted that some expansion of this type occurred in Baltimore immediately following World War I, when African American population increases combined with a suburban boom in whites-only housing to produce an episode where some of the tactics that came to be associated with blockbusting were employed.[6]

What made the episodes of blockbusting and the resultant racial change in American cities during the 1950s and 1960s so significant, however, was their extent and scale. Rather than marginal ghetto expansion, entire neighborhoods and broad sections of cities were transformed from predominantly all-white to predominantly all-African American in a relatively short period of time. In Baltimore, charges of blockbusting were voiced in the midst of massive episodes of white flight and rapid racial succession, primarily in the northwestern and western sections of the city (the Reisterstown Road, Liberty Heights Avenue, and Edmondson Avenue corridors) and to a lesser extent on the near northeast (along lower Harford Road and The Alameda, and in sections around Lake Montebello). In Chicago, a comparable process occurred with particular intensity on the south and west sides, where inhabitants referred to the work of "panic peddlers" in triggering white flight and producing large-scale racial change in such neighborhoods as Lawndale and Austin. The same term was applied to operatives in Washington, D.C., in the midst of racial change which occurred there in dramatic proportions. And the process apparently was much the same in the New York borough of Brooklyn, where the pre-World War II concentration of African Americans and Puerto Ricans in a section of Bedford-Stuyvesant expanded substantially during the postwar decades.[7]

In a number of cities—Boston, New York, Chicago, Philadelphia, Baltimore, and others—blockbusting sometimes targeted Jewish neighborhoods, prompting extensive Jewish to African American succession. Jews and African Americans, both excluded from equal access to the housing market, whether by such legal mechanisms as restrictive covenants or by discrimination entrenched in custom, often lived in close proximity yet with clear lines of social separation. While Jewish communities often exhibited rare degrees of tolerance, they also were disproportionately singled out by speculators and frequently proved vulnerable to such manipulation. Hillel Levine and Lawrence Harmon have made a convincing case that older Jewish neighborhoods in Boston were victimized through the collusion of the city's financial, real estate, and political leadership, for example.[8] However acute such episodes, the phenomenon of blockbusting as a trigger for white flight transcended religious and ethnic identification. Baltimore's Edmondson Village area, for instance, consisted of a rather even mix of Protestants and Roman Catholics, and numerous other cases similarly illustrate the broad susceptibility of communities to blockbusting tactics.

Sometimes the residential turnover accompanying blockbusting occurred in older, inner city neighborhoods, when speculators carved up large housing units into multifamily tenements and profited from charging excessive rents to new African American tenants. This process characterized the experience in Cleveland's Hough section during the 1950s, for example.[9] But in other instances, blockbusting and rapid racial change extended into areas that in the process became the "secondhand suburbs," where the housing stock was only several decades old, single-family dwellings predominated, and resident home ownership was the prevailing pattern, as was the case in Edmondson Village. In these circumstances, speculative profits resulted when housing, typically bought low from fleeing whites, was sold to African Americans at higher than market value and on terms arranged to benefit the speculator, not the buyer.

In retrospect, the 1950s and 1960s represented the zenith of blockbusting and the kind of rapid racial change it generated. During these decades the cracks in the edifice of the segregated housing market became more visible. The World War II period produced unprecedented population growth in urban centers, but little expansion in the available housing stock. At war's end, suburban development opened up a new housing frontier for white Americans, but the walls of de facto segregation continued to hem in an African American population feeling severely cramped by inadequate and rigidly limited housing. Pressure upon housing alone might have forced change. But expectations were rising as well. In part these resulted from improved economic opportunities available to some African Americans in the wartime and postwar economy. In part they were spurred by the formative stages of the civil rights movement, which gained ideological steam from a war fought against racism to produce a more vocal challenge to the racial status quo. One prop of the dual housing market was struck down in 1948 when the Supreme Court ruled that states could not enforce residential restrictive covenants. Rising expectations and a sense of changing times led some African Americans to consider active choices to improve their housing opportunities and neighborhood amenities.

In spite of these mounting pressures—perhaps because of them—mainstream private and governmental institutions sought to hold a firm line, resisting the voices of change and making very few concessions to accommodate the new circumstances. Much the same must be said for white public opinion. Nowhere was reluctance to confront change more evident than on the domestic front, the province of home. In older inner city neighborhoods white residents frequently had to accept degrees of social diversity regarding class and ethnicity, but race was another matter. Faced with the prospect of African American settlement, residents of such neighborhoods sometimes resisted racial change forcefully, even violently, especially in instances where ethnic ties and social class combined to reinforce internal cohesion and to repel outsiders. In other cases, they viewed African American entry as another sign of neighborhood powerlessness, and flight ensued.

Outer city neighborhoods had been developed on the implicit promise of social homogeneity inherent in the suburban ideal in its various late nineteenth- and twentieth-century versions. In these suburban havens, whether older or newer, whites constructed what they considered to be a safe and secure social world, depending upon covert mechanisms to assure racial restriction rather than upon traditions of overt resistance. Therefore, white residents of most outer city neighborhoods typically refused to consider the possibility of racial integration. During the decades in question many communities remained immune to change, whether due to geographical or social, political, and economic factors. Overt resistance occurred occasionally, as was the case in the Brooklyn section of Canarsie, where Italians and Jews, once displaced from older sections of the city, dug in their heels to defend their neighborhood's identity, attempting to maintain the community as a "fortress, a fenced land."[10] In some instances, residents tried valiantly to make integration work. Chicago's Oak Park community, for example, developed a national reputation for its systematic efforts to stem the tide of white flight and to promote racial balance.[11] But in many communities, when residents were confronted directly by the challenge of African American settlement, they succumbed to racial fears and moved on. When the process was abetted by blockbusting, as in Edmondson Village, flight often assumed dramatic proportions.

Flight on such a scale traumatized whole communities, leaving its mark on those who left as well as upon those who took their place. While fleeing whites may have contributed to their own victimization through their collective behavior, they nevertheless faced the many difficulties associated with hasty relocation: the loss of community ties, the uncertain prospects of new settings, and—for many—the substantial financial penalty that blockbusting extorted. The social and economic toll for African American newcomers was often even greater. They gained housing options they had been illegitimately denied but at exploitative prices that strained their economic resources—necessitating new and sometimes onerous family strategies to meet the financial demands—and on terms that left them extremely vulnerable and insecure. Sometimes the instability of rapid racial change continued unabated in unstable patterns of residential turnover. Incoming residents often complained that commercial and governmental services declined in the wake of white flight and racial change. Given the exploitative mechanisms involved in blockbusting and the instability that episodes of white flight engendered, it is no wonder that many whites and, indeed, many African Americans feared that the result would be slum creation. All too often, the prophecy proved accurate. That some succession communities such as Edmondson Village could weather such circumstances with measures of stability and viability is a tribute to the perseverance and resiliency of African American pioneers, not in any way a refutation of the social trauma involved.

Since the late 1960s, egregious forms of blockbusting have been less common, partly as a result of changes in attitudes and institutional structures. The 1968 Fair Housing Act, for instance, explicitly forbade blockbusting, discrimination in multiple listings, and steering, though enforcement has proved problematic, and some forms of these abuses continue to exist, usually in much more subtle fashion than before the act was passed. The rate of racial change also has cooled substantially. Yet, recent scholarship on racial residential segregation has found it to be persistent both in central cities and in suburbs, with the strong likelihood of resegregation in racially mixed areas and with very little change in that pattern over time.[12] Nationally, the percentage of African Americans living in suburbs actually declined during the decade of the 1960s, and the much-heralded increase in African American percentages during the 1970s and 1980s often has represented "ghetto spillover" racial resegregation patterns.[13]

The scholarly literature on race and residency in twentieth-century America harks back to the pioneering work of the Chicago School of Sociology, whose ecological analysis of metropolitan change posited a model of "natural succession" to account for socioeconomic evolution in urban neighborhoods. Perhaps adequate as a description of the changing composition of Chicago communities in the early decades of the century, this model failed to pay sufficient heed to the role played by institutional forces in maintaining the status quo or in manipulating the change process. In the post-World War II period, accelerating racial change led sociologists to focus debate on the concept of a "tipping point" for racial change, giving rise to a flurry of studies seeking to determine the particular circumstances that might account for and predict white flight. However, a universally applicable social scientific model proved elusive. Over the past several decades, some studies of the large-scale white movement from central cities to suburban areas since World War II have downplayed the causal role of white flight. One argument suggests that nonracial factors were largely responsible for the racial changeover of neighborhoods; a second contends that white avoidance, not white flight per se, has been the chief explanation for neighborhood change.[14] Both lines of argument have contributed to a broader understanding of the complexity of the dynamics involved. The former quite rightly called attention to factors other than race that attracted whites to new suburban settlement; the latter demonstrated that the interruption of normal patterns of in-migration can profoundly affect neighborhood balance by accelerating the racial change process. However helpful these considerations, they all too often have been presented as either/or explanations. While white out-migration certainly resulted in large measure from the pull of the suburbs, there is no denying that racial fears interpreted as the push of a changing city also served as a powerful force. Moreover, the mathematics of white avoidance still cannot discount the salience of white flight as the primary contributor to rapid racial change and resegregation. Furthermore, neither explanation has paid particular heed to the special dynamics of blockbuster-induced residential turnover during this traumatic historical moment.

What occurred in Edmondson Village was a particularly acute form of white flight fueled by blockbusters who preyed upon white fears to induce panic selling. Two broad questions are central to this investigation of the Edmondson Village case: First, why did whites there so readily succumb to blockbusting? And, second, what was the legacy of blockbusting and white flight for the succession African American community?

To try to answer the first question one must seek to understand who Edmondson Village's white residents were, what kind of community they had created for themselves in social character and cultural style, and why

The Trauma of Racial Change

the entrance of African American settlers was perceived as so threatening to their conception of community. Moreover, since communities do not exist in isolation, the story necessarily involves an exploration of the larger forces of the nation and the metropolitan area that undergirded their social world, as well as consideration of the changing dynamics that challenged it so profoundly at mid-century. These broader perspectives provide the necessary context to address the primary issues about the nature of white response to racial change in Edmondson Village: What were the specific mechanisms of blockbusting that were applied in this case? Why was this particular community susceptible to such manipulation? How did these circumstances produce the panicked, massive white flight that ensued?

The second focus of this study is the experience of African American pioneers. Since white response was shaped by assumptions about race and by perceptions that African American settlers deviated in substantial ways from previous residents, it is important to examine the social character and expectations of the new group to determine whether in terms of socioeconomic status and aspirations they resembled or differed from their rowhouse neighbors who so rapidly abandoned the area. Of course, the circumstances under which African American pioneers acquired their housing did contrast vastly with those of their white predecessors; therefore, the impact of blockbusting and associated speculative activity upon the new residents deserves special examination. Finally, what kind of community emerged for African Americans in the wake of blockbusting and white flight? Such conditions seemed unpropitious for community well-being—to contemporaries on both sides of the racial divide, as well as in retrospect—but the social record of Edmondson Village needs to be investigated systematically to examine this assumption and to make some determination about the African American experience of "secondhand suburbanization." This study will consider the first quarter century of these pioneers' tenure in a neighborhood characterized by such dramatic upheaval.

The Edmondson Village story affords a case history of the process of massive residential racial change that contributed in such profound ways to the radical reconfiguration of urban space and experience in twentieth-century America. Though the special circumstances involved in this rowhouse community in west Baltimore deserve exploration and delineation, the attitudes and social mechanisms at work there were not unique. Since prevailing assumptions about the likely consequences of racial change often have become self-fulfilling prophecies, and the unresolved legacy of these dramatic episodes continues to shape behavior and policy, it is essential that we come to terms with this traumatic chapter in our recent past.

Studying Community

A key concept in this study is community, a somewhat elusive quality in modern American urban culture. Kai Erikson, in *Everything in Its Path*, provides a useful model for conceptualizing community in his effort to interpret the individual and collective dimensions of trauma that a cataclysmic flood produced in the settlements along Buffalo Creek, West Virginia, in 1972. Analyzing a situation in which the sense of community had been particularly intense, Erikson noted that the people of Buffalo Creek had been "held together by a common occupation, a common sense of the past, a common community, and a common feeling of belonging to, being a part of, a defined place."[15] While the circumstances of urban living differed for the people of Edmondson Village from those in Erikson's Appalachian communities, the effort to understand the trauma of racial change requires a similarly broad, profound, and sensitive conception of the complex dimensions of community.

Taking cues from Erikson's example and from a rich tradition of scholarly literature, my study defines community as a relatively small area with defined boundaries shared by a population whose sense of common space, form of social interaction, and broad consensus regarding morality and values provide the basis for a common identity. Therefore, the dimensions of shared physical setting (place, including both the natural and the built environment), social structure (the nature of social status and social interaction) and symbol (the realm of shared identity, beliefs, and values) establish the analytical framework for considering community in Edmondson Village and for gauging its social and cultural character over time.[16]

There is always the possibility that the concept of community may be posited to assert a nostalgic distortion of an urban past or present. While locally based identifications are important in the twentieth-century metropolis, recognition always must be given to the patterns of physical mobility and social identification that transcend the local context and to the pervasive influence of national culture as mediated through forms of mass communication and commercialism. The suburbanization process also has contributed to the erosion of traditional forms of community. By establishing socially homogeneous residential areas, suburbanization has served to heighten social distinctions, such as class and race, thereby defining community in quite narrow terms. The depth and durability of this form of suburban-style community is one of the underlying questions of this study.

Socioeconomic status represents a second important concept in the evaluation of the process of racial change in Edmondson Village. Social class always has been real but relative in the American experience, defying most attempts at precise categorization yet unmistakably a factor in perceptions and in social behavior. The Edmondson area's initial rowhouse residents typically fell somewhere at the social mid-point; in popular parlance this was a broadly middle-class community. By many sociological definitions, especially those focusing upon occupation, the whitecollar/blue-collar mix of the labor force might have been viewed as a combination of lower middle class and upper working class. However, rather than attempt to assign what inevitably would be an arbitrary—and perhaps stereotypical—classification, I have chosen to cast the present analysis in terms of descriptors of socioeconomic status, such as occupation, income, and education, and to look closely at such other demographic factors as conditions of residency, age, and family type. By describing socioeconomic status rather than categorizing it too glibly, this study seeks to provide a social profile of the community as a basis for comparison over time.[17]

The special relevance of socioeconomic status centers upon two considerations. First is the assertion that American suburbanization has been inextricably linked with social class and race, typically resulting in socially homogeneous communities. Secondly, a critical factor of interpretation regards the socioeconomic status of the neighborhood's whites and of the African Americans who sought to settle there—critical both in perceptions at the time and for analysis of racial change in retrospect. In instances of racial change whites often take race as a marker of class and make the assumption that incoming African Americans represent decline in socioeconomic terms; this contention needs to be examined carefully against the possibility that African American pioneers may resemble prior white residents more than they differ from them. A careful analysis of perceptions and attitudes, on the one hand, and of objective evidence regarding socioeconomic status, on the other, is necessary to try to unravel the social realities beneath this particular instance of rapid racial change.

This study is based upon both qualitative and quantitative data. The former consists primarily of oral history interviews conducted with approximately thirty respondents, including whites who resided in the neighborhood for various periods from its initial development in the late 1910s to the point of racial change in the 1950s and 1960s, and African Americans, both those who were pioneers in the process of racial change and more recent settlers. An effort was made to include a diverse sample of both populations, taking into consideration such factors as age, gender, location within the neighborhood, and period of residence. To protect the privacy of interviewees who have offered their views on an episode so recent and with aspects potentially controversial, pseudonyms have been used in all cases except where the public role of individuals (as elected or appointed officials, developers, or entrepreneurs, for instance) makes their identification a necessary and appropriate part of the historical record.[18]

Oral history interviews are not necessarily objective. Rather, they constitute thoughtful reflection by participants in the evolution of the community experience, filtered through the perspective of the present and their own constructions of the past. They do, however, offer extremely valuable perceptions of social reality. Though subjective by nature, such perceptions shape human behavior and therefore take on a social significance of their own. People act upon what they *believe* to be true, whether objective or not. As Italian social historian Alesandro Portelli has observed: "The first thing that makes oral history different . . . is that it tells us less about events as such than about their meaning."[19] This perspective was extremely helpful for a study of the complex and controversial dynamics involved in racial change, since it provided a way of helping to interpret apparent contradictions between the qualitative evidence of the interviews and the quantitative evidence derived from other data. As I have noted in an earlier reflection on the significance of this disparity regarding white perceptions of the racial change process, "oral history testimony points most clearly to the central social reality at the heart of the neighborhood experience, and it is that reality which the data on social characteristics must help us to understand, not the other way around."[20]

Quantitative data provides the second baseline for analysis, always in dynamic tension with the qualitative oral history sources. Federal census tract reports, which included limited details in 1930 and more extensive tables from 1940 forward (through the 1990 census), supply considerable information regarding social characteristics at the neighborhood level.[21] They provide the basis for compiling a rather thorough profile of the social character of the community at each decade point. However, the tract data reports afford little information for the period before 1940. Moreover, they do not permit the tracing of particular individuals or

The Trauma of Racial Change

households over time. These shortcomings necessitated the development of a block reconstruction method for this study. My sample block survey provides a profile of households on ten sample blocks at ten year intervals, beginning in 1920. It draws upon city directories, tax records, and (for the later period) telephone directories to determine such information as place of prior and subsequent residence, tenure of residence, home ownership, and occupation.[22] While the aggregate figures from the census tract data afford a systematic social portrait of the community at fixed points, the residential case histories of the sample block survey help to trace patterns of stability and change over time.

Rowhouse Suburbia

In the late nineteenth century and through the first half of the twentieth, rowhouse suburbanization made relatively new housing on the urban periphery available to a broad segment of America's middle class in cities like Baltimore. In doing so, its developers sought to capitalize upon an ideal of suburban living that evolved in tandem with the transportation innovations of the nineteenth and twentieth centuries to promise a combination of the convenience of the city with a more natural setting associated with the countryside.[23] Exclusive and costly detached housing developments set the initial tone for the suburban ideal. In the Baltimore area, for example, Roland Park (begun in the 1890s) and Guilford (begun in the 1910s), laid claims as upper income preserves on the basis of the size and architectural distinctiveness of their dwellings, their extravagant use of space, and their attention to landscape design. Both projects of the Roland Park Company and based upon plans drawn up by the prestigious firm founded by Frederick Law Olmsted, they were designed, in the unabashed words of promoter Edward Bouton, to "catch the whole of the better class suburban development of the city."[24] Clearly suburbs of this ilk promised a social elite not only elegance but privacy and exclusivity as well.

Rowhouse suburbia made more modest claims than these upper income versions, offering an affordable suburban ideal for the mainstream.[25] Builders like James Keelty, who began large-scale development in the Edmondson Avenue area of west Baltimore in the 1920s, recognized the attraction of a housing alternative that appealed to the suburban ideal by combining the benefits of the city—transportation and opportunities for jobs, education, shopping, and recreation—and evocations of the country— fresh air, light, trees, and green grass. Beginning in the late 1910s, the in-

Figure 1. The Edmondson area: rowhouse suburbs, 1938. Rowhouses line the streets on the Edmondson Avenue hillside, as construction of Hilton Parkway, a boulevard transversing Gwynns Falls Park, dominates the foreground. The James Keelty Company began building rowhouses, many of them the newer daylight type, on this lower portion of the hill in the 1920s. By the 1950s the hillside had been filled with Keelty-built houses. (The Peale Museum, Baltimore City Life Museums)

creasingly popular rowhouse version they proffered was the "daylight style," an adaptation of the traditional urban rowhouse, redesigned with more spacious proportions to provide an outside window for each room. While the Tudor-style adornments of Keelty's finest Edmondson Avenue rowhouses in the Wildwood section could only faintly echo a Roland Park or Guilford, nevertheless the housing package afforded by the daylight rowhouse was spacious, solidly constructed, and reasonable in cost. And, while the density of population in rowhouse suburbia more resembled the tradi-

The Trauma of Racial Change

Figure 2. The view up the Edmondson Avenue hill looking west from the vicinity of Hilton Street, 1954, shows the central role played in the early years by streetcar accessibility, as well as the increasing importance of auto and truck transportation by the 1950s. Keelty-built daylight rowhouses in 1920s styles are evident on the right side, as are important community institutions: the Edgewood Theater, Christ Edmondson Methodist Church, and St. Bernardine's Roman Catholic Church (with its golden dome). (Collection of the Maryland Historical Society, Baltimore)

tional city than the elite suburbs, it appeared to afford a version of the latter in its implicit promise of a family-oriented, socially homogeneous residential preserve, relatively free from the commercial and industrial functions of urban life and differentiated along lines of class and race from the diverse population groups of the evolving metropolis.[26]

While the suburban ideal offered an attractive package for housebuilders and their clients, the predilection for more homogeneous communities drew support from other quarters, including the ranks of housing reformers and planners interested in expanding the suburban option beyond its more upscale versions. The historian Robert Fairbanks has argued persuasively that in the first decades of the century the views of these two groups converged in a common diagnosis of urban ills that suggested that the congestion, disorder, and heterogeneity of the city could be cured by the creation of improved housing in community settings. He notes that these views received codification in 1931 when the President's Conference on Home Building and Home Ownership, convened by Herbert Hoover, concluded that federal housing policy should be guided by the goal of establishing "homogeneous communities," a conviction that subsequently undergirded New Deal housing programs.[27] Indeed, it was not the homogeneity of the suburbs—elite or more modest—to which reformers objected but the tendency for suburban residents to live what Harlan Douglass, in his 1925 volume, *The Suburban Trend*, called "bi-focal" or "lopsided" lives. Douglass, who felt that suburbs represented "the hope of the future city" because of the prospect for decentralization, was troubled that suburban residency tended to separate the personal domain of home from the public realm of the larger metropolitan area. Acknowledging the social and economic selectivity characteristic of such communities, Douglass believed that there was nothing wrong with homogeneity if a more "all-sided" notion of civic responsibility could be cultivated and if more diverse housing options for suburban living could be made available to larger numbers of people. Indeed, his enthusiasm for decentralized suburbs led him to exude: "Even the relatively slight acceleration of the suburban trend by such means of social control as are in sight, may set up changes in the structure and relationships of modern society which, when sufficiently reinforced, may save the day for the human race."[28]

The new suburbs were not only homogeneous in terms of class but in terms of race as well. A pervasive system of Jim Crow extended the invisible color line of discrimination to all aspects of social life—schooling, employment, public accommodations, and housing. Like many other border and northern cities, Baltimore had developed a rather clearly defined, racially segregated ghetto by the opening years of the twentieth century.[29] As the African American population began to increase substantially, white response typically took two forms: racial restriction in the housing market and white flight. The former found its most vivid illustration in the attempt during the 1910s to enact residential segregation ordinances (what Garrett Power has called "apartheid Baltimore style"). In 1917 such legal restrictions were ruled unconstitutional because of the limitation they placed upon property rights (not because they were discriminatory). They were, however, replaced by a pervasive and systematic set of mechanisms for accomplishing de facto what could not be done de jure, ranging from informal private pressure to institutional discrimination involving the real estate industry, state law, and lending agencies—both private and governmental.[30]

The second mode of avoiding residential mixing was white flight. A 1911 British report on "The Cost of Living in American Towns" observed regarding race and housing patterns in Baltimore: "In those areas of the city which are inhabited by the wage-earning classes a general segregation by race or by colour is discernible. . . . It often happens, especially in the better parts of the city, that when a coloured family is able to secure a house in the center of a row hitherto exclusively occupied by whites, the latter will remove at the earliest moment, even at a pecuniary loss."[31] Flight, of course, was an admission that the mechanisms limiting African American residency had failed. However, through the interwar decades they generally tended to hold, despite some modest change in the post-World War I years. By 1940, when African Americans constituted nearly one-fourth of the city's total population, the line of de facto racial segregation was firmly drawn around a spatially limited ghetto area more than 75 percent African American. (See map 1.) Even during World War II, under conditions of unprecedented population growth, as both African Americans and whites flocked to cities to take advantage of war-fueled employment opportunities, the artificial restrictions on living space persisted—though they were coming under intensive pressure.

Through the first several decades of the twentieth century the silent conspiracy on race and residency proved remarkably durable. However, Baltimore's African American community played an important role in the evolving assault upon segregation and discrimination, which eventually would take the form of a powerful national movement. In the 1930s the dormant Baltimore branch of the NAACP had been revived, and by the end of World War II it was one of the largest and most active in the country, spearheading efforts to secure gains for African Americans in schooling, voting, employment, and public accommodations.[32] Housing opportunity remained a difficult challenge, but the surge in African American population during the 1940s made it one of the greatest pressure points as the decade progressed. In the late 1940s and early 1950s the old neighborhood racial division lines began to be breached, gradually at first, then with greater speed and volume, as what one local African American interviewee called "the evacuation" by whites began to occur on the city's near west side. Suddenly, the undercurrents of change threatened to become a tide.

African American housing pressure, white racism: the tinder only required the match of the blockbuster. When it was applied in the Edmondson Village area between 1955 and 1965, it touched off an intensive wave of white flight, rapidly and systematically creating near total population changeover in an entire section of the city. Repeated in varying forms in urban areas across the nation, the era's dramatic episodes of racial succession rewrote the demographic maps of American cities. So much part of the social landscape, yet so little understood, this story represents one of those critical points at which our collective past bears so importantly upon our collective present.

2
The Making of a Rowhouse Neighborhood

> Because of the electric railway, the very modest wage earner, no less than the prosperous business man, might leave his wife to breathe fresh country air and his children to romp over green fields, and yet not be further removed from them in point of time than if they were crowded into some sunless, damp court.
> —William A. House, president of Baltimore's United Railways (1912)

In his now classic study of Boston's late nineteenth-century streetcar suburbs, Sam Bass Warner, Jr., observed that developers had not built communities; they had built streets of houses. Yet, as Warner made clear, the results were neighborhoods whose social and economic structures distinctly differentiated them from older sections of the previous walking city. The new suburban metropolis of Boston by 1900 functioned as a "selective melting pot" in which "people were separated by income and mixed together with little regard to national origin."[1] The heyday of the streetcar era in the first decades of the twentieth century and the advent of the auto in the following two, urban housing pressures related to race and immigration, and larger-scale development strategies by countless builders combined to hasten the process in city after city, from Boston to Baltimore. Yet we have few case studies that examine the social and cultural character of these newly established communities, which rapidly encircled the older urban core during the first half of the century, profoundly transforming the American metropolis, eventually to be eclipsed by new, even larger waves of suburbanization and engulfed by massive social or racial change in the post-World War II period.

This chapter traces the history of the late streetcar/early auto rowhouse suburb that took root in the Edmondson Avenue corridor of west Baltimore in the early decades of the twentieth century, experienced the housing boom of the 1920s and continued growth thereafter, and created a new community with its defined turf, distinctive social character, and patterned culture only to succumb totally and rapidly to white flight in the late 1950s and early 1960s. In numerous communities in urban centers like Baltimore and elsewhere, such a scenario was not untypical for the era, yet its very "typicality" deserves investigation. It poses a two-fold question: 1) what was the social and cultural character of these new, highly differentiated middle-income urban neighborhoods, and 2) why did they respond as they did to the prospect of racial change? This chapter focuses on the first question, hoping to find some clues from the community's early evolution for later consideration of the second.

Two factors stand out in the formative stage of the Edmondson community's growth from 1915 to 1945: first, the process of development and settlement interacted to produce a social definition that remained remarkably consistent over the decades, functioning as a cushion for considerable degrees of social change; second, the differentiated conception of community provided the appearance of stability and security but in reality was quite fragile, proving to be an inadequate basis for adaptation to change, which it could not contain. Even if developers built houses rather than communities, the social and cultural structure of the communities that emerged was not simply a matter of happenstance but rather a complex interplay of individual aspirations and collective forces we must consider if we are to understand the complexity of the twentieth-century American city at the neighborhood level.

A word about the Edmondson area's earlier history and character: with its western boundary near the crest of the uplands that ring Baltimore on the north and west (along a line that had become the city's new border in 1888), the Edmondson area sloped downward to its eastern terminus, the Gwynns Falls, site of earlier mill enterprises. The ravine formed by this small river cut a deep natural border separating the district distinctly from the developing urban areas to its east and from the city center a full three and a half miles away. Prior to 1910 the only immediate access for vehicular traffic between countryside and city lay along Edmondson Avenue, which bisected the tract and crossed the Gwynns Falls on a narrow trestle bridge constructed by Baltimore County in 1879-80, just ahead of the city's annexation in 1888. As late as 1910 the Edmondson area still consisted primarily of farmland and woods, the preserve of farm estates, a character reflected both in contemporary maps and in the federal manuscript census of that year. While some of the landowning gentry class were year-round residents like Hugh Gelston of Gelston Heights, others maintained country residences primarily for summer habitation, as was the case with Mary Frick Garrett Jacobs of Uplands and E. Austin Jenkins of Hunting Ridge, who owned the two large estates that bounded the area just west of the city line.[2] Smaller landholdings were in the hands of a somewhat lesser status gentry group, working farmers, or those engaged in entrepreneurial occupations.

The gentry clearly continued to set the social and economic tone of the area in 1910 as it had in the past, but two other broad social groups were clearly identifiable in the social equation. First, there were those whose livelihood was primarily related to the area's rural environment, whether farm workers on the larger estates, performers of rural-related crafts and services, or operatives and laborers in such enterprises as quarrying. The second and newer group, who settled in two brick duplexes and a short line of rowhouses along Edmondson Avenue at the bottom of the hill, differed substantially from the others and represented a harbinger of imminent change. For them the Edmondson area provided a country suburban residence for households whose employment was primarily urban. A milk route dairyman, a slaughterhouse butcher, an engraver, a superintendent in a furniture factory, they—and those who would join them shortly—were commuters to the offices, business establishments, and factories east of the Gwynns Falls in the settled portions of the city. Altogether the three groups numbered only ninety-seven,[3] yet their presence could be linked with other signs of impending change: the Ellicott City streetcar line, which had begun electric service along Edmondson Avenue in 1899; the new bridge in 1910; the new shingle suburban cottages built along Walnut Avenue in Rognel Heights just west of the city limits, beginning in 1909; and the additional construction along Edmondson Avenue of several sets of brick duplexes and rows between 1910 and 1914, expanding the tiny nucleus at the bottom of the hill and initiating a new one near the top.[4] By 1914 the rowhouse builders were offering a housing package for a new middle-class urban commuter that promised "all the conveniences of the city with all the advantages of the country."[5] The suburban ideal had arrived on the Edmondson hillside.

The Keelty Rowhouse and the Suburban Ideal

Between 1910 and 1930, the Edmondson Avenue area west of the Gwynns Falls experienced a population surge from 97 to 8,991, much of it coming in the single decade of the 1920s. In retrospect, it appears clear that the market existed for new housing for particular types of people and that developers emerged who were ready to meet that need with housing that suited the clientele. Though there was little that seemed to dictate how

Blockbusting in Baltimore

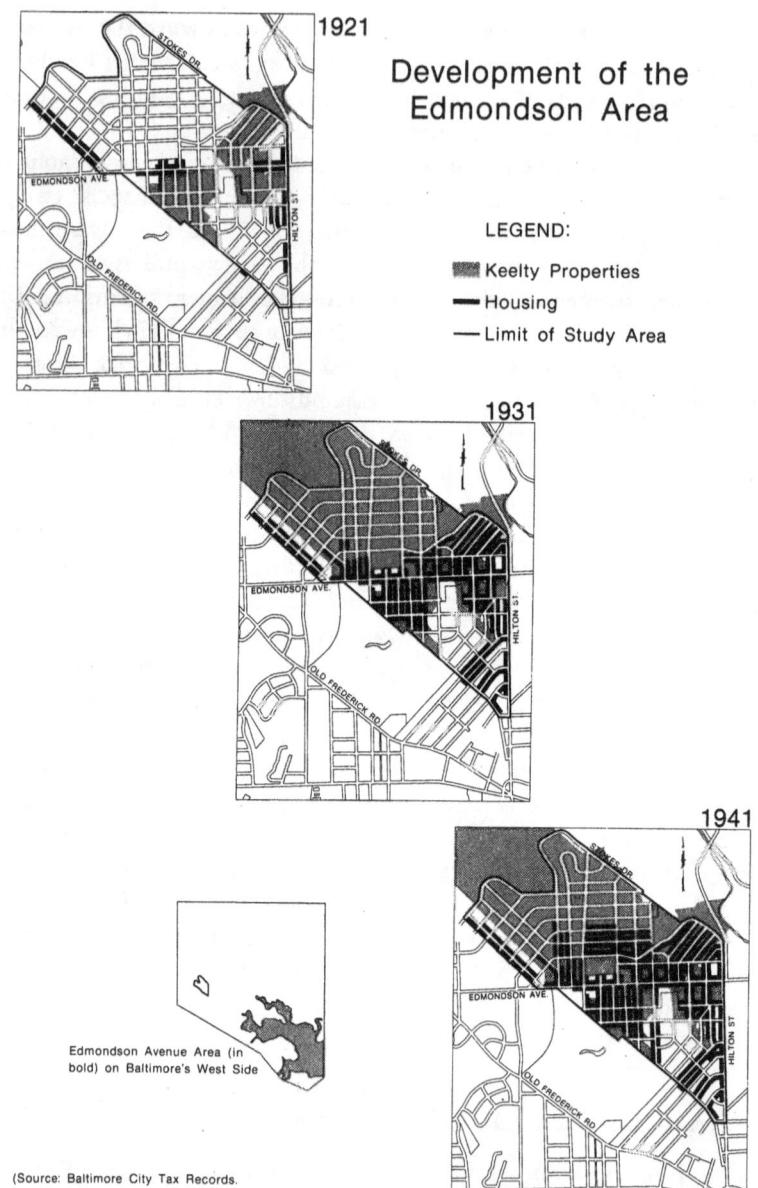

Map 3. Development of the Edmondson area, 1921-1941 [street network as of 1982]. (Compiled by the author from Baltimore City tax assessment records; map by UMBC Cartographic Services)

The Making of a Rowhouse Neighborhood

the developer, housing type, and new residents would interact, by 1930—and certainly by 1940—the social character of the community was firmly set. Much of the responsibility was due to James Keelty and his "daylight-style" rowhouses.

Beginning in 1916, Keelty made a series of purchases that outflanked the existing developments at the top and bottom of the hill. By 1922 he had gained control of most of the undeveloped land along Edmondson Avenue, in 1926 he acquired the entire Gelston estate on the north, and in 1928 he purchased the old Lyndhurst estate on the northwest.[6] With these acquisitions, Keelty accumulated two-thirds of the land for the future rowhouse community.

In advertisements for his houses, he proudly referred to himself as "James Keelty, The Builder." Born in Ireland in 1869, brought to Baltimore by his parents as a child of age ten or eleven, and educated in the Hibernian Free School, Keelty started off as a stonemason but soon began to build two-story rowhouses on his own. After completing his first projects along Calvert Street and Greenmount Avenue in the central portions of the city, in 1908 he turned to the western side, constructing two-story, buff-brick swell fronts in the 2300 blocks of West Fayette and West Baltimore streets before moving farther out to the growing Poplar Grove area (along Mosher and Dukeland Streets and Riggs Avenue) in the 1910s, where many of his houses had stone porch fronts and upper bays. Having purchased the land along Edmondson Avenue on the next hill to the west, Keelty began to develop it in the early 1920s. By 1930 Keelty houses occupied approximately fifty square blocks of the Edmondson area; ten years later most of the section's 1,584 housing units had been constructed by his company.[7] (See map 3.)

While Keelty's developments were substantial, there was nothing particularly unique about either his enterprise or his product. Rather, Keelty houses of the 1920s and 1930s represented the apex of Baltimore rowhouse design, the "daylight" or "sunlight" house. Soon daylight houses were all the rage, with one builder trying to capitalize on the fad in an advertisement by having a wife coo, "Oh, Dickie, dear, let's buy one of these 'bright in every corner' houses."[8] The distinctive feature of the daylight house style was that each room indeed did have at least one outside window. Conventional, earlier two-story rows had one or two "blind" rooms in the center, though sometimes a skylight was added to give light to a central room upstairs. Houses of the older type built on the west side just prior to the new innovation typically had fourteen-foot widths and depths of forty-five to fifty feet.[9] In contrast, a typical Keelty daylight of

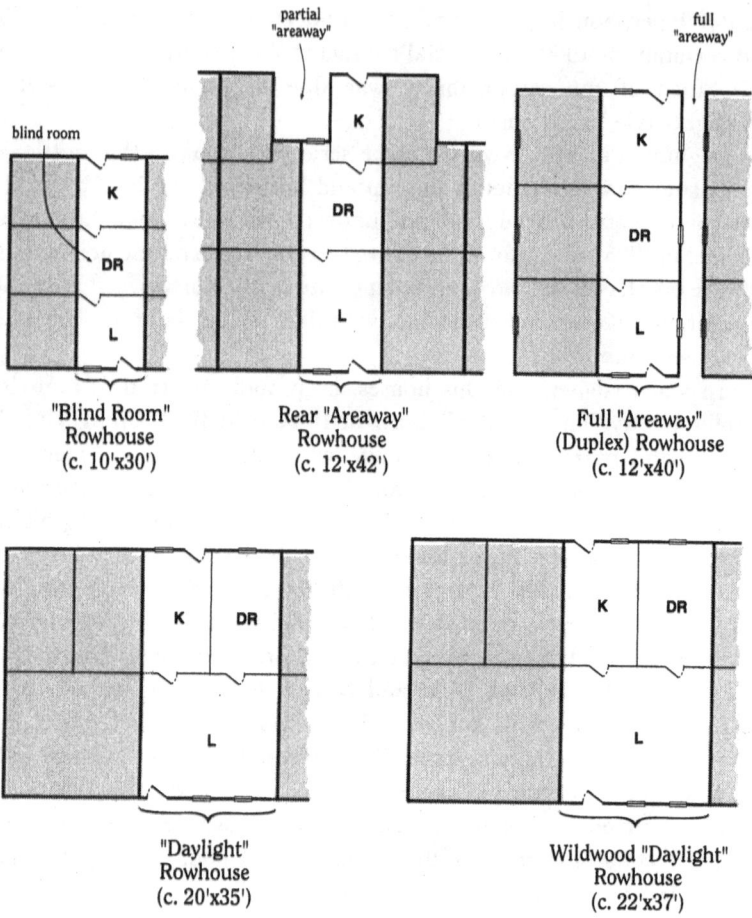

Figure 3. Rowhouse Styles (Designed by the author; graphic by UMBC Cartographic Services)

the early 1920s had a front twenty to twenty-two feet wide and a depth of approximately thirty-five feet. Upstairs, each of the three or four bedrooms had at least one window, while downstairs an entry hall with stairs and a spacious living room occupied the front, and the dining room and kitchen both had windows to the rear. (See figure 3)

For the consumer, the daylight modification of the rowhouse meant a spacious, pleasant housing interior at a modest cost that made home ownership possible for middle-income people. For the developer, the slight decrease in density (in the Edmondson area, for example, two daylights

The Making of a Rowhouse Neighborhood

occupied approximately the same amount of frontage [forty to forty-four feet] as three of the conventional rows [forty-two feet]) still allowed many of the economies of rowhouse construction—shared walls, common utility lines, and simultaneous erection. Sherry Olson has pointed out that progressive-era concern about older, narrower urban housing designs with their lack of light and air had created a climate of opinion receptive to the wider, daylight styles as a housing reform, a trend underwritten by a series of progressive municipal building codes.[10] When demand for new housing became intense in the post-World War I period—the building of new housing having been virtually halted during the war—it was the new daylight form that consumers demanded.[11] Just beginning his Edmondson area development at precisely the moment these several trends converged, Keelty switched to the new style, daylight rows marching up the Edmondson hill, block by block. (See figures 4 through 8.)

Though Keelty's Edmondson rowhouses of the early to mid-1920s were solid and spacious, if modest, adaptations of the daylight type, his crowning version came in the late 1920s and the 1930s in Wildwood, the name he gave developments on the extensive land tracts that had been the Gelston and Lyndhurst estates. Designed as an upgraded form of the basic daylight box, these dwellings were billed as English type, distinguished from the earlier homes primarily by slightly more spacious dimensions (some were twenty-two by thirty-seven feet, with an additional half-story in a gabled attic), quality features (such as slate roofs, copper spouting, tile porches, and fireplaces), and architectural variation (gabled roofs, red Tudor-type brickwork, and architectural variety within the row). (See figures 9 and 10.) John Carpenter, whose family moved into a Keelty-built house on Norman (later Normandy) Avenue in 1921, recalls his reaction as a boy to the new Wildwood homes across Edmondson Avenue: "The houses in Wildwood, we heard at the time, were supposed to be Keelty's best. I guess he started and made money, and then when he got to Wildwood, he upgraded the houses. I had a couple of boy friends who were in the Scout troop [and lived] there, and I can remember going in their houses, and they had a third-story attic that was finished off, and I thought this would be great, to have a play room or study up there, which our houses didn't have."[12]

Keelty ads for Wildwood, "Baltimore's newest suburban development," once more evoked the suburban ideal: Wildwood, they boasted, was "splendidly convenient to the cars [streetcars], churches of various denominations, schools, stores and banks, and but a quarter hour's drive to the city," yet enjoyed the benefits of nearby parkland and a ridge-top

Figure 4. "Areaway" houses, among the first rowhouses on Edmondson Avenue, built in the period 1911-1914. These houses were 14 feet wide by 45 feet deep, with a narrow space ("areaway") in the rear between every two pairs to allow light to inner rooms. (See the layout of the "areaway" style rowhouse in Figure 3.)

location—"standing on the front porch of these homes you can see all over the city"—a combination representing a "truly suburban atmosphere."[13] If Keelty's housing type was right, his timing may have been unfortunate; begun in 1928, development of Wildwood was slowed by the onset of the Depression.[14] By the mid-1930s it had accelerated again, only to experience the abrupt halt that World War II caused here, as elsewhere.

The rapid pace of Keelty's development from the early 1920s onward hinged not only upon his land acquisition and construction methods, but also upon the provision of essential urban services. Rognel Heights, just west of the city line prior to the 1918 annexation, had been developed in 1909 with the provision of a private water supply system. By the early teens, however, expansion of the city water supply and sewage systems permitted extension of both services into the Edmondson section on Baltimore's far western side.[15] In contrast to these new municipal facilities, privately financed transportation in the form of the United Railways and Electric Company's Ellicott City streetcar line had been in place since 1899, when electric service was initiated on the tracks along Edmondson Avenue. Keelty ads, like those of the earlier developers, stressed the convenience of streetcar transportation, assuming right up to World War II that prospective buyers would be coming *by* trolley *out* from the city

The Making of a Rowhouse Neighborhood

Figure 5. James Keelty Company daylight-type rowhouses, built in the early 1920s. With front widths of 20 feet and depths of 35 feet, these houses could offer a window in every room.

(though one further quality feature of the Wildwood houses, recognizing changing times, was the provision for a garage).[16] In 1932 Baltimore City officials opened an additional span over the Gwynns Falls, the new West Baltimore Street concrete bridge, Mayor Howard W. Jackson noting the connection between public works and private investment: "The opening of this bridge marks an important step in the further development of this section of the city. The Gwynns Falls Valley for many years has been a natural barrier to quick communication between the older section of the city to the east of the valley and that evergrowing section to the west."[17]

Keelty not only built rapidly and extensively, he also apparently built well. "Keelty-built" homes became a hallmark of quality construction on the west side, a trademark "The Builder" prided himself for. No absentee landlord, he continued to maintain his office within the community throughout the period. Demonstrating a paternalistic interest in the new neighborhood he had built, he contributed the cost of the sanctuary for the new St. Bernardine's Roman Catholic Church as a memorial to his recently deceased young daughter. (See figure 11.) One striking feature of Keelty's developments was the high rate of home ownership, a point to be developed later. And it is generally conceded that he offered a quality product at a relatively low cost. Creation of ground rent aided greatly in the process, a mechanism in Maryland state law that benefitted both the consumer, by reducing the amount of the mortgage, and the developer, for whom it often represented the margin of profit.[18] (See figure 12.) But rowhouse developers like Keelty were not simply selling houses; they were selling a "housing package." Location, cost, house type, and size—all were determinants of the market whose housing needs would be met and, therefore, also determined the social character of the community that would form.[19] In many ways the most telling promise of Edmondson's "suburban atmosphere" was more apparent in result than in billing: a remarkable degree of social homogeneity. Keelty had built a community whose social character was as regular as the brick fronts of his two-story houses.

The Social Character of the New Rowhouse Community

If the Keelty daylights represented the apex of urban rowhouse living for middle-income residents, their appearance on the market right after World War I could not have been more opportune in terms of population growth and housing needs. During the decade from 1910 to 1920 the city's population had increased precipitously at a rate of 31 percent, producing consequent pressure upon housing. Janet Kemp's 1907 study of *Housing Conditions in Baltimore* chronicled a growing urban housing crisis, documenting in particular the degree of overcrowding and unhealthy conditions in districts where African Americans and new foreign-born immigrants were concentrated.[20] In the early 1910s, concern for such conditions led to passage of a series of racial residential segregation ordinances by Baltimore's city council and its politically "progressive" mayor, though the legislation subsequently failed constitutional tests. These circumstances presaged a sizable white exodus to the periphery, including the large portion of land added to the city after the annexation of 1918.[21] Housing developments such as those along Edmondson Avenue would function to siphon off from older, densely settled areas that segment of the urban populace able and willing to make the move. In this late period of streetcar suburbanization, physical space increasingly corresponded with social class.

For the Edmondson area, change was the order of the day as the community absorbed high rates of population growth. During the 1920s the total population there quadrupled, and even during the economic hard times of the 1930s it experienced a 31 percent increase. As John

Figure 6. Daylight houses in the 500 block of Normandy Avenue built by the James Keelty Company in 1921. These were 21 feet by 35 feet. (See the Sanborn fire insurance map in figure 8 for the configuration of comparable housing on nearby N. Loudon Avenue.)

Carpenter put it, "there were people moving in all the time; . . . they were always building houses." Not only was in-migration strong and steady, but a substantial number of settlers were in the young family-forming stages, so that new births added to the total. Population gains from these two sources more than offset the losses due to death and the steady, normal out-migration rate (29 percent per decade) during the same period.[22]

Just as remarkable as the degree of change was the degree of residential longevity. In 1930, for example, 68 percent of those on the sample blocks had lived there for five years or more, and 82 percent were first residents in their dwellings; by 1940 a strikingly high 92 percent had lived in their present homes for five years or more, 62 percent were first residents, 38 percent second, and no housing had yet turned over to a third resident.[23] While this degree of residential permanence suggests an apparent high level of satisfaction, it also contributed subtly to change in the long run, since the eventual result would be a maturing population, a factor still masked in this period by the continuing in-migration of young adults and expansion of the housing stock.

Figure 7. One of the Normandy Avenue houses, which were distinctive for the dormer window on the small front mansard, behind which was a main roof sloping slightly to the rear. Marble lintels and stone porch fronts were among the "quality" features of these 1920s-era daylights.

In a setting of considerable movement and flux, however, the social homogeneity of the new settlers provided a clear definition of the community and acted in a powerful way to provide a sense of stability, the overwhelming retrospective perception of those interviewed for this study. If new settlers lacked prior contact, they nevertheless shared remarkable similarities when it came to such matters as age and family status; home ownership; place of origin and prior urban experience; racial, ethnic, and religious identification; and occupational level. These were the ingredients that seemed to provide a basis for community in the new context.

By population count young adults (aged twenty-five through forty-four) predominated in the new community, setting the norm as one of modest-sized nuclear families. Though their children represented a sizable contingent in the neighborhood and gave it a youthful cast, those from birth to age twenty actually numbered fewer than their parents' generation, both in 1930 and in 1940. In that latter year census data showed that 58 percent of all households consisted of three to five members, while only 3 percent were composed of one person and only 10 percent of more than five.[24] Relatively youthful with small families, many of the Edmondson settlers shared a common stage in the life cycle and a

The Making of a Rowhouse Neighborhood

similar family type as an adaptation to their social and economic circumstances.

Keelty and the lesser developers in the Edmondson area produced housing for a community of single-family resident homeowners. In 1920 all of the houses on the sample blocks developed to that point were owner-occupied. Ten years later, after the rapid housing and population expansion of the 1920s, home ownership in the sample blocks stood at 86 percent, and even after the worst of the Depression in 1940 it was a high 80 percent. Census data for 1940 showed a somewhat lower 63 percent, but by 1950 the census figure had climbed to 73 percent (while in the sample it was a striking 96 percent). By comparison, citywide figures for an urban area usually considered distinguished for its high rate of home ownership showed 39 percent of the dwelling units to be owner-occupied in 1940, while in 1950 the figure had increased to 50 percent.[25] Of course, many of the Edmondson residents listed as homeowners were, in fact, only in the process of buying their homes, a financial burden they shared in common and one that sometimes led them to refer to the area as "Mortgage Hill."[26]

The Depression challenged the American dream of home ownership and employment for many Americans. In Baltimore, unemployment reached twenty percent in 1933, and home ownership fell by one-fifth during the decade, even as the city administration resisted New Deal programs intended to help victims of the Depression. But Edmondson area residents were cushioned from the direct impact of hard times, as employment and home ownership levels remained relatively steady throughout the period.[27]

Residents also shared somewhat similar places of origin and urban experiences. Not newcomers to the city, most were moving from prior residence in older Baltimore neighborhoods. In a sizable number of cases, residents in the early period migrated from older neighborhoods nearer the center city that had been impacted by considerable population growth during the 1920s (and subsequently), sometimes by the numbers of African Americans or European immigrants. The sample block data for 1920, 1930, and 1940 shows relatively even streams of migrants from 1) areas of West Baltimore immediately east of the Edmondson district, 2) Old West Baltimore (from the city's center to Fulton Street), 3) South Baltimore, and 4) East Baltimore.[28] With population density producing pressures upon the aging housing stock in those areas as well as creating new strains of heterogeneity, movement was one solution—but one available only to those able to afford to purchase a single family dwelling, even at a modest cost.

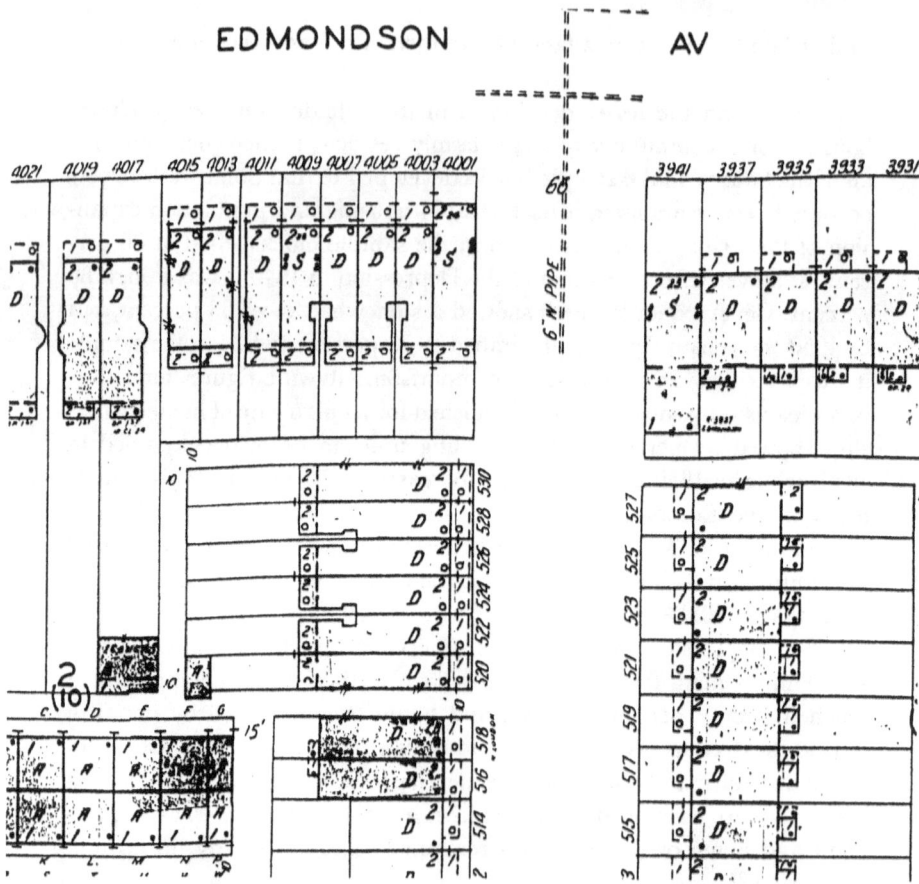

Figure 8. The Edmondson Avenue area, depicted on this 1928 fire insurance map, exhibits the mixture of rowhouse sizes in one of the sections of early development at the corner of Edmondson Avenue and N. Loudon Avenue, the latter a typical side street. Houses in the 4000 block of Edmondson Avenue and numbers 520-530 along the west (left) side of N. Loudon are of the "areaway" type, with the passage separating the rear of the houses between every pair. 4017 and 4019 Edmondson Avenue are duplexes, separated from adjoining houses by a narrow passage extending the length of the entire house. Both types share the narrow fronts and long depths of the earlier rowhouse styles. In contrast, the houses on the odd side (to the east, or right) and in the 3900 block of Edmondson Avenue are daylights, wider and less deep. Comparison of the two indicates that the ratio of frontage required for the daylights as opposed to the older types was approximately 2 to 3. Note the garages (marked "A") on the lower left; located in the middle of some of the blocks in this section, these could be purchased or rented by the minority of residents who had automobiles. (*Insurance Maps of Baltimore, Maryland,* Sanborn Map Company, 1928; used with permission)

Regarding race, the social definition of the new neighborhood was near absolute: new residents were white. In 1930 only forty-four of the total population in the two census tracts were African American, and in 1940 that small number had shrunk even farther to thirty-four (while white population grew from 8,947 in 1930 to 11,745 in 1940). Moreover, census block data for the latter year shows that the handful of African American households were located on the margins of the two tracts, with none occupying the new brick rowhouses.[29] As Madge Cooper recalls: "The only blacks lived on Hilton Street—almost to Frederick Road. There were two—or maybe three—homes; then on the other side of the railroad . . . there were a few; but those people had lived there for many, many years—probably before we came; and they never bothered us, and we never bothered them. But there was no real socializing—and the children, of course, didn't go to our school; I have no idea where they went to school."[30] Or, in Marilyn Simkins's recollection: "You just didn't see black people in the neighborhood, except women who came in to do day work or delivery men, or something like that. They just didn't live in the area then."[31]

Indeed, the racial exclusivity of white neighborhoods like the new Edmondson area was undergirded by a web of mechanisms that served to assure residential segregation. In addition to long-standing patterns of individual prejudice and custom were the controls exerted by powerful institutions: the real estate industry (the statement by the National Association of Real Estate Brokers deemed it improper to introduce members of another race into a neighborhood), state law (restrictive covenants, though not necessarily used in this section of the city, were upheld by the Maryland Court of Appeals in 1938 and not ruled unconstitutional by the U.S. Supreme Court until 1948), and the financial establishment (where private lending institutions and the government mortgage agencies established by the New Deal federal administration typically discriminated against African Americans).[32] These mechanisms worked with such apparent effectiveness that racial diversity simply was not an overt issue within the confines of the community.

If race was an absolute definer, religion was less so, and ethnicity only a trace. The emerging community was overwhelmingly Roman Catholic and Protestant, congregations of the latter established within the boundaries being from such main line denominations as Lutheran, Methodist, and Reformed Episcopal. Conspicuous was the absence of Jewish residents, whether because of choice or exclusion. Among the early settlers German names stand out slightly more prominently numerically,

Figure 9. Early Keelty "English-type" daylight rowhouses in the Wildwood development, advertised in 1928. These are in the 600 block of Wildwood Parkway.

with Irish perhaps second, but in most cases ethnic ties appeared not to be strong. Very few settlers were first generation immigrants; while some were second generation, most would have been third and beyond. Where ethnic ties once had been important, they had been left behind in the old neighborhood.[33]

A high level of home ownership; similarities in place of origin and prior urban experience; racial, ethnic, and religious homogeneity—all contributed in important ways to the social definition of the emerging rowhouse community. Yet, no factor was more important in that definition than occupational level. Social historians in recent years rightly have been cautious about hierarchical rankings of occupation as well as about judgments regarding upward and downward mobility based upon those rankings.[34] Occupational level however, clearly has a variety of consequences, not least of which is income. And income and occupation, taken together, may have far-reaching influences upon such other dimensions of social life as social status, lifestyle, aspiration, and opportunity.[35] At the very least, the occupational profile of a neighborhood provides some indication of its socioeconomic diversity or homogeneity. Moreover, comparison of occupational level and of changes in a given community with trends in the national and metropolitan workforce may provide some indication of how residents of that neighborhood fit in the larger social and economic context.

The Making of a Rowhouse Neighborhood

Figure 10. Architectural variations such as dormers, gabled porches, and sloping slate roofs characterized the "English-type" daylight rowhouses. With dimensions of 22 by 37 feet, these included a half-story attic and a garage in the rear.

What is most striking about the new Edmondson rowhouse community was the concentration of occupational types in several middle-level categories and the way in which that configuration persisted over time with little change, even as older families matured or moved away and new families moved in. Perhaps no other social factor contributed so greatly to the perceived stability of the neighborhood: individuals might come and go, but occupational types remained the same. The occupational profile that emerged with the first household heads in 1920 (in the sample block survey) was one strongly concentrated in four areas: sales, clerical, crafts (skilled trades), and manufacturing. On the one hand, there were few in credentialed professional or upper managerial capacities, though there were some in middle management; on the other, Edmondson was not a community of laborers, service workers, or domestics.[36] With only slight variation, this was the occupational pattern that persisted for the rest of the community's history—even into the later period of racial change.

According to the sample block survey, during the 1920s the percentage of residents in managerial positions increased somewhat and those in positions as craftsmen to a greater extent, but after the Depression decade of the 1930s the balance evened out once more. While the block study is only a sample limited to household heads, census tract data for 1940 on all persons in the neighborhood confirms the pattern, though it shows even more level distribution among sales-clerical (grouped together in that report), craftsmen, and operative categories (the latter being somewhat underrepresented in the sample block data).[37] Perhaps more clearly than the sample, the census emphasized the middle-level occupational profile in the neighborhood.

Most women did not participate in the community's paid workforce. For the early period the sample block survey (limited to household heads and based primarily upon city directories) suggests only a few instances where widows or adult daughters living at home were employed, though city directories do not provide an adequate picture of women's employment.[38] The 1940 census tract data paints a more complete portrait of women's role in Edmondson's paid workforce, one that apparently had begun to increase. In that year women constituted 28 percent of those employed, a figure not differing substantially from the citywide average for white women. While the percentage of women working outside the home represented a distinct minority, their involvement indicated that Depression economics, changing norms regarding women's work, and a gap between middle-class aspirations and rowhouse realities may have made an impact on the hillside community. Two-thirds of women's jobs were concentrated in the sales-clerical category, and women were very thinly represented in other types of jobs: women constituted only 2 percent of professionals, 2.5 percent of managers, and 4.2 percent of operatives, while women working as domestics were only .5 percent of the total paid workforce.[39] As a general norm, the pattern for women was work within the home, not paid labor outside, and this was especially true for married women and mothers.

The 1940 census also provides an opportunity to compare the Edmondson area workforce with that of the city as a whole. At first glance, the very middle-level profile of the neighborhood is reflected in the way that it closely mirrors the citywide averages. In this sense Edmondson might be considered a typical Baltimore neighborhood. Yet, in a city where place of residence was becoming highly differentiated along lines of race, class, and religious or ethnic identification, neighborhood occupational profiles were likely to be much more skewed toward certain categories than others. Therefore, the concentration of Edmondson's jobs in the center illustrated its own peculiar identity rather than its typicality. Together with other developing rowhouse and detached house communities, it played a middle-level role increasingly set off from older, more hetero-

The Making of a Rowhouse Neighborhood

Figure 11. St. Bernardine's Roman Catholic Church, c. 1929, Edmondson Avenue and Mt. Holly St. Begun in 1928 and completed the next year, the sanctuary of the new church was contributed by James Keelty and his wife as a memorial to their deceased daughter. (The Peale Museum, Baltimore City Life Museums)

geneous neighborhoods by a social definition in which occupation and social class were closely linked.[40]

Two related phenomena were operating upon the workforce in cities like Baltimore, both with consequences for neighborhood structure. First, rapid growth across the spectrum of occupational possibilities had expanded the total number of urban jobs considerably, particularly on the eve of Edmondson's initial development.[41] Had no other changes occurred at all, this expansion would have provided a pool of residents who might have spilled over from older, existing neighborhoods into the newly developing rowhouse suburbs. Insofar as occupation and income were correlated, the cost of new housing would have acted as an economic filter channeling the expanded workforce into particular new residential choices. But, accompanying workforce expansion was a major shift in the character of the workforce. The transition to mass, machine production not only required large numbers of semiskilled operatives; it also fed a new consumer

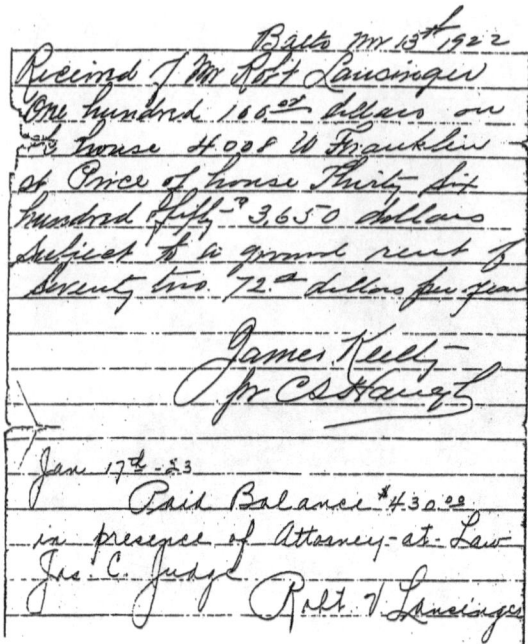

Figure 12. Handwritten receipt for the $100 downpayment on a James Keelty rowhouse costing $3650 in 1922. The house had been purchased by Robert Lansinger at 4008 W. Franklin Street. (The family of Robert Lansinger)

economy that necessitated dramatic growth of the bureaucratic, marketing, and consumer-service sectors. Most of Edmondson's workers filled these latter ranks. Sellers of goods, middle-level managers, clerks in large establishments (both business and government), repairers and installers of consumer goods, or foremen and managers who facilitated the production process—by and large, these were neither the skilled artisan producers of the past nor the semiskilled mass production operatives needed in such large numbers at that time. In this sense Edmondson's residents were indeed a new middle class, a mix of those engaged in the sales, clerical, crafts, and manufacturing positions of an increasingly consumer-oriented economy.[42]

If they constituted a new, expanding occupational profile, were they themselves newcomers to those job categories? The sample block survey indicates that throughout the period under consideration those moving into the Edmondson area had not made a recent change in occupational category. The majority of new residents simply were settling in a neighborhood where occupational level was remarkably similar to their own. For the minority who had made a recent change in work, it usually was a modest one, in almost all cases along a continuum from unskilled to skilled, from manual to nonmanual, or from employee to supervisor or manager—all in a direction that a middle-class culture would have inter-

The Making of a Rowhouse Neighborhood

preted as "upward" mobility.[43] Once settled, the same pattern held during the period of tenure for Edmondson residents: 1) a predominance of occupational stability, and 2) a tendency for change, when it occurred, to proceed along the same continuum, almost never the reverse.

Opportunity for occupational upward mobility tended not to increase over time, however; if anything, it may have declined slightly during the period, not surprising during the Depression decade but somewhat more significant in the postwar boom era.[44] Even though actual rates of opportunity for change may have been leveling or lessening over time, the perception of occupational stability and upward mobility no doubt contributed to the image of a stable, prosperous neighborhood.[45] Both were consistent with the national faith, and both were more likely to be privileges of the middle class than of those whose occupational experience was more marginal.

Amidst the considerable change attributable to rapid and substantial development, it was the social homogeneity of the new neighborhood that gave it definition and that contributed in a significant way to the sense of stability. Young family heads, homeowners, first-generation suburbanites, sharing similar social identifications, Edmondson residents were representatives of a new and growing class in cities such as Baltimore. While the particular occupational mix gave some definition that may have distinguished the housing on the hill from other developing sections of the city, in general the middle-level occupations prevalent in the Edmondson area were those of a new consumer-oriented economy, and Edmondson's workers were its functionaries. Even as older residents moved away or died and newer residents took their places, the social character of the settlers in the Keelty-built neighborhood remained remarkably the same.

Community and Culture in the New Rowhouse Neighborhood

In many ways the streetcar epitomized the character of the new rowhouse community's culture. Every morning most men took it out of the neighborhood to their places of work; once a week or so women rode it downtown to do their major shopping; and when children reached their early teens, they traveled on it to high schools elsewhere in the city. Work, shopping, school, home—to a great extent these functioned as separate spheres, segregated along lines of gender and age and operating in distinctly defined physical spaces. Just as surely, the physical isolation of the new neighborhood and its social homogeneity walled it off from the diversity as well as the historic roots of the larger metropolitan area, only a short streetcar ride away.[46] If the Edmondson area was a version of the emerging middle-class equation, then differentiation seemed to be one important corollary.

As a brand new residential area, the streetcar suburb lacked many of the historic bases associated with community cohesion. Indeed, as might commonly be expected with any new development, one is struck by the general absence of community organizations and institutions (other than the churches), even commercial activities, a lack paralleled by the corresponding absence of collective rituals and traditions. Nevertheless, social homogeneity mirrored an apparent sense of cultural homogeneity. The new Edmondson residents appeared to share levels of collective identity, common understandings, and shared values, which, taken together, functioned to provide some of the structures for coping with the segmentation and novelty of the community.[47] They felt the community to be stable and themselves to be secure because in many ways they were like one another. An exchange with a former resident illustrates this perception: "We moved there in the spring, and in the fall I started to school, and I only went to school three days, [before] they were building the houses on Edgewood Street. [Did that change the neighborhood much?] No, because you knew those people, too."[48] Yet, as a basis for community, social homogeneity—and its reflection in cultural homogeneity—was extremely one-dimensional. And in an urban area where an increasing number of people were socially and culturally "not like us," its premises would be profoundly challenged.

Names and boundaries both are significant for the way in which they reveal levels of collective identity and identification.[49] Interviews with former residents from the period under consideration produce no single, commonly agreed upon name prior to the erection after World War II of the Edmondson Village Shopping Center, which eventually provided a widely accepted appellation. Portions of the development were given names by the developers—Lyndhurst and Wildwood by Keelty, and Allendale by another builder—but for some reason none of these seemed to stick, nor were the boundaries between them all that distinct. The following interchange with two early residents was characteristic:

Orser: The area where you lived, did it ever have a name?
Wallace: No, it never had a name of a development, you mean.
Morgan: But the improvement association we came under, was that the Lyndhurst Improvement Association?
Wallace: The only thing my mother ever joined was the women's civic league, because she was still trying to get that alley.
Orser: But if you told people where you lived, what did you say?
Morgan: I always just said Edmondson Avenue—I always would say just above Hilton Street, because most people know where that is.
Wallace: On the other side of the bridge.
Morgan: Yes, that's it . . .[50]

The Making of a Rowhouse Neighborhood

But if the community's name was vague, its outer boundaries were quite clear in people's perceptions. Natural barriers to the east and north (the wooded ravine cut by the Gwynns Falls valley, which had been designated parkland) and a cemetery on the southwest distinctly limited areas where rowhouse settlement touched adjoining inhabited areas. Due south, where such barriers were absent, social distinctions differentiated the area from the older streetcar suburb of Irvington; similarly, to the immediate west, Rognel Heights, with its frame detached houses, was considered somewhat distinct, but more so were the spacious lots and larger houses of Hunting Ridge and Ten Hills beyond. For an area so clearly demarcated in people's perceptions, its lack of a clear name is surprising. Did it suggest that the new community lacked historical connection with its past (as indeed it did); a natural, physical meeting point or focus, such as a major crossroads or village center (as indeed it did); any strong political or social organizations (as indeed it did); or a degree of self-sufficiency socially and economically (as indeed it did)?

While in many ways Edmondson community culture mirrored the larger national culture, mediated through such increasingly important channels as popular mass media, and perhaps did not differ substantially from other urban variations, it nevertheless is instructive to consider the particular shape cultural beliefs took in a newly formed community with such clearly delineated social characteristics. To a great extent, this was a culture in which gender and age groups each had their defined roles, spheres, and institutions—distinctions undergirded apparently by widely shared norms.

Men's role was employment, and employment universally took them out of the neighborhood. There they encountered the diversity of urban types not present in the residential community, but they did so from a vantage point marked by relative occupational stability, even security. If few would make dramatic occupational changes that might be interpreted as advancement, fewer would view their career as downward occupational mobility. Most worked in relatively large corporate settings, as part of the bureaucratic or the industrial process. Typical employers included McCormick's Spices, the Baltimore and Ohio Railroad, the Baltimore Gas and Electric Company, Chesapeake and Potomac Telephone, Baltimore Transit, Hutzler's Department Store, Sun Life Insurance, and the U.S. Post Office. A minority of residents worked in small shops or businesses or, in the case of craftsmen, in the construction and repair trades, though usually not in a business of their own. Almost none were independent artisans, proprietors, or professionals.

An interview from the latter years of this period suggests that men's work was something not widely shared with other family members, and that, indeed, considerable deference might be paid to the father upon his return home from the career world. As Alice Hughes recalled:

> In the summer when everybody would be outside playing, about 4 o'clock in the afternoon, not only my mother but most of the mothers would round up the children and bring us in and make us take baths, wash hair, and put on clean clothes, so that when our father came home we looked presentable—because they very much believed that if the father had to go out all day and put up with whatever he had to put up with, which was never mentioned, by the way—you assumed that your father was somehow really suffering at his office, whatever he was doing, you knew that he worked all the time, every minute, he was really in there slugging away—and when he came home at the end of the day, the least you could do was look presentable for him.[51]

Apparently, men's roles in the community were defined by a rather clear cultural ideal.[52]

For women, the cultural norm was equally explicit, especially pronounced in the prescribed role for married women with children. The following interchange with two interviewees who grew up in the 1920s and 1930s is a typical illustration:

Orser: Now, what about both of your mothers; did they work at home, or—?
Morgan and Wallace: Home!
Wallace: Home, my gracious!
Morgan: Mothers didn't work back then. My mother didn't work—ever.

The vigor of the response evokes a traditional middle-class ideology that large numbers of households were able to maintain. In many cases Edmondson residents had come from neighborhoods where some women worked outside the home or from family backgrounds in which female members may have had to do so. Clearly, the housewife role was a privilege not available to all socioeconomic classes, and it appears to have been interpreted as a badge of middle-class status by Edmondson's populace.[53]

If widely held as an ideal, especially in the instance of mothers of young children, the limitation nevertheless was far from absolute in practice, and the exceptions were noteworthy. For example, daughters typically continued to live at home for a relatively short period of time after completing school, usually until marriage, and it was generally acceptable—even expected—for them to work outside the home. It also was not uncommon—though apparently less desirable—for women to continue to work after marriage until childbirth. These variations also pointed toward some generational change. While the two women cited above could not have imagined their mothers working outside the home as they grew up, both of them took secretarial courses in high school and found employment in clerical jobs until they were married (and afterwards, in one of the cases). The fact that a substantial minority of Edmondson women did work outside the home suggested economic exigencies, alternative choices, or degrees of latitude that broadened the avowed ideal.

If father's province was the workplace, mother's was the home.[54] Supposedly freed from any prospect of outside employment, she was to devote full time to housekeeping, childcare, shopping, and volunteer activities such as church and school. The same two interviewees reflected on how totally their mothers regarded the kitchen as their preserve:

Wallace: My mother never allowed me in the kitchen. When I got married, I didn't even know how to make a cup of coffee. She never allowed me in the kitchen.

Morgan: Mother . . . used to say, it's too much trouble, let me do it, and when I'd measure anything, she would say, you don't have to have a [measuring] cup; just take any cup. And I'd say, but it's not the same. Oh, my heavens, she just laughed at me, and she'd say, oh, I'll never learn. And even when I got married, she would let me cook, but she'd say, now when you're ready to make the gravy, you don't know how to make it, so I'll make it. She always said that.

Living within a somewhat isolated residential area with few facilities or activities available within its boundaries, women had very limited opportunities for contact that transcended those of block and community.

The Edmondson community had a predominantly young family profile, and children were a substantial ingredient in community life as well as a correspondingly important element in the cultural definition of roles. Elementary and junior high schools were neighborhood-based, but public and parochial institutions reinforced divided religious affiliations, to some degree channeling friendship patterns. It was not until high school that Edmondson area young people left the local environs for an educational setting that brought them into contact with those from other neighborhoods, usually on a basis segregated by gender, race, and, to some degree, class. Though leisure activities were an increasingly important phenomenon of a developing teenage culture, there was "nothing to do" in the neighborhood, a void only partially filled by sports activities and the opening of a local movie theater. It was primarily the churches that stepped into the breach, maintaining recreation or teen centers.[55] In this period the teenage role ended abruptly at the conclusion of high school education, with employment, marriage, and an independent household as expected norms.[56]

If roles were highly differentiated across lines of gender and age with significant portions of individual experience relegated to separate institutions, physical spaces, and sets of social contacts, it was the family unit and the community that somehow had to draw these together. It is difficult to evaluate how well either performed this task, but several observations are in order. First, families, by and large, were somewhat isolated from nearby kinship networks. Second, except for the fledgling churches, there were few established institutional supports for the family unit and few social outlets for men, women, or youth within the community. Finally, in a brand new residential neighborhood, there were few precedents, traditions, or guideposts to set the tone of community life. It might be assumed that these factors, taken together, would place considerable responsibility, even pressure, upon the nuclear family.

Yet, it is the uniformity rather than diversity of cultural norms and values that stands out in the examination of this formative period in the rowhouse community's history. Since these norms and values did not derive from the particular place, we must assume that they were the distillation of common experience, influenced by such factors as mass culture, family background and experience, and prior cultural experience, applied in a particular setting in a similar way by people sharing a common social definition that found expression in a set of shared values.

To a great extent, the community the new families brought into being and whose shared culture gave them sustenance and support was a mirror of themselves and their collective experience. Seeking new residence in a new suburban locale, physically set apart from other sections of the city, they found it in the clearly defined physical and social boundaries of the Edmondson area. First generation suburbanites with prior urban experience in older neighborhoods, they discovered others with similar backgrounds. Middle level on the occupational continuum in a Baltimore economy where their ranks were swelling, they settled into houses next to neighbors who were more likely than not to share very similar job types and economic status. Predominantly young and family-forming, they could expect others on the street to share the same stages of the family cycle. The consequence of so much shared experience and situation was a community whose culture represented a strong strain toward consistency and uniformity—even conformity. That tendency was particularly evident in the steadfastness with which gender and age roles were defined in this formative period. It was as if an unwritten cultural code provided stability and security in a situation that, in fact, was novel and ever-changing. In this community culture, similarity bred familiarity:

Morgan: Oh yes, we knew everybody. I knew people in her block, the 3300 block, and all the people across from us, and on our side, I knew those people. We knew everybody's name.... We even knew people that lived way down on that other side.

Wallace: Everybody was so helpful. If anybody would get sick, you'd always go and help them out. And I know at our house at Christmas we always had open house, and my mother on her dining room table would have this big punchbowl of eggnog, and everybody would go to Elsie's for eggnog for Christmas. And you always visited your neighbors for Christmas. Every neighbor would give a party. But my mother always had hers on Christmas day, because she had to be home; all the family would be coming. But we were very close, all the neighbors.

Simkins: They would get together, for example, on the fourth of July in the backyard.... She was friendly with her neighbors, and on Christmas day it was the tradition, on my block at least, that you went to visit your neighbors—you went to church, and when you came home you went to visit your neighbors, and had a toddy, or something; and then you went home and had your afternoon and evening with your family.

It is always difficult to measure such qualities as closeness, particularly when viewed in considerable retrospect. Yet, streetcar rowhouse living in the new Edmondson area appears to have engendered a degree of neighborly relations and a common culture that was an important and satisfying context for area residents.

The high degree of social homogeneity and the strain toward uniformity that had characterized the neighborhood from its inception reached its zenith during the decade following World War II, when the demand for housing and commercial services spurred the culminating physical development of the area and ushered in an era of apparent suburban satisfaction, the subject of the next chapter. Ironically, these same persistent qualities contributed in significant ways to the rapidity with which the community crumbled in the face of the challenge of racial change at the end of this postwar interlude. In retrospect, the process of urban differentiation that gave birth to the Edmondson area as a white rowhouse enclave provided a social definition that residents took to be the basis for a shared sense of stability and security. In many respects, the Keelty-built rowhouse neighborhood offered a satisfying and rewarding lifestyle, the basis for the strong note of nostalgia that infuses many interviewees' memories. At the same time, however, this definition proved to be not only narrow but—ultimately—fragile and illusory, because it allowed little room for inclusion of others or adaptation to change. Perhaps this one-dimensional concept of community was the greatest cost of the outer-city residential sections Keelty and numerous other developers erected to meet the needs of an expanding metropolis in the first half of the century.

3
Continuity and Undercurrents of Change

> Those were the gold old days.
> —David Graff

> Without a doubt Edmondson Village was the most beautiful shopping center around.
> —Edgar Raines

When the Edmondson Village Shopping Center opened its doors in 1947 on the site of the former Hunting Ridge estate at the top of the Edmondson Avenue hill, it seemed to represent the culmination of the suburban ideal to which residents of the area had aspired. Almost overnight, "the Village" gained acceptance as the community's focal point, providing both a commercial center and a point of reference—not just for shopping, but for meeting, for "hanging out," for identifiability. Significantly, the name gained rapid acceptance as a designation for the community as a whole. Edmondson Village was now complete, as if the addition of the commercial cluster to the residential section fulfilled the image of suburban community life. For white residents of the area during this period before the moment of racial change, these were Edmondson Village's "golden" years.

But they were golden in other senses as well. It was during this period that the postwar construction boom surged to fill up the remaining open spaces within the community, completing the area's physical growth. As if to symbolize this completion, the Keelty Company expanded its rowhouse fiefdom then quietly sold off undeveloped sections and exited the community it had built. By the mid-1950s, the Edmondson Village area was fully developed, with little vacant space remaining for housing or for anything else.

As the postwar housing boom surged beyond outer city neighborhoods like the Edmondson section into new areas outside the city's boundaries, the suburban ideal took on new forms—not rowhouse, but ranch-style. The circumferential beltway provided a new main street for these suburbs, opening prime locations for housing and commercial de-

Continuity and Undercurrents of Change 49

velopment and setting the pace for white middle-class tastes. The Edmondson Avenue area no longer stood as the epitome of the suburban ideal; it was becoming distinctly urban, settled, obsolete—old.

For those coming of age in Edmondson Village in the 1950s these were the golden days of adolescence, and hanging out at the shopping center became a way of teenage life. But if teens set the era's tone, they were by no means preponderant in the population. Indeed, the satisfaction with the area's rowhouse style of living produced a very stable, settled population. After the war, new housing contributed to a degree of rejuvenation and a parallel population surge, but it also masked the fact that this was a distinctly maturing populace. Moreover, the stability of residents' economic status not only was an indication of relative security; it also suggested a possible leveling off of prospects for upward social mobility. Often, when socioeconomic advancement did occur, it produced a decision to move to the newer outer suburbs.

Golden, too, was the community's social character, increasingly precious in the midst of major social changes in urban areas during the postwar period. During the 1940s Baltimore City's African American population grew by more than 25 percent, while the boundaries of segregation expanded hardly at all, placing extreme stresses upon a limited, aging housing market. Not only did Baltimore still hew to a dual housing market; its school system remained segregated, Southern-style. An emerging civil rights coalition was beginning to challenge the foundations of the traditional racial status quo, but its efforts were rumblings seemingly beneath the surface. White suburban rowhouse communities like Edmondson continued to serve as social enclaves, defined by race and class, and there were few signs from within these perimeters that anything would ever be different. Therefore, the entry of the first African American students into the neighborhood's junior high school in 1954 as the result of the city's new desegregation plan, followed the next year by the settlement of the first African American residents in the southeastern corner of the community, produced shock, consternation, and resistance. Change was afoot, yet the narrow social definition of the Edmondson Village community—so consistent and stable over the years—allowed no room for it. As powerful outside forces impinged on the neighborhood's suburban ideal while residents resisted change, their gold appeared to be the work of an alchemist.

The Edmondson Village Shopping Center and the Suburban Ideal

On May 7, 1947, large crowds attended the opening of the Edmondson Village Shopping Center, "a suburban shopping center of harmonious

Figure 13. The Edmondson Village Shopping Center in its early years. The photo was taken by Jerome Adams in 1952. Note the brick wall screening the parking lot from Edmondson Avenue. (The Peale Museum, Baltimore City Life Museums)

design, said to be unique in American city planning," in the words of the Baltimore *Evening Sun*.[1] Advanced billing by the developers, Jacob and Joseph Myerhoff, proclaimed that Edmondson Village would be "the only planned, integrated shopping center in Baltimore, under one ownership and management" with control over the design and construction of the entire project. The announcement boasted of the architectural consideration that had gone into the undertaking: "The Village is in one of the finest residential districts in Baltimore, and with this fact ever in mind, it is being created in a mode of architecture reminiscent of the charming atmosphere of colonial Williamsburg." Recognizing that the postwar period would be the era of the automobile, the developers took pains to point out the care that had been taken to assure adequate parking in a manner harmonious with site and community. The center would consist of a major area department store branch (the second branch of the downtown Hochschild, Kohn firm) as the anchor for as many as forty smaller shops.[2] (See figures 13 through 16.)

The new shopping center occupied approximately ten acres on the site of the former Edward Austin Jenkins estate, Hunting Ridge. The sale of the estate and the intended razing of the house represented the belated end of the earlier gentry era, as the Baltimore *Sun* noted in Sep-

Continuity and Undercurrents of Change 51

Figure 14. The Hochschild, Kohn Department Store rises above the roofline of other shops in the Edmondson Village Shopping Center, shortly after it opened in 1947. Architectural variation was employed to alleviate the straight line of the strip layout. In 1949 an additional section was completed to the east (far right), containing a movie theater and a bowling alley. (Baltimore *Sun*)

tember, 1945: "Another landmark of old Baltimore is about to make way for the modern city. The last bit of Hunting Ridge, pre-Revolutionary estate, has been sold. . . . And so Hunting Ridge bows to modern progress and a new community will come to life."[3]

Edmondson Village Shopping Center partners Jacob and Joseph Myerhoff were major players in post-World War II residential and commercial development in the Baltimore region. Joseph, who was brought to the United States in 1906 by his Russian Jewish parents, got his start as a housing developer in the 1920s and 1930s with projects in northeastern and northwestern Baltimore (Govans, Loch Raven, Northwood, and Falstaff). In 1936 brother Jack (Jacob) joined the business. During World War II the team built an apartment house in the southern section of the city (Brooklyn) with FHA backing, and at war's end they turned to large-scale housing development in the Essex-Dundalk area of southeastern Baltimore County. Edmondson Village was their first shopping center, though later under a separate company Joseph was to build the Westview and Eastpoint centers as well.[4]

The most striking aspect of the center—and the one that won it immediate accolades—was its handsome Williamsburg-style architecture. Essentially a strip in concept, its facade nevertheless provided sufficient variety—with irregular roof lines, bays, dormers, and gables—to evoke its village claim. (See figures 13 and 14.) These architectural features, the creation of architects Kenneth Miller and James Edmunds, masked the actual regularity of the layout. Large chimneys also were borrowed from the colonial Williamsburg prototype, adding charm and variety but serving primarily an ornamental function. Restrictions on the size and placement of signs, requiring them to be flush with the building line and to employ lettering consistent with the architecture, enhanced the traditional appearance.

Though the use of colonial architecture in a suburban shopping center appeared to be novel, the style had been popular throughout the 1930s nationally, in part as a response to the restoration of Colonial Williamsburg with Rockefeller largesse.[5] Builders responded to this trend. For example, in the Wildwood and Lyndhurst residential sections adjacent to the future center, James Keelty introduced local rowhouse colonial adaptations in the 1930s, a style the company continued in its postwar development in the Wildwood section (along Kevin Road and elsewhere). The colonial motif took other west Baltimore manifestations in duplex and detached house form, such as in Hunting Ridge, to the immediate west.

The shopping center's colonial Williamsburg-style design received wide praise from professional critics and the public alike. The Urban Land Institute, for instance, concluded its review with the judgment that the architectural plan gave the effect of "a series of individual buildings, . . . adding considerable charm and distinctive character to the project."[6] Architectural character not only had aesthetic benefits; it served to draw the public as well. This point was not lost on the center's management, which in 1950 noted with pleasure: "Small wonder that so many thousands of Baltimoreans have made Edmondson Village a regular shopping habit . . . [and] that Baltimoreans make it a point of pride to bring out-of-town visitors to Edmondson Village, a landmark of Baltimore progress."[7] With its Williamsburg tone, Edmondson Village had become more than a retail center; it was a west Baltimore attraction.

The second most notable design element was provision for the automobile. Trolley tracks along Edmondson Avenue featured prominently in the foreground of news pictures of the opening in 1947, but the parking

Continuity and Undercurrents of Change 53

Figure 15. Crowd gathered for the dedication of the Hecht Company Department Store on the south side of Edmondson Avenue across from the Edmondson Village Shopping Center, October 15, 1956. The new building did not conform to the colonial architecture of the center, its Williamsburg-style lines visible in the distance. The photographer was John Stadler of the Baltimore *News-American*. (Jacques Kelly)

lots—visible just beyond—were a major consideration in the plan. To accommodate parking for some 550 cars in front, the center was set back on a secondary access road paralleling Edmondson Avenue at a distance of two hundred feet. Considerable care was taken to minimize the visual impact of the parking lot, depressing it below street level (which the Urban Land Institute said "lessens the apparent distance of the buildings from the main highway"); dividing it into three sections, each enclosed with decorative brick walls; and bordering it with shrubbery and trees— all steps intended to be "in keeping with the district in which the Village is located." While usually mentioning convenient trolley access, advertising emphasized the automobile: "All Roads Lead to Edmondson Village" trumpeted a 1951 ad.[8] One-stop shopping was essentially a car-oriented concept.

When Edmondson Village opened in 1947 it boasted the Hochschild, Kohn department store (with two stories; a third was added in 1951) and twenty-nine shops and stores ranging from auto supplies to hardware to shoes to gifts to ice cream to drugs to food—"the most complete shopping selection in Baltimore," in the words of a 1951 flyer.[9] But the developers clearly wanted Edmondson Village to be a center serving multiple functions. The original set of buildings included a clubhouse for community organizations and activities, complete with a seating capacity of 250, a stage, and a kitchen. In 1949, recreational facilities were enhanced by the opening of a movie theater seating 1,250 and a twenty-three-lane bowling alley below. These additions insured that Edmondson Village would become a multipurpose center for the area.

From its inception the center clearly aimed at serving a large region not simply the nearby Edmondson Avenue community. A 1950 flyer proclaimed, "In terms of time, Edmondson Village is really a shopping center for all Baltimore," and a 1951 ad, claiming that "parking is a dream," traced automobile routes from all points of the western side of the city and county.[10]

In 1956 the addition across the street of a Hecht Company branch department store, not bearing the Village's colonial architectural style, further enhanced the regional appeal of Edmondson Village, which to that point had no real competition on Baltimore's west side. (See figure 15.) However, the center's pre-eminence was short-lived: in 1958 Joseph Myerhoff's firm built the Westview Shopping Center some two miles west at the intersection with the new beltway, the first in a series of developments in adjacent suburban Baltimore County that signaled the end of the Village's distinctive but brief period of commercial hegemony.

People who patronized the Edmondson Village Shopping Center during those early years inevitably cite its uniqueness, sometimes insisting that they were told it was the first shopping center in the country, or in the East, or, closer to the actual truth, "the first suburban shopping center on the East Coast."[11] Even the latter claim requires qualification, though the perception of the Village's special status said much about people's feelings toward it. While the suburban shopping center was especially a creation of the postwar era, and Edmondson Village was one of the first of the new breed, it actually was an idea that had been some time in coming. Baltimore had its own early version in the small English Tudor group of stores erected in Roland Park in 1896.[12] On a scale more comparable had been the Shaker Heights Center near Cleveland (early 1920s); Country Club Plaza in Kansas City (begun in 1923); and the Highland

Continuity and Undercurrents of Change

Park Shopping Village in Dallas (1931). The latter most nearly appears as the prototype for centers like Edmondson Village (and several developed in the Los Angeles area just prior to it), with stores grouped away from the street, provision for parking courts to permit maximum access by auto, a scale of forty stores for "one-stop shopping," and a distinctive, harmonious architectural style (in that case Spanish), which lent itself to the village designation. In the Washington, D.C., area and elsewhere the immediate postwar period gave birth to a number of small suburban strip groups of stores with small amounts of parking in front, but Edmondson Village might make fair claim to being the first regional, suburban shopping center of harmonious design on the East Coast—a string of qualifications that area residents found unnecessary.[13]

The Village quickly changed both shopping habits and lifestyles. In an area of such dense residential development, yet with no retail outlets other than the small corner stores—most of them groceries, with a scattering of drugstores, cleaners, and bakeries—the Village offered a range of shopping opportunities that began to wean shoppers—women in particular—from the weekly trolley trip downtown. Moreover, its Food Fair supermarket produced the first competition with the downtown food markets (principally Lexington) and the corner groceries. Marilyn Simkins's mother's shopping habits had been typical for Edmondson area women prior to the Village:

> Wednesday was shopping day for downtown—usually every week or every other week. She went by the #14 streetcar to Howard and Lexington. We had accounts at all the big department stores—Hochschild's, Hutzler's, Hecht's, Stewart's; you could get anything you wanted downtown. She would get clothing or things for the house; or maybe it was just an afternoon for herself. She would wear a dress. . . . You were used to having personal service in your local [grocery] store. You had your weekly order—and you didn't always pay for it either; you had your bill, and you paid it by the week or by the month. I very rarely carried money; if we needed bread, I would trot on down and get the bread, and it was just put right on the ticket; and then my father would pay the bill.

But the opening of the Village changed all that:

> After my father died—he died when I was eleven—when I was thirteen she got her driving license, and that made her more mobile. And the shopping center was open at the Village, and she started to go out to Food Fair to shop and out to Hochschild's, and it widened her scope—having her own car. . . . Hochschild's looked like a wonderland. . . . You could go into Hochschild's and get just about anything you wanted; it was very well stocked, very well maintained. And Hess Shoes was there; and the hardware store; Clayton's Women's Shop; Reamer's

Figure 16. Christmas lights outlining the trees and store fronts at the Edmondson Village Shopping Center, 1958. The photographer was Fred G. Kraft of the Baltimore *News-American*. (Jacques Kelly)

Men's Store. You could go to Edmondson Village and get just about anything you needed, if you preferred not to go downtown. And then Hecht's opened up, and that gave you two choices. . . . I didn't know what a supermarket was until Edmondson Village opened up with Food Fair for the first time.

Not only did shopping habits change, however. The Village provided a much needed community center for a large residential area lacking any natural gathering point. It became a place for meeting people and socializing, whether in the adult mode where such needs could be ascribed to "shopping," or in the teenage and childhood style of "hanging out," aspects to be discussed more fully later. In an area lacking other entertainment facilities, it served that function too. The Edmondson Village Theater soon became the regional cinema, while the older Edgewood Theater was now perceived as a neighborhood movie house. As Joe Slovensky, a teenager in the 1950s, recalls: "The Edmondson Village movies—I never saw a theater that beautiful inside. I mean when we walked in there—where we got the tickets—that was all marble. . . . You walked in the lobby—I mean, that was a lobby, man! And they had big curtains that closed until the next show was ready. And they had the big bay windows that looked out on the parking lot, and that would be open, except at show time, and they would close them. That was a beautiful place!"[14]

In addition to commercial entertainment—the theater and the bowling alley—the Village provided a site for public entertainment functions.

Continuity and Undercurrents of Change

Particularly popular attractions were record hops in the parking area. The center included other drawing cards, two of which elicited frequent mention in interviews: the monkeys in the shoe store window and the lights at Christmas. Bertha Roberts was one of many who recalled the former: "Hess's Shoe Store was on the corner, at the far end. They had a cage with monkeys in it—they were darling. The mamas would take their children to get their shoes, and the children wouldn't misbehave, because they could watch the monkeys."[15] Since Hess also had a barbershop, the monkeys served the same diversionary function for itchy youngsters in the barber's chair. At Christmas the roof lines of the shopping center's buildings were lined with lights, and lights were hung in the trees planted around the parking lot. (See figure 16.) Eunice Clemens echoed the memories expressed by many interviewees: "I remember at Christmas they used to put little Christmas lights on those trees around Edmondson Village. And one time my nephew took us out, and it was so crowded you couldn't even park, so many people came just to see those trees."[16]

The Edmondson Village Shopping Center filled a vacuum, both in the physical development of the Edmondson Avenue rowhouse area and in the lifestyle of its residents. Seeking a village-like atmosphere in their suburban quest, they found it in this cluster of colonial-style shops and stores that gave a sense of completion to their residential environment, not only filling their shopping needs but serving as meeting places and entertainment as well. That there may have been a vacuum is suggested by the rapidity with which Edmondson Village became the focal point for the area, providing it a point of reference, an identity, and a name. Technically Edmondson Village was the shopping center itself, but increasingly the term was used to refer to the community as well. Soon real estate listings pointed out that their properties were "near Edmondson Village Shopping Center," and as early as 1949 they began to label the location simply as Edmondson Village. Early references bearing this appellation were primarily to the immediately adjacent streets; soon real estate listings used the name for the entire hillside rowhouse area. If Keelty provided much of the housing for the developing neighborhood, the Myerhoffs gave it a commercial center: the suburban village seemed complete.

Baltimore's Second Housing Boom

At the end of World War II, the Edmondson area began to experience its second housing boom. Census figures show that from 1940 to 1960 the housing stock of the two census tracts nearly doubled, with the primary

Map 4. Post-World War II Develo[p]ment of the Edmondson Avenue Area, listed by developer or build[er].

1. D.J. Pistorio (late 1940s);
2. Keelty Company (1940s);
3. Edmondale Building Company (late 1940s);
4. Edmondale Apartments (c. 195[0]
5. Wildwood Section 10, Keelty Company (early 1950s);
6. Wildwood Section 10, portion developed by the Kevin Company (1954-1955);
7. Uplands Apartments, Ralph Ch[ ] (c. 1950);
8. Edmonson Village Shopping Center, Joseph and Jacob Myerho[ff] (1947/1949).
(Compiled by the author; map by UMBC Cartographic Services)

growth occurring in the late 1940s following the end of the wartime building moratorium, and in the early 1950s. During the 1940s the portion north of Edmondson Avenue (tract 1608) increased its housing units by 43 percent, and during the 1950s by another 19 percent. South of Edmondson Avenue (tract 2007) expansion was on a slightly smaller, but still impressive, scale: a growth rate of 25 percent during the 1940s, and 16 per cent during the 1950s.[17] Moreover, development of the extensive triangle in the neighborhood's northwest (census tract 2804, just beyond tract 1608) added to the very substantial spurt of new housing. Virtually all of the new housing was rowhouse in type, with the exception of apartments on the community's margins in Edmondale and Uplands. The net effect of this postwar boom was that by 1955 the entire area had been filled in, as densely developed as rowhouse layout would permit. (See map 4.)

The James Keelty Company continued to be the prime mover, though now without its founder, who died in 1944.[18] Continuing as a family firm (under James, Jr., who was joined after the war by younger brother Joseph), the company completed the development the elder Keelty had begun. Few periods in Keelty's earlier operations exhibited the speed and scale of the company's postwar development. The standard Edmondson area rowhouse of this era was colonial in its architectural style, essentially a simple adaptation of the six-room daylight version that Keelty had built in the Edmondson area beginning in the 1920s.

Keelty's colonial daylights from the late 1930s and the postwar period represented a distinct retrenchment from the commodious two and a half-story English-style Wildwood daylights that had run afoul of Depression economics.[19] The slightly smaller and more modest design signaled a market decision to downscale Edmondson area housing, an eventuality with significant consequences for the community's postwar growth and social character.

Many colonial-style features were structurally superficial—old brick, tall windows, white fascia boards. The early colonials (those built until approximately 1950) were characterized by full gabled slate roofs, porches with matching slate, lower front bays at intervals, and varied front door lintels.[20] Many of the colonial rows continued to enjoy the greater distance from the street and the resulting larger yards that had characterized the Wildwood section, but the newer developments omitted garages. An important construction innovation was the use of concrete block as a backing for the brick façades, which Joseph Keelty maintains "was a labor-saving and cost-saving device, without any sacrifice in quality."

However, by 1950 the colonial adaptations were downscaled further. Keelty Company colonial daylights built in the final stages of development represented a simpler version, with a low slate mansard front roof (which masked a nearly flat roof) and a concrete front entry slab (instead of a full covered porch). Moreover, these colonials had smaller overall dimensions.[21] The gradual alteration of the postwar colonials suggest cost-cutting measures and a reversal of the company's earlier pattern of continuing to upscale its housing product in the area, not simply adaptations to changing architectural tastes and building methods.

Edmondson's postwar house-building boom benefited from new mortgage opportunities, just as did new housing elsewhere. Long term FHA-guaranteed mortgages, a product of New Deal Depression-era innovations, provided more protection for consumers while permitting builders to secure construction loans that would roll over into permanent savings and loan financing, thereby freeing up capital for additional new development. After the war, VA financing provided further federal assistance for new housing. Joseph Keelty observed: "There hadn't been any [new housing] built in four years, and people had money—G.I. Bill financing enabled a lot of people to buy houses." As in the prewar period, a high level of home ownership continued to characterize the Edmondson area; 73 percent of the Edmondson housing stock was owner-occupied in 1950.[22]

In the late 1940s the Keelty Company sold off a portion of its undeveloped land. The section north of Wildwood was purchased by developer Leonard Stallman, whose Edmondale Building Company proceeded rapidly to erect its own version of colonial-style rowhouses and the area's first large apartment complex, the Edmondale Apartments. While some Edmondale houses featured the gabled slate roofs of the earlier colonial style, most represented a considerably more spartan version that exhibited few of the architectural embellishments that had made the Keelty colonials distinctive.[23] In 1949 Edmondale houses were advertised as selling for $8,590 [plus a ground rent of $90], "only $890 down for vets." These less expensive colonials were presented with the familiar lure of the suburban ideal: "Everything about Edmondale is aimed at making the family's health, well-being, and happiness go up, up, up! They'll be near schools, churches, playgrounds, the Edmondson Village Shopping Center. They'll be in a modern, sunshiny neighborhood away from the roar of mid-town . . . but only 20 minutes from downtown by streetcar."[24] The Edmondale Apartments, a significant deviation from the otherwise uniform rowhouse character of the area, consisted of two- and three-story buildings, the taller exhibiting front columns as a bow to the neighborhood's colonial theme. By 1950 much of the Edmondale development had been completed, a sizable component of Edmondson's postwar building boom.

In 1950 the Keelty Company began construction in its remaining undeveloped portion of the Wildwood tract—the northwestern triangle along Kevin and Wicklow and their cross streets. (See map 4.) The 1950 master plan for the section (Section 10, Wildwood) indicated dense rowhouse development, providing for 366 new dwellings. (See figure 17.) In 1952 the Keelty Company advertised some of these (Kevin Road) houses in the following manner:

Check the location, the features, the value of the beautiful Keelty-built homes, Edmondson Avenue section, on Kevin Road . . . facing beautiful Gwynns Falls Park. . . . One of the highest elevations in Baltimore—with all suburban advantages and all city conveniences. Near St. Bernardine's Catholic Church and School, a fine elementary school, shopping centers, and transportation. . . . Three large bedrooms—gas-fired automatic hot-water heater—modern kitchen units—tiled bathroom—good sized closets—all modern conveniences and finest trimwork. . . . These homes are selling fast because the price can't be beat for homes of this quality. Only $9800—ground rent $96—on terms as low as $950 down, $72.70 a month to qualified veterans.[25]

Abruptly, however, the Kevin Road development changed hands; in 1954 Kevin Road rowhouses were being advertised by the Kevin Company for

Continuity and Undercurrents of Change 61

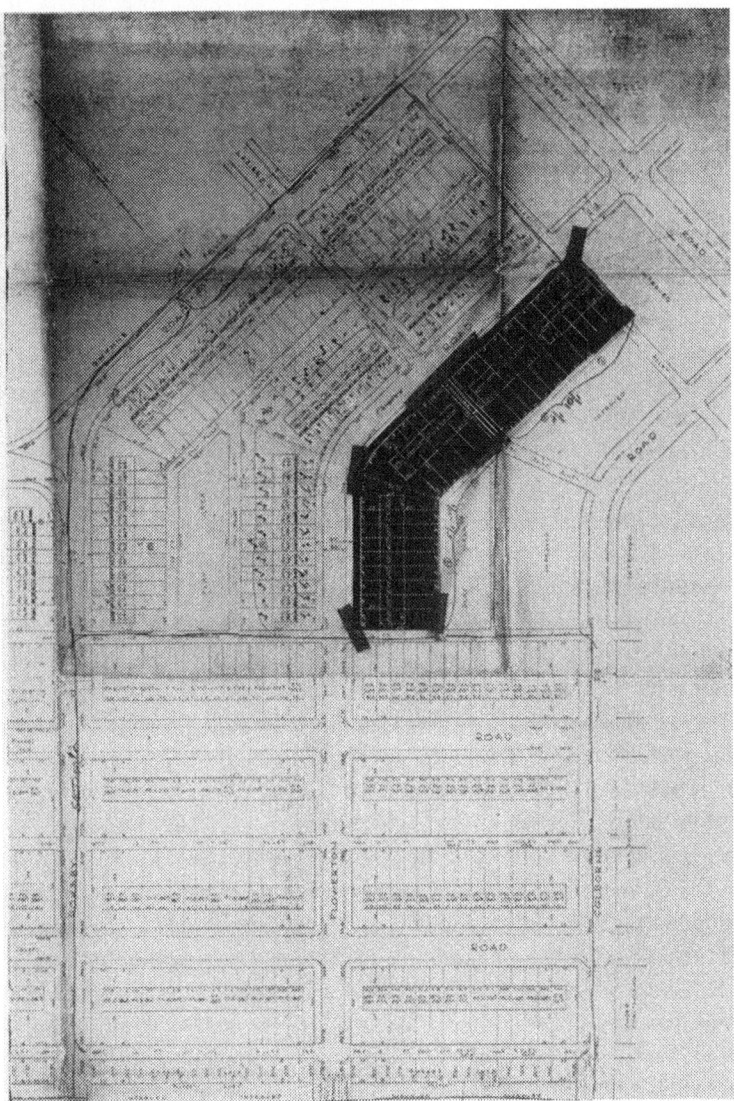

Figure 17. Group Homes Development Plan, Wildwood Section 10, James Keelty Company, November 27, 1950. Lots and house layouts have been planned to accommodate the bends of Flowerton Road and Rokeby Road at the top of the map; note the small tracts, otherwise unusable, designated as "play area." In the lower section the streets are Kevin Road (above) and Wicklow Road (below); adjacent portions of Kevin and Wicklow (to the left [NW] of the section shown here) were sold to the Kevin Company for development in 1954. (Joseph Keelty)

$9500.[26] The Keelty Company had sold its last project in the Edmondson area, where operations had been underway since the early 1920s. The area's prime developer had built a community and moved on before completing the final phase of its plans.

From the early 1930s onward the Keelty Company increasingly had become involved in development beyond the confines of the Edmondson section. During the 1930s and 1940s Rodgers Forge, just north of the city limits in Baltimore County, emerged as its showpiece for rowhouse development, a northern suburban counterpoint to its finest Wildwood rowhouses. In the early 1950s, on the eve of the company's exit from the Edmondson area, development in Rodgers Forge continued strong. In 1955 the Keelty Company announced a new rowhouse development on the west side, beyond the city limits (Frederick Heights). But the firm was about to make a dramatic shift from rowhouse to ranch-style detached house, a move initiated with Colonial Gardens, farther to the west in the Catonsville area of suburban Baltimore County. Split-levels, ranchers, and two-story cottages—these house styles represented considerable upgrading in terms of type and cost, and they appealed to a more affluent clientele.[27] The Keelty Company had adopted a new version of the suburban ideal. Joseph Keelty reflected on the company's change of direction and its eventual abandonment of westside development altogether: "Yes, we finished up Wildwood—sold the last lots there and didn't build it—I would say in the middle fifties. Then we moved up into the Catonsville area; we did several on Frederick Road—Medford, Frederick Heights. Then we did a couple of individual house [developments]—we got away from the rowhouse—one was Keeper Hill [off of Rolling Road]; some in Colonial Gardens. It was probably in the latter fifties that we didn't have any more land out in that area and mainly concentrated in the north end, from Rodgers Forge north."

By the mid-1950s, the Edmondson Avenue area's available parcels of land had been filled in, almost entirely with dwellings of the rowhouse type, and the neighborhood now bordered its own new regional shopping center. The final phases of the postwar housing boom brought some downscaling of the new housing stock and the exodus of the major developer. In retrospect, both eventualities signaled a new era for the community; for the moment, they simply pointed to completion of three and a half decades of development.

The postwar housing boom was not unique to the Edmondson area, of course, but part of a major phenomenon in metropolitan areas nationwide. Fueled by the opportunity for wartime work, large-scale migration to the country's industrial and commercial urban centers induced severe housing shortages. This hiatus, exacerbated by the virtual moratorium on

Continuity and Undercurrents of Change 63

new house construction during the national emergency, produced enormous pressure on the existing housing stock and created an insatiable demand for new housing at war's end. When the postwar period turned out to be an era of prosperity rather than the predicted economic depression, the demand for housing reached unprecedented proportions. The policies of federal lending agencies, which gave preference to new rather than existing housing, helped underwrite the shift to the suburbs.

An important dimension of postwar suburbanization, though one seldom acknowledged explicitly, was the factor of race. In Baltimore and many other cities where African American population had increased significantly during the war but where housing space had remained virtually the same as the result of traditional walls of segregation, African American housing needs intensified. In response to the twin forces of postwar residential expansion and the challenge to traditional racial patterns, the white middle and working classes experienced the proverbial pull and push of suburbanization: the attraction of new housing in a suburban setting, the push of groups from whom they sought social distance.

These social forces combined to produce a wave of suburbanization to eclipse all previous versions. That surge not only fed Edmondson Village's housing boom and accounted for the completion of its development; it also passed it by with a new form of tract home and ranch-style suburbanization that left the city limits behind. The streetcar had been the vehicle of the Edmondson area's early development; the auto ferried the new outer suburbanites.

The halt in new housing during the war made a bad situation even more desperate. Reporter Louis Azrael noted in a 1946 Baltimore *News-Post* column that Baltimore ranked first among the seven largest cities in the dilapidation of its housing stock: "Our housing situation, even if it should return to peace-time levels, would still be worse than in any other of the nation's biggest cities."[28]

At war's end the problem of dilapidated housing remained unaddressed, but the boom in new suburban housing took little time getting underway. Two factors stand out in the postwar figures: 1) the enormous magnitude of new housing activity, and 2) the shift from city to suburban county development. Between 1940 and 1950 the housing stock of the metropolitan area as a whole (SMSA) expanded by 31 percent—much of it occurring in the latter 1940s—and between 1950 and 1960 by an additional 39 percent. Figures for Baltimore City alone, though showing growth rates of 17 and 18 percent for the two decades, respectively, were less dramatic.[29] Increasingly, Baltimore City's development was leveling off or declining as available areas filled up, and nearby county suburban areas were the hot spots for residential development. As Frank Henry observed in a 1950 *Sun* article on the role of developers in the creation of new neighborhoods: "For the house builders it has been a long, gigantic game of leapfrog, going forward by fits and starts. They build one neighborhood on the city's perimeter and leap over that to build another beyond. And now that little land is left within the city for mass housing developments, the contractors have gone into Baltimore and Anne Arundel counties."[30] Relentlessly, the developing edge of the urban area was moving beyond the city's political boundaries.

By 1949 the postwar building boom was in full swing. "New Homes for 72,000" blared a headline in the *Sun*, which estimated that twenty thousand new living units in the metropolitan area in 1948-49 would be enough to house the entire population of Silver Spring, then considered Maryland's second largest city. A water bureau official expressed the belief that the number of dwelling units being erected "must equal or exceed the number undertaken in the boom years of the twenties."[31] In 1950 the *Sun* noted "Heavy Moving Underway," citing estimates by overworked moving companies that the current volume of housing relocations represented "the biggest mass movement of tenants since World War II broke out."[32] An interviewee involved in the real estate industry during this period observed that the combination of pent-up demand, reasonable prices, available financing (including FHA and VA loans), and new housing opportunities created an unprecedented housing market; as he put it, "The 'Open House' replaced sex and baseball as the national pastime."[33]

Though the rowhouse continued to be a popular housing choice, it was being challenged by apartments and by newer detached housing styles. Carroll Williams, *Sun* real estate reporter, estimated that one-quarter of the new units were apartments, mostly of the garden type, meaning that they were two or three story structures, accessible by stairs rather than elevators.[34] In 1950 he reported that some thirteen thousand apartment units were recently completed or underway, enough to house fifty thousand people. The largest such project, Westland Gardens, lay just beyond the city limits on the southwest side in Baltimore County. The second largest, Uplands (built by Ralph Chiaro), adjoined the Edmondson Village Shopping Center, occupying a portion of land formerly part of the Uplands Estate from which it took its name. The smaller Edmondale Apartments project on the other edge of the Edmondson Village section contributed to the great increase in apartment availability on the west side, though Williams commented that a great deal of the apartment development activity was on the city's northern fringe.[35]

Demand for the ever-popular Baltimore rowhouse continued to be strong, primarily the daylight "group home" version, which departed from the earlier uninterrupted row by clustering groups of rowhouses and provided for front yard set-back. As the *Sun* noted: "Well-lighted, well-ventilated and with trees on their lawns, they were a far cry from the blind-roomed dwellings of the turn of the century."[36]

But most popular in the rapidly developing suburban areas at the city's edge and beyond were detached houses. Tract frame bungalows offered the most economical version. More desirable, if they could be afforded, were what Carroll Williams referred to in 1949 as "ramblers": "the West's sprawling, squat, ranch-type houses."[37] By the late 1950s Williams was claiming in *Sun* articles that new house construction was almost evenly divided between the rowhouse (or group house) and detached houses (bungalows, ranchers, or ramblers). The trend, he said, was toward larger versions, with design reflecting the interest in "outdoor living with inclosed gardens, covered patios, ornamental fences, ponds and pools, barbecue pits and outdoor fireplaces"—and carports![38] Clearly 1950s-style suburbanization was leaving Edmondson's rowhouses behind in style, space, and cost.

Highway expansion struggled to keep pace with the new wave of suburbanization and provided it with fresh impetus. When Baltimore County community associations resisted plans for a metropolitan beltway in 1953-54, highway officials countered that the proposed road was not intended primarily as a bypass but that instead it was needed to reduce congestion in the rapidly growing suburban sector, contending that 85 percent of the traffic would be intracounty, not interstate.[39] The highway, begun in 1954 and finally completed in 1962, indeed contributed to a "boom around the beltway"; as one regional publication put it: "The new beltways for motor vehicles around Baltimore and Washington were conceived mainly as by-passes but have in fact fundamentally altered the real estate and business structures of the two metropolitan areas."[40] A 1965 study by the James Rouse Company concluded that the Baltimore Beltway, the first circumferential highway completed under the federal interstate program, had generated "fully two-thirds of all major retail development in the Baltimore area in the past five years."[41]

The Racial Geography of Housing in Postwar Baltimore

While suburban development was streaming beyond the Edmondson Village section on the western side, equally significant social and economic pressure was building up to its east. Between 1930 and 1950 Baltimore City's African American population increased by nearly 60 percent (from 142,106 in 1930 to 165,843 in 1940 to 225,099 in 1950). Yet, during the Depression decade and the World War II years the racial boundary of Baltimore's African American district remained virtually unchanged. On the west side in both 1930 and 1940 it ran along Fulton Avenue south of Edmondson Avenue and along Pulaski Street north of Edmondson; by 1950 there had only been modest movement, shifting the four additional blocks west to Pulaski below Edmondson Avenue.[42] (See map 1.) Although Pulaski Street was only a mile from the Edmondson area's eastern edge, this relatively small degree of change may not have appeared to represent a fundamental alteration in the racial geography of housing. Even as the ghetto boundary began to ease westward, residential segregation continued to prevail. In 1950 seventeen census tracts in the westside ghetto had African American percentages over 75 percent (5 more than in 1940), while three had more than 50 percent. North or west of the new line no census tract had as much as a 25 percent African American presence.

Residential segregation not only limited the geographical options available for African American residency in Baltimore but restricted African Americans to some of the oldest, poorest sections of the city as well. In the early 1940s plans for an expressway to run west from the city's center along the Franklin-Mulberry streets corridor, right through the heart of the west Baltimore ghetto, were justified both because the highway would provide relief from automobile congestion and because it would aid in "the rehabilitation of blighted areas." Writing on behalf of the Commission on the City Plan, J.D. Steele argued: "This highway will cut through the heart of the worst slum area, demolishing in the west half of the freeway approximately 2500 dwelling units, and a trip afoot, making detours into the alleys, will be sufficient to convince most people of the need for cleaning out these slum areas."[43] In a series of articles on the proposed expressway and its impact in the *Sun* in 1944, Frederick Kreller noted that along the route one found some white residents whose "homes are well tended despite their age." He observed however,: "As the [proposed] freeway passes beyond Fulton Avenue, and into the section occupied by Negroes deterioration becomes more evident. Homes are very badly in need of repair and paint; dead rats lie in the street where they were crushed by automobiles; alleys are littered with debris and foul-smelling garbage; lots where homes formerly stood are covered with a thick layer of ashes. . . . Many of the houses in this section are unfit for humans."[44] That same year the Citizens Planning and Housing Association released a report estimating that between 1940 and 1944 there had been "a continuous in-migration at an average rate of 300 to 400 Negroes a month," yet during the same period "only one additional dwelling unit for each fifteen additional Negroes" had been added to the housing stock.[45]

One postwar response to the acute conditions portrayed by such assessments was the erection of public housing projects, a solution that eliminated slum housing through urban renewal while it perpetuated the segregation of the ghetto. By 1955 the Housing Authority of Baltimore announced plans for three major public housing complexes designed to accommodate 1,668 families. In 1957 work began on one of these projects on the city's west side, Lexington Terrace, with one fourteen-story and four eleven-story apartment buildings.[46] In the early 1960s another major complex, the George P. Murphy Homes, was erected nearby. These highrise dream projects of the 1950s and 1960s all too soon would become the new slums of later decades.

The war years and their aftermath produced ambivalent economic prospects for African Americans. While many suffered from dislocation and traditional limitations on job opportunity, a sizable number benefited from employment expansion in such formerly restricted areas as industry and government.[47] Moreover, the antitotalitarian and antiracist ideology of the war effort helped to foster a climate for a formative civil rights challenge to segregation and discrimination. These changes heightened expectations for African Americans, yet hopes remained unfulfilled in the area of housing, even for those whose improved economic status provided them the financial means to seek new opportunities. Carroll Williams, writing in the *Sun* in 1955, called attention to the continued neglect of African American housing needs: "The Negro population of Baltimore has always lived in hand-me-downs." Since the dramatic postwar boom in new house construction was for whites only, he argued, African Americans with improved economic status had no alternative except to try to push into secondhand housing in surrounding white areas. Williams felt that the relationship between African American housing needs and a whites-only building boom was direct: "When the history of home building in this decade is written, it will be seen that the improved status of the Negro is one of the chief factors behind our huge home-building boom. For though practically all of the home building has been undertaken with white occupancy in mind, it has been the pressure of the Negro population on the older houses of white occupancy, that has made such a ready market for the new."[48]

As racial change began to occur on the west side, it conformed to familiar patterns of residential race relations in the dual housing market. When African Americans settled on formerly all-white blocks, whites followed long-time Baltimore patterns through either resistance or flight. The former was evident, for example, when in 1948 the *Sun* reported on a home on the west side (in the 1400 block of West Fayette Street, near Franklin Square) that had been vandalized when an African American family moved in, its windows broken and the letters "KKK" smeared on the outside.[49] Flight appeared to be more common than overt resistance. For instance, in that same year the congregation of Christ Methodist Church, located at North Avenue and Retreat Street since 1895, sold its building to an African American Baptist church and merged with the Edmondson Avenue Methodist Church, an action clearly signaling the expansion of African American residency into a section on the northern fringe of the prewar racial boundary and the flight of the white congregation's members westward.[50] While flight may not have been on a large scale from a metropolitan perspective in the late 1940s and while it may still have seemed distant to residents of Edmondson Village, it nevertheless could be dramatic in those sections directly affected. One African American interviewee, Samuel Brown, recounted the first postwar movement of African Americans westward and the panicked white response:

Black people started moving out of the confined areas somewhere around forty-seven or forty-eight, but what would happen was that whites would evacuate a block or two blocks, and black people would move in. The evacuation would take place first. I remember streets like Fulton Avenue, Monroe Street—they were once totally white, and they went through the transition and changed somewhere between forty-six and forty-nine—that was the time I was in service—when I went in, there were no black people and when I came out they were black streets. . . . But it wasn't integration . . . in the early phases, it was an evacuation.[51]

A survey of real estate advertisements in the Baltimore *Sun* reflects the changing residential pattern on the west side.[52] The immediate postwar years brought an increase in listings for houses for sale under the designation "colored," as real estate firms either reflected or created changing residential patterns in choosing to market houses under this rubric. Often ads noted that the house already was vacant, confirmation that evacuation indeed had taken place. The specification of vacancy implied there need be no direct contact between former (white) residents and new buyers, whether aspirant African American homeowners or those wishing to invest in African American-occupied housing.

Continuity and Undercurrents of Change

The year 1950 marked a watershed in the racial geography of the west side, if one is to use the ads as an indicator. Prior to that year few listings advertised any housing west of the Fulton Avenue/Pulaski Street boundary as "colored." However, in 1950 the line was breached with notices for houses in the 2200 block of West Saratoga Street immediately to the west, while farther to the northwest notice was served of "Colored Homes—Walbrook Specials." A year later housing in the 2500 blocks of westside streets (Edmondson Avenue, West Fayette Street, West Lanvale Street) was advertised as "colored," and in one more year the same was true for the 2700 and 2800 blocks (Edmondson Avenue, Ellicott Driveway, Harlem Avenue). In 1953 a house in the 3000 block of Lanvale Street was referred to as one of "Walbrook's Outstanding Colored Buys." Walbrook, the next neighborhood to the east of the Edmondson Village area, suddenly was experiencing massive racial change. Within a period of only two to three years the city's racial boundary had shifted nearly a mile westward. Significant African American settlement was now occurring on the adjacent hill just across the Gwynns Falls ravine from the Edmondson area's boundary.

Challenges to the Racial Status Quo

The breach in old lines of residential restriction represented a visible sign of changing times at the moment when a variety of forces were coalescing to challenge the racial status quo in Baltimore and elsewhere. While initially these seemed little likely to impinge on the rowhouse preserve where notions of social insulation prevailed, they represented a significant undercurrent in the postwar social climate.

Compared to some cities, Baltimore had a long tradition of civic activism and political involvement among its African American population.[53] By the turn of the century the shift from earlier residential patterns of dispersion to increased ghettolike concentration on the near west side had helped to make the section called Old West Baltimore the base for a number of important institutions, particularly churches, which served as the center for community cohesion and action. The desperate conditions of the 1930s provided fertile ground for challenges to the social and economic manifestations of segregation and discrimination, launching a civil rights movement that continued its assaults for the next several decades. Karen Olson and others have called attention to the important working coalition established in the 1930s between Lillie Carroll Jackson, who was elected president of the dormant Baltimore branch of the NAACP in 1935;

Carl Murphy, Jr., publisher of the locally produced *Afro-American*, which provided publicity for the movement; and the Interdenominational Ministerial Alliance, a politically powerful association of African American clergy. Under Jackson's leadership and with the support of the other two partners, the Baltimore branch became an energetic grassroots organization, its membership by 1946 making it the largest chapter in the country.

During the 1930s and the years of World War II this coalition, sometimes joined by white progressives, launched a series of assaults on segregation and discrimination. In the early 1930s protests were mounted against stores in the African American community that refused to hire African Americans, rallying around the slogan, "Don't Buy Where You Can't Work." Effective voter registration campaigns dramatically increased the size and influence of the African American electorate and helped secure the victory of Republican candidate Theodore McKeldin as mayor in 1943; McKeldin in turn appointed African Americans to important positions in the city administration and opened some jobs in city employment. Protests against lynchings on Maryland's Eastern Shore galvanized the African American community in the 1930s, as did demonstrations against brutality by the Baltimore police force during World War II. The Baltimore branch of the NAACP filed suit against residential restrictive covenants; though the case was lost in the Maryland Court of Appeals in 1938, the U.S. Supreme Court ruled against the constitutionality of such state-sanctioned discrimination ten years later.

Educational opportunity remained a central concern, especially for Lillie Carroll Jackson, whose own political activism stemmed in part from the indignation she felt when her own daughters were denied admission to Maryland institutions of higher education. Beginning in the 1930s the NAACP's legal counsel, Baltimore-born Thurgood Marshall, initiated a series of suits against educational discrimination that eventually proved successful in challenging the segregation of professional and graduate schools at the University of Maryland (including the School of Law, to which he himself earlier had been denied admission) and laid the groundwork for the landmark 1954 Supreme Court *Brown* decision.

In the postwar period the campaign found new energy; the coalition expanded to include broader white participation and added newer organizations, such as CORE. Targets of protests and demonstrations in Baltimore included downtown theaters, department stores, and eating establishments, with breakthroughs eventuating on all three fronts by the mid-1950s. Further employment progress occurred in 1953 with the ending of racial discrimination for jobs in the city's fire department.

Education again took center stage as the strategy of mounting a national legal attack on segregated schooling had its local counterpart in challenges to racial separation in the Baltimore City schools. In 1945 the Baltimore branch of the NAACP demanded a parallel African American administration if the school system remained segregated, but in subsequent years its efforts focused upon gaining entry for qualified African American students to specialized programs currently available only to whites and where no parallel Jim Crow program existed.[54] This strategy challenged the "separate but equal" doctrine; the potential cost of providing such programs on a divided basis upped the financial ante and caused moderate whites to question whether the price of segregation was worth the trouble. The approach bore fruit in 1952 when the Baltimore Board of School Commissioners confronted the issue posed by sixteeen young African American men who had applied to Baltimore Polytechnic Institute, the public school system's well-regarded selective male-only secondary school for math and engineering. As the board saw it, the questions posed were twofold: 1) whether the youth qualified by Poly's admission standards, and 2) whether a comparable program could be established at all-African American Frederick Douglass High School. When the board was advised that ten men qualified, the debate focused on the issue of comparability, and on these grounds the board on a 5 to 3 vote decided to admit the ten to Poly, a decision supported by the president of the board (an appointee of the mayor, Thomas D'Alesandro, Jr.) and Governor McKeldin. Integration of Poly proceeded with little fanfare, and subsequent challenges were mounted for African American admission to other selective programs at all-female Western High School and at Mergenthaler Vocational and Technical School.[55]

These developments meant that the May 17, 1954, Supreme Court ruling that segregation in schooling was unconstitutional did not come as a complete surprise in Baltimore, and local officials, pressed by the civil rights coalition, moved quickly to address the issue. At its regular June 3, 1954, meeting, the board received the opinion of the city solicitor that the Supreme Court decision took precedence over state segregation statutes, and the School Board, with little debate, unanimously adopted a resolution endorsed by School Superintendent John H. Fischer and Board President Walter Sondheim that "our system should be conformed to a nonsegregated basis to be in effect by the opening of schools in September of this year." The provision for immediate implementation of the open enrollment plan gave Baltimore the distinction of being the first segregated school system to approve a plan to integrate, and the following fall 3 percent of the city's African American children elected to enter formerly all-white schools. Clearly the growth of a broad-based civil rights coalition and the support of key city elected officials and administrators were essential elements in these developments.[56]

While the 1954 Supreme Court decision and the subsequent Baltimore School Board action may not have been unexpected for careful followers of civil rights issues, the inevitability of successful challenges to the prevailing racial status quo, so apparent in retrospect, was by no means a given at the time for many white residents of Baltimore in communities such as Edmondson Village—or elsewhere in the nation, for that matter. In what seemed to be a golden era of postwar prosperity and well-being, the prospect of fundamental changes may have appeared distant and remote, rumblings beneath the surface with little likelihood of altering familiar patterns. Yet, the suburban housing boom and challenges to the racial status quo represented twin forces of metropolitan change occurring in the postwar era with potentially profound consequences for the rowhouse neighborhood.

The Demographics of the Village's Golden Age

The postwar Edmondson Village community experienced the paradox of simultaneous stability and growth. The sense of stability resulted from the strong tradition of residential permanence and the general persistence of the neighborhood's social character. Yet, population growth, a consequence of housing expansion and the baby boom, provided a sense of youthfulness, vigor, and vitality.

Population bulged in the years during and following World War II, increasing overall by nearly 40 percent between 1940 and 1950 (from 11,779 to 16,388 in the two tracts); a more modest 10 percent growth (to 18,074) occurred between 1950 and 1960.[57] Moreover, development on the northwest (the triangle between Walnut Avenue and the old city line west of Woodington, not included in the two census tracts) further contributed to the population surge of the contiguous Edmondson rowhouse area.

As communities elsewhere, Edmondson Village experienced a baby boom. Between 1940 and 1950 the number of children under five years old more than doubled, and the number of those age five through nineteen increased substantially, though less dramatically. The growing numbers of young residents helped to give the community a youthful cast and provided the basis for a suburban-style teenage culture in the 1950s. At the same time, a substantial proportion of the population was maturing. For

Continuity and Undercurrents of Change 73

example, between 1940 and 1950 those over age fifty-five also increased significantly in number (from 1,684 to 2,655), while their fraction of the total remained at a relatively constant one in seven.

The sample block survey provides some insight into this dynamic of stability and growth. Blocks settled prior to World War II remained remarkably stable residentially into the late 1940s and early 1950s. In 1940, for instance, 62 percent of residences in the block study sample were inhabited by their original householders and 38 percent by second householders. In 1950, first householders still constituted 56 percent and second householders 33 percent on the sample blocks, suggesting a high degree of residential stability.[58] The 1950 census, which did not discriminate between new and existing housing, found that in Edmondson Village 86 percent had resided in the same house the previous year, close to the percentage (84) for the city as a whole. Given such residential tenure, new housing construction provided the major opportunity for younger residents attracted to the area.

Edmondson Village's newcomers continued to follow the same migration paths as their predecessors. In 1940 and 1950 their places of previous residence were virtually identical; almost entirely from the Baltimore area, most either moved from neighborhoods on the west side closer to the city or from other parts of Edmondson Village. However, shortly after the war's end the direction of out-migration changed markedly. While most moves during the 1940s continued to be to other parts of Baltimore City, during the 1950s most were westward to suburban county areas.[59]

As housing expanded and population grew, the occupational character of the Edmondson Avenue area's wage earners remained remarkably consistent. In 1940, 57 percent were in white-collar occupations; ten years later the percentage was 56. Among men, slightly more than half had white-collar occupations in 1940; slightly less than half did so in 1950—but the difference was insignificant.

In 1940, at the end of the Depression decade, 29 percent of Edmondson area women were in the paid labor force (women constituting 28 percent of the total). No doubt the war years brought some increase (census data provides no basis for making this determination with certainty, though there is little indication that Edmondson Village women were likely candidates for roles as "Rosie the Riveter"), but in 1950 female labor force participation had risen only slightly to 32 percent (30 percent of the total). However, the continued pattern of work outside the home by a substantial minority of women suggested that the traditional norm was not so absolute as community ideology would have it. Most who did so were employed in lower level pink-collar positions; in 1950, for example, approximately half of women workers were in clerical occupations.[60]

Also remaining consistent was the strong rate of home ownership, which had been a high 63 percent even at the end of the Depression decade in 1940 and rose to 73 percent by 1950. Housing values declined during the Depression, but rebounded in the postwar period. The estimated median value of homes in tract 1608 in 1940 had been $3,528; ten years later it stood at $9,142. In 1940 the estimated value for Edmondson Avenue owner-occupied houses was 18 percent above the city median; in 1950 it was 22 percent higher.[61]

Finally, to this portrait of relative stability amidst change must be added the ingredient of race. Edmondson Village's rowhouses were still white-only. In 1950 just forty-four African Americans resided in the combined tracts—living on the margins of the area—the exact number as twenty years previously in 1930. (See map 2.)

Rowhouse Culture in the Postwar Years

Until World War II, suburbanization typically took two forms. One was represented by elite developments such as Baltimore's Roland Park and Guilford, which promised elegance, privacy, and exclusivity for a social elite. Rowhouse suburbanization constituted the other principal option. Built on a much more modest scale, with a high degree of density and without the parklike setting of the classical suburban ideal, rowhouse developments nevertheless offered an analog to the more affluent version in their promise of a family-oriented environment, social homogeneity, and respite from urban life. And they did so at a cost that a broad middle-income cross section could afford.

Post-World War II suburbanization, however, offered new alternatives to this polar choice. As buses replaced trolleys and as private automobiles proliferated, the density of rowhouse suburbia was at once less necessary and less appealing. Bungalow developments in the immediate postwar years departed from the attached row to provide detached dwellings set on surrounding yards, though often on an extremely modest scale, as if developers only timidly recognized the potential to be tapped by expanded house and yard size. By the early 1950s, however, ranch-style suburbanization realized this opportunity, providing greater floor space (frequently on a single-floor or split-level plan, which eliminated the stair-climbing of traditional two-story rowhouse and detached house design), larger yards, and accommodations for the automobile—driveways,

Continuity and Undercurrents of Change 75

carports, garages. While postwar ranch-style suburbanization had its wide variety of cost and class, compared to the rowhouse suburbs it more closely resembled the earlier, upper-class version in its appeal to space, amenity, and differentiation. Privacy was another matter. Physical separation of housing, large yards, and frequently isolated settings afforded conditions conducive to social distance, but life cycle considerations (the prevalence of young families) and the common circumstances of suburban pioneering (cut off, for instance, from family networks) often promoted a passion for togetherness that became a 1950s stereotype.[62]

Edmondson Village, with its own early postwar housing and youth booms, in some respects mirrored these postwar suburban trends, its rejuvenation and family oriented-lifestyles resembling newer outer suburban versions. Moreover, Edmondson Village continued to offer the suburban assurance of social homogeneity. In these respects, therefore, postwar Edmondson Village shared in the burgeoning suburban culture of the late 1940s and early 1950s, its lifestyles and social patterns congruent with the white middle-class mainstream whose economic prosperity and social satisfaction seemed to set a golden tone for the era. The realities, of course, were that rowhouse suburbanization would have a hard time competing for upwardly mobile aspirations. Moreover, the social and economic barriers that had insulated outer city rowhouse suburbs from the changing demography of the inner city would prove transitory and illusory. Still, the logic of suburban differentiation went virtually unquestioned—in Edmondson Village, as in the rest of white suburban America.

It is not surprising, therefore, that many white interviewees recall the postwar period as a golden era for Edmondson Village. Life in the Village sufficiently resembled trend-setting suburban styles to make Villagers part of the mainstream, and the prospect of change seemed remote enough to have played little role in the collective consciousness. In these respects, retrospective interviews with residents recalling this era no doubt closely resemble perceived social reality. At the same time, however, such recollections may exaggerate the degree of satisfaction and well-being interviewees associate with the period, not only because of the inevitable aura of nostalgia that must be sifted when considering any oral history narrative but particularly because many interviewees participated as young parents or as youth in the dominant family-oriented suburban culture that they view as the hallmark of the period. Further, there can be no doubt that the trauma of eventual massive racial change has contributed substantially to the memory of the period immediately prior as a golden, yet lost, epoch.

Interview recollections portray a postwar reaffirmation of the suburban version of traditional family values and gender roles that had characterized the community's aspirations since its establishment as a rowhouse preserve in the 1920s, as discussed in chapter 2. Elaine Tyler May has argued that in the aftermath of the Second World War, middle-class America embraced a resurgent domesticity through young marriages, parenting, and traditional roles for women as housewives and men as breadwinners: she attributes these trends to the dominant preoccupation of the period with security and containment.[63] Edmondson Village seemed in the mainstream of these trends, displaying its own version of an ideal of domesticity that considered it normative to send men into the city each day to provide income for their families and to assign women, as wives, the care of home and children.

For both men and women, the increasing expectation was the completion of education through high school. Few Edmondson Village youth of either gender went on to college. Joe Slovensky commented on the expectations for young men in the immediate postwar period:

A lot of them quit school and went in the service. That was a thing to do then—oh, to heck with school. But you know back then if you had a high school diploma it was like a college degree. So nobody said to me, well, what about college? That wasn't even mentioned. If somebody went to college, it was somebody who had money, or something, back then. . . . So, I would say maybe 50 percent of us quit school and went in the service. That was *the* thing. And then come back, and wear your uniform up to the Village. Go up the bowling alley and show off your uniform.

While Slovensky may have overestimated the high school drop-out rate for young men in an era when secondary school completion was becoming normative, clearly the expectation of college education was not widely shared. Among Edmondson Village's adults (25 years and older) in 1940, only 3.4 percent had attended four years of college, and in 1950 the percentage had risen to only 5 percent.[64] The unlikelihood of college education was even greater for young women, in the view of Edith Romaine: "Especially with the girls, there was no way in my mind I wanted to go to college. It wasn't talked about that much. Not many of us did, the women. . . . There were a few who went [to work]. I did work a year before I was married, and the only reason was because he [her fiancé, who was in the service] wasn't here; most likely, if he was here, I'd have gotten married even younger. See at that time we weren't exposed to as much as today—you know, the careers, especially for women."[65]

After high school, men entered the labor force directly, while women might work outside the home until marriage, or possibly until childbirth, but generally not thereafter. For many families, the pattern of separation of roles by place that had characterized the prewar era was reasserted in the postwar period. As one interviewee recalled her own family life:

> My mother was a housewife, and my father was an accountant downtown. He went to work everyday on a bus. . . . We did not own a car until I was seventeen, so everywhere we went we either walked, went by cab, or went by bus. [We] rarely left the neighborhood. I can't remember needing a car—it was not essential in those days. My father had a three-block walk to the bus stop—he thought it was good exercise. If we went shopping, we walked to the Village. If we went downtown, we took the bus. On those occasions when we had to go out of the neighborhood—like to a doctor or relative—we took a cab, but . . . that didn't happen real often. Most of the time we stayed in the community.[66]

The reassertion of the community's traditional separation of work roles according to gender was reflected in the fact that the percentage of women participating in the labor force increased only marginally between 1940 and 1950. A significant percentage of the three in ten of Edmondson area women who were employed outside the home were in their early adult years prior to probable marriage, or young married women prior to likely childbirth. For example, Madge Cooper, who had been in the business course in high school, observed:

> Oh, yes, we didn't really have an option [except to work], I don't believe, at the time—until we were married. Ultimately, we hoped that when we married we wouldn't have to work again, because we didn't at that time aspire to real careers. I worked until I was married about a year, and then my husband went into the military, shortly after we were married, because he was part of the Korea [contingent], and I went off to live with him for a year, and when I came back I probably fully intended either to be pregnant or—When I came back I probably really wouldn't have considered going back to work—but I did, on a part-time basis, so we could buy our first house, and I believe that's where most of us were at that time; when we worked, we worked for a specific reason, and when we had attained that goal, then we stopped working.[67]

Some who worked outside the home were married women with children, but usually the circumstances were considered special. Marilyn Simkins, for instance, reported that her mother always worked as a nurse, largely due to her father's poor health. Agnes Malone recalled several sisters who were "maiden ladies" and worked in department stores but contended that it was "just automatically accepted" that wives, particularly those with children, should stay home, except in what were considered atypical situations: "There was one woman down the street with children, and she worked, but she was a single parent. That's the only one that I remember. Everybody else's mothers were at home."[68] While these various special circumstances apparently did not represent a fundamental deviation from past conventions, they indicate that after a decade and a half of Depression and war, the prevailing norm could nevertheless accommodate broad exceptions. Still, the dominant note in Edmondson Village's postwar experience was the reassertion of traditional patterns as part of the return to normalcy, and the era's relative prosperity made the norm attainable for many of the area's families.

Housing and population growth produced expansion for institutions that provided for family-centered needs, such as churches and schools. For example, Edmondson Methodist Church in 1946 reported a severely overcrowded Sunday School facility and in 1951 dedicated a new educational building to serve these needs. Its congregational membership reached an all-time high in the early 1950s.[69]

For families and their young members, the churches served as hubs both of religious and social life, their youth centers especially seeking to address a need not otherwise provided by institutional means in the community. Though the populace was relatively evenly divided between Protestants and Roman Catholics—a division that separated some young people not only in church but in school—it was the Catholic Youth Organization at St. Bernardine's that most successfully attracted a broad spectrum of community youth, Catholic as well as non-Catholic. As Marilyn Simkins, whose family belonged to Christ Edmondson Methodist, recalled:

> Now, I was not Catholic—most of my friends were—I went to Christ Edmondson, which offered little for young people. . . . St. Bernardine's had a very active CYO, one of the best, if not the best, in the area. They had a lot to offer kids—they had girls' and boys' basketball teams . . . I think it was the priests, the rector—Msgr. Vaeth—he loved kids. They were scared of him, but he really liked kids, and I think he liked to have a very active parish. . . . As far as social life, for myself as a teenager, St. Bernardine's was it—for Edmondson Village. . . . So I danced at St. Bernardine's on Saturday night, and worshipped at Christ Edmondson on Sunday morning.[70]

Schools experienced overcrowding, and school construction lagged considerably behind need. In the early postwar years Lyndhurst Elementary School gained an annex, which housed a gym, cafeteria, and additional classrooms. By the early 1950s high school enrollment, until this point accommodated entirely by citywide schools outside the neighbor-

Continuity and Undercurrents of Change

Figure 18. Parishioners of St. Bernardine's Roman Catholic Church spill out onto Edmondson Avenue and across the streetcar tracks for the dedication of a memorial to members who had served in the armed forces. The ceremony was photographed on August 23, 1948 by Albert D. Cochran of the Baltimore *Sun*. (Baltimore *Sun*)

hood, reached such proportions that planning was initiated in 1954 for the area's first community-based comprehensive high school. Edmondson High School was completed in 1957 and, almost immediately, enlarged in 1959. In the late 1950s its attraction may have been largely a function of the desire to avoid racially changing public schools in other parts of the city.[71]

Edmondson Village teenagers participated in an emergent youth culture that became an important feature of the era, finding expression in the nation's popular culture even as national popular culture shaped it. Such social commentators as Robert and Helen Lynd had identified the rudiments of youth culture in their study of Muncie, Indiana, in the 1920s and 1930s, a product of the changing economic role of teenagers and the impact of the mass media.[72] A self-conscious youth culture, deferred by the Great Depression and World War II, even as those successive crises in some respects laid a basis for it by undermining adult authority and heightening age-based affiliations, found new expression in the prospering postwar period at the grassroots as well as the national level.

The development of Edmondson Village's commercial facilities played an important role in the form a patterned youth culture took in the postwar community. The movies, the bowling alley, drug stores, and ice cream shops all provided places not only for consumption but for gathering. The shopping center management facilitated this role by furnishing facilities for a teen center and sponsoring dances hosted by popular media disk jockeys on the center's asphalt parking lot. Edith Romaine recalls: "At Halloween up in the Village, they used to block off part of the parking area. They had Buddy Dean, you know, who was on television. . . . They used to have dancing contests. They would block off a whole section of the parking area. You'd be dancing right there, and cars would be passing by on Edmondson Avenue, and see all these kids dancing. That was nice."

Commonality and togetherness are central themes in retrospective accounts of growing up as young people in Edmondson Village in the 1950s. Within a context where everyone could be presumed to be pretty much alike, subtle forms of differentiation relating to age or personal tastes developed, as friends spent time together, walking places and "hanging out." In a peer-oriented youth culture, such groupings defined identity and status. They also mirrored national cultural phenomena, indicative of the growing influence of mass media—especially films, television, and records—as translated at the local level, complete with distinctive language and clothing styles.[73] For example, Edmondson Village in the early to mid-1950s had its "drapes" and "squares," and recollections represent a veritable taxonomy of teenage behavior and dress. Joe Slovensky said, "A 'drape' was a bad guy—long hair—a D.A.—and he had pegged pants, usually black, with a pink stripe up the side." Edith Romaine described "drapes" as having "hair that curled down, just flopped down. They had the leather jackets. And the girls that were considered 'drapey' wore their hair long and pinned it right behind the ear with bobbie pins. They wore it real long. Now, see the squares would look like this: plaid, khaki pants, crew neck sweaters, shorter hair. . . . I guess I was more square, but every now and then I would dress a little bit, maybe, that way. And see, the guy I was going with at that time definitely was on the drapey side."

Drug stores and ice cream shops drew particular crowds who "hung" there and provided a changing social map of peer relationships. The shifting social definitions applied to such neighborhood commercial hangouts as the Edgewood Pharmacy, Whalen's, the Arundel, and the Greek's in the following interviews suggest variations in experience as well as changes in perceived social reputations over time:

The place we went to in Edmondson Village was the Arundel. Down in my neighborhood at the corner of Allendale and Edmondson there was a place called the

Continuity and Undercurrents of Change

Greek's; they had a soda fountain and a jukebox. . . . When you were little you went in Voshell's but when you were old enough to be in the teenage group, you went to the Greek's. I think the people were Greek—and they called it the Greek's.—Agnes Malone

The Village was a hangout. The library was there—that was always a good excuse. You'd go meet your friends. A lot of people hung out at the Arundel and at Whalen's Drug Store and the bowling alley. . . . It would be just whoever was there. Now, I didn't hang around the Village all that much; my hangout was the Edgewood Pharmacy. But you could go in and find no less than a dozen kids in the Arundel at one time, or there might be only two or three. I knew some of them by name or sight, but I usually stayed around the Edgewood Pharmacy—that's where my friends hung out. At the Greek's the people who hung out were greasers, drapes—we called them drapes in those days—and I was very scared of them. . . . They were three to five years older than I—I was terrified of them. Some of them were bad. But now that I look back on them I think it was funny. I would walk up Edmondson Avenue, then I would cross the street for about a block, and then cross back over again. I wouldn't walk by them; I was afraid. There were girls who hung out there too, but I don't remember them; I remember the guys. They had slicked black hair, black leather jackets, peg pants, a couple of them had those crazy long key chains—the typical stuff you would see in the movie "Grease." But some of them were worse. Although now they're grown and have their own families, and they're not quite so foreboding as they were then. . . . The Edgewood Pharmacy was where the squares were—how they got that name, I don't know. They had a regular pharmacy department in the front, and a soda fountain in the back. We'd just go there and have some ice cream or a Coke and kill some time.—Marilyn Simkins

We didn't go up there [to the Arundel]; those guys were too old for us; we used to hang down at Whalen's. I used to just go to the Arundel, get an orange sherbet, and leave. Yes, we were afraid of that place. That was where the big boys were. . . . The Greek's, well I never went there. . . . People like "the Fonz" would hang down there; you didn't go there.—Joe Slovensky

We'd go to the Arundel and have a Coke or a milkshake. You'd usually go up to the Village and meet other people you knew. . . . The Greek's was a corner soda shop—back in the early to mid fifties, the local drapes and drapettes—that was a term that was given them—would go there. They would be the people you would consider greasers today, I guess; the people with the black leather coats and D.A. haircuts who rode motorcycles. They were considered the bad people of the neighborhood. They were the unruly, incorrigible teenagers that no decent person was allowed to go near. People were very much more willing to divide people into good and bad in those days—I think we've come a ways since then. I was definitely not allowed to go to the Greek's. That was also one place my brother couldn't go. I had to walk by there almost every day. I did slip in there once just to find out why it was off limits. And I recall girls sitting around in very tight, low-cut sweaters, with lots of hair and lots of lipstick—totally scornful of anyone who would walk into the place who wasn't in their crowd—but I was a good bit younger than those people. I recall them as being very pushy people and very aggressive and loud—people who would cuss a lot. . . . I remember one day I had a fight with one of them—what had actually happened was that I had had a disagreement with one of these person's twin sisters, and they went home and got their older sister to come after me, and she did—she must have been six years older than me and quite a bit bigger. And this girl just beat me up and down.—Alice Hughes

Such social differences seldom resulted in open conflict, as in the latter instance. Indeed, interviewees testify to the general safety and security young people felt and the general freedom permitted them by their parents as long as they remained within the extended neighborhood's confines. However, sometimes parental prohibitions suggested concern about groups of people considered less than desirable. In the following account, told by Alice Hughes, apprehension may have resulted as much from age and gender differences as from genuine social distinction or threat: "I know that the people at the bowling alley were not people we were supposed to associate with—I don't know why, maybe because they were faster than the people my mother wanted me to hang around with. We would go there to bowl, but my mother was very much opposed to us going to the bowling alley to visit. I guess you could say that if there were different groups of people, there were the ones who went to the bowling alley and those who didn't. But by the time I was a teenager, Edmondson Village was changing." Gender differences also patterned norms in subtle, but significant ways, as Alice Hughes recalls:

There were a lot of people, including my brother, who would go up there and hang out—stand on the corner, and do whatever you did—talk and smoke cigarettes and whistle at the girls—but I never hung out there. I would just go there for a place to go, and browse. He would go up there for the evening; I would go up there for as along as it took to have a Coke and see if I knew anyone. I might go for an hour; he would go for three hours. I would be walking the whole time, and he would be standing in one spot. I guess that would be the difference.

If drapes and squares represented local variations of cultural types within the national phenomenon of teen culture, they did not appear to correspond in any significant way to socioeconomic differences within the community. Indeed, interviewees suggest that "drapes," for instance, came from throughout the residential area, not from one particular section deemed socially different or deviant. Rather than signaling a challenge to the community's social homogeneity or to its common cultural values, these distinctions seemed relatively transitory, symptoms of incipient intergenerational cleavages but not fundamental rebellion or challenge. Indeed, teenage life in Edmondson Village was a sheltered existence. The community's young people, like their parents, had little exposure to genuine social diversity and, like their white suburban counterparts elsewhere, were little prepared to accept it.

Certainly this was true when it came to race. Within the community there was virtually no contact with African Americans, except the occasional "A-rabbers" or hawkers who sold their wares from horse-drawn wagons in the alleyways. Baltimore public schools continued to be segregated until 1954, as were the community's churches and its shopping district. In one sense, then, African Americans didn't exist for Edmondson Village residents, at least in terms of immediate experience. However, in another and very real sense they did, for interviewees testify that prejudice was a significant feature of their upbringing, a topic to be considered more fully in chapter 4. Beneath the "gold" of the Edmondson area's postwar rowhouse suburban boom and its flourishing family-oriented lifestyle was the reality that the suburban ideal allowed little room for change or for social diversity, and such assumptions were about to be challenged profoundly.

4
A White Community Responds to Change

> I think the only thing that might be similar to it would be the Three Mile Island thing—something that would create such a fear.
> —David Graff

Pressure for racial change was building up on the community's borders, yet white residents of the Edmondson Village area continued to believe that their neighborhood was insulated and secure, a suburban haven. Nevertheless, in approximately 1955, the first African American settlers took up residence in rowhouses in the southeastern corner. (See map 2.) By 1960 the area south of Edmondson Avenue (census tract 2007) had changed from its 1950 count of 6,662 whites and 13 non-whites, to a population of 3,528 whites and 5,714 African Americans. In 1970 the same tract totaled 9,276 African Americans, 841 whites. North of Edmondson Avenue (in census tract 1608) the racial line remained virtually intact in 1960; in 1950 population totals had been 5,089 white, 21 nonwhite, and in 1960 they stood at 8,708 whites, 96 African Americans. But during the decade of the 1960s, nearly twenty thousand persons exchanged places in tract 1608, as the population changed dramatically to 11,007 African Americans and 390 whites by 1970.[1] Census years make the process seem more prolonged than it was; in fact, the change proceeded block by block at an incredibly rapid rate, too fast for consideration of a "tipping point" to be either measurable or meaningful.[2]

Triggering this episode of racial change was the systematic activity labeled blockbusting, the intentional action of a real estate speculator to place an African American resident in a house on a previously all-white block for the express purpose of panicking whites into selling for the profit to be gained by buying low and selling high. Blockbusters stepped into the artificial void maintained by the dual housing market, relying upon African American housing needs and white racial fears to manipulate the process of racial change for their own ends. In doing so, they provided a commodity to African Americans that they previously had been illegitimately denied. But the transaction typically was exploitative, victimizing both sellers and buyers. Edmondson Village illustrated just how pervasive the process could be once the seeds of a blockbusting activities had been sown.

The Social Context for Blockbusting

As noted in chapter 3, the postwar years brought unprecedented suburban expansion, typically on a white-only basis. The century's second housing boom produced renewed development in outer city rowhouse neighborhoods such as Edmondson Village, where the Keelty Company and other developers completed their work of filling the remaining vacant land with residences but brought even more impressive growth to the newer suburbs beyond, where apartments, group homes, and ranchers acted as magnets for the postwar white middle class. In the 1950s, the Keelty Company itself recognized this trend by shifting its operations from filling in older areas to constructing new suburbs, playing the game of suburban leapfrog like many other developers.

The World War II period and the immediate postwar years also produced immense pressure upon housing for Baltimore's African Americans. While population increased substantially, the areas of African American residential concentration expanded only marginally. Moreover, overcrowding and slum conditions only became worse. For those whose financial status had improved from expanded job opportunities and whose expectations regarding social progress had been raised by a formative civil rights movement, limited housing opportunities remained a major source of frustration. Shut out of the suburban housing market, their only option was to seek "hand-me-downs" (as *Sun* reporter Carroll Williams called them) in adjacent white areas.[3] Yet, they continued to meet resistance from white residents and from the powerful but informal mechanisms of the dual housing market. Questionnaires surveying the policies and practices of Baltimore real estate brokers in the 1950s indicated that most were unwilling to sell to African Americans in predominantly white sections of the city. Mainstream firms belonged to the National Association of Real Estate Brokers, whose 1950 revised code of ethics contained a clause listing as unethical "the introduction of a character of property or occupancy whose presence will clearly be detrimental to property values in the neighborhood." While on the surface this 1950 reformulation referred only to use or class rather than specifying race or nationality, as had been the case since 1924, it nevertheless could be understood to continue to imply these exclusions, if one assumed—as many certainly did—that the entry of new African American residents into previously all-white residential areas necessarily would lower property values or have other negative consequences.[4] Similar patterns of discrimination and assumptions about the soundness of neighborhoods as the basis for policy decisions prevailed for local banking institutions, as well as for such federal governmental mortgage agencies as FHA and VA. The redlining policies of these two pillars of residential financing excluded African Americans from access to broad sectors of the housing market.[5]

While this silent conspiracy characteristically took the form of refusal to do business with African Americans seeking housing in white areas, in some instances it resulted in a carefully orchestrated charade that permitted mainstream real estate firms to benefit from racial changeover without being directly involved. Mal Sherman, a well-regarded member of the Baltimore Real Estate Board, testified to the U.S. Civil Rights Commission about his company's activities on the northwest side of the city in the early 1950s:

For the period fifty-one to fifty-five we were making black sales in areas of the city that were all-white, but we didn't have the nerve to make them ourselves, so we were doing it on the basis of listing houses with black brokers and getting one-third referral fee. In other words, if we have a owner that wanted to sell to black [sic], we would refer it to a black real estate broker, and we would get a referral fee, and we were not making the house sales ourselves because in those days, it was considered that this was a block and if a real estate broker put a black in place on that block, he was called a blockbuster, and we did not have the guts to participate in making black sales that we wanted to make ourselves. So rather than get that kind of label, we worked through black brokers.[6]

In this case the etiquette of the dual housing market was maintained through referral to an African American broker. However, in the context of what one real estate insider active during this period described as "the hottest real estate market I had ever seen," the potential for lucrative profits attracted speculators ready to breach the conspiracy, and mainstream realtors prepared to look the other way.[7] The former typically had operated on the margins of the real estate market, acquiring properties others no longer coveted, picking them up at bargain rates. Their more aggressive role in the post-World War II period might have been resented and resisted by mainline realtors, except that the latter now stood to benefit by white relocations to existing housing in the outer ring and to new house sales in the exploding suburbs beyond. As pieces of the proverbial pie expanded for all segments of the industry, speculative activity intensified and its scale increased exponentially. In the process, a handful of operators became major players in the racial turnover of neighborhoods.

While the general climate created conditions ripe for such activity, the tactics associated with blockbusting provided the wedge. Early instances occurred in the period immediately following the war. For example, in 1945 white residents in the Fulton Avenue section on the near west side complained of "the practices of some real estate operators to 'break' a block" and insisted that further "encroachment" should stop. The charge that Jewish operatives were involved in some of the transactions in this area led to intervention by the Baltimore Jewish Council, which admonished the offending parties but objected to the emphasis placed upon their Jewish identity, insisting that this was a larger civic problem.[8] As broad sections of older neighborhoods adjacent to the wartime boundaries of the African American ghetto changed racially in the following years, similar episodes occurred. The issue suddenly received widespread public notice in 1955 and 1956 when a flurry of newspaper articles called attention to systematic instances that had occurred in various parts of the outer city, primarily on the northwestern and western sides, as well as in certain areas to the northeast. In these press accounts the term "blockbusting" often was put in quotation marks, suggesting its relative novelty to the general newspaper readership.[9] By early 1957 the Maryland Commission on Interracial Problems and Relations was expressing alarm that "the in-migration of Negro families into formerly all white neighborhoods was becoming the most troublesome area of friction between the races." Asserting that "block-busting" was at the root of the rapid changeover process, the commission went on to lament that there was "no legal means of deterring the real estate dealers from their offensive and highly lucrative practices."[10]

In the public discourse of the mid-1950s, the term blockbusting often was used to refer to any real estate practice that introduced an African American household into a formerly white residential area for the purpose of provoking panic-driven racial turnover. Institutional voices found it necessary, however, to try to delineate more precisely the specific practices that should be labeled unscrupulous, unethical, or illegal. Since blockbusting challenged many of the implicit assumptions of the dual housing market, public agencies—like the race relations commissions—found themselves forced to consider whether *any* introduction of an African American household into a racially segregated neighborhood constituted abuse per se, or whether such an interpretation was too sweeping an appeal to de facto segregation. Therefore, statements from this period reveal the search for formulations that were more precise in their identification of the specific practices deemed inappropriate. Recognition of this need for delineation was evident, for instance, in the 1956 statement by the Baltimore Commission on Human Relations that "'block-busting' is not caused merely by Negroes moving into white neighborhoods, but by the practices of 'certain unscrupulous real estate operators of both races.'"[11]

These more qualified interpretations of blockbusting focused principally on three areas of alleged abuse: the manner and mode of solicitation, the alleged characteristics of the new residents, and excessive profits. Solicitation was neither illegal (in state or local law) nor unethical (under the Real Estate Board code of ethics), though when applied to a targeted neighborhood systematically and repeatedly, with veiled and not so veiled references to impending racial change and lowered property values, it clearly could be a powerful destabilizing force.[12] One real estate broker, Stanley Greenberg, asserted in an interview that the major speculators singled out neighborhoods and saturated them with solicitors, typically assuring the desired results of panicked sales. Not until 1966, after another decade of intensive blockbusting activity in broad sections of the city, did the Baltimore City Council pass an ordinance forbidding real estate activity that involved "general door-to-door solicitation, in person, by telephone or mail, or by the mass distribution of circulars." The Real Estate Board of Baltimore opposed the law, contending that the organization was capable of dealing with such abuses through its own procedures, although these clearly had not been effective, nor were all who engaged in such activities necessarily members of the board.[13]

A second aspect of the effort to delineate the illegal or unscrupulous elements of blockbusting focused on the type of resident to whom real estate operatives rented or sold in the initial stages of racial turnover. On this point the tendency was to specify as inappropriate the introduction of residents who were "undesirable"—typically the term was not precisely defined—for the purpose of provoking panic. The 1956 statement by the Baltimore Commission on Human Relations, for instance, charged that "these speculators buy houses in stable neighborhoods and rent them to undesirable tenants, relying on a 'fear campaign' to force other home owners to sell out in panic."[14] The Maryland Commission on Interracial Problems and Relations sought to distinguish the unethical elements in blockbusting along similar lines: "Numerous complaints were received at our office from home owners and also from officers of improvement associations about the unscrupulous real estate dealers who were buying up properties in certain neighborhoods and putting in undesirable tenants with a view to frightening the residents into selling their properties at panic prices."[15] In 1958 the Baltimore Commission went so far as to assert that there often was little difficulty if African Americans moving into formerly all-white neighborhoods were "of the same economic and cultural background as the former residents" but that "the true block-buster is a speculator who buys a house in a stable neighborhood and puts in tenants at little or no rent—the type of tenants who would be undesirable neighbors no matter what their race, religion, or origin."[16]

In some instances blockbusters indeed rented to African Americans with little capacity to pay or sold houses on newly broken blocks to African Americans without the financial resources to handle the steeply inflated prices.[17] For instance, in 1958 and 1959 in the nearby Ashburton neighborhood, a real estate operative was accused of fraudulent sale to an African American to create the appearance of purchase and thereby to panic whites. Newspaper coverage of the incident noted: "[Residents] charged that Manning-Shaw had moved Mr. Carter, a Negro, into the house and erected a 'sold' sign in an attempt to frighten white neighbors into selling their homes. This is a key technique used by blockbusters."[18] Sometimes, especially in sections with larger homes, blockbusters might divide a newly acquired property into smaller units rented by people with lesser economic means than area homeowners, thereby profiting from the revenue as well as creating a situation of overcrowding that area whites viewed with alarm. Baltimore *Sun* reporter Douglas Connah, Jr., for example, contended that in the 1950s "houses once occupied by single families [were] bought by speculators, stuffed with poor people, and 'milked.'"[19]

On the other hand, not all African Americans who were the first of their race on formerly all-white blocks fit this pattern, nor did they necessarily differ in terms of class from their new white neighbors. As unscrupulous and exploitative as the methods and goals involved in the blockbusting process may have been, the interpretation that blockbusting necessarily involved the introduction of "undesirable" tenants was problematic in its substitution of class as a marker for race.

The fact of the matter is that in the racial climate of the mid-1950s it took only a relatively few instances of real estate transactions resulting in African American settlement to induce panicked white flight. Blockbusting depended upon white bias, which—protestations to the contrary—often rejected settlement by any African American, regardless of class. As one writer of a letter to the editor of the *Sun* noted in 1955: "The real villains are prejudice, which makes a whole neighborhood flee because of one Negro family, and the monopoly in new homes which the white citizens enjoy."[20] Therefore, assertions that the first African American settlers in the blockbusting process were *necessarily* of a lower class status blurred the reality that race tended to be the primary determinant of white response. Moreover, such interpretations presented African Americans as *necessarily* unwitting tools, victims in the process. They tended to obscure the active choices most initial African American settlers were making about their housing status—choices made in spite of risks, both known and unknown. They also failed to recognize that the victimization African Americans experienced stemmed primarily from their exclusion from access to normal real estate and financial mechanisms, exclusion that left them vulnerable to the exploitative and insecure terms they were forced to accept from blockbusters and speculators. Therefore, efforts to portray initial African American settlers as victims often tended to justify the dual housing market without questioning its underlying assumptions—rather than to demonstrate genuine sympathy and understanding for the circumstances pioneers faced.

The third contention regarding blockbusters was that their activities were designed to produce exploitative profits. Complaints about blockbusting practices frequently contained references to "panic prices" and "lucrative practices." The principal pattern prevailing in blockbusting involved purchase prices below market value from whites who had been panicked into flight and the resale of properties to African Americans at prices above the market value. Typically the blockbuster might be willing to make an initial purchase on an all-white block at an unusually high price on the assumption, proved correct time and time again, that the first African American presence (even the rumor of such presence) could reap a harvest of severely depreciated prices from the remaining whites on the block. In acute instances of heightened blockbuster-induced panic situations, houses might be bought for as little as 50 percent of the prevailing market value, then sold for as much as 50 percent above. Even discounting the attendant real estate costs and risks in such procedures, a markup on the order of 100 percent might indeed be deemed exploitative.[21] Ironically, the depression in prices whites received for housing in panic situations fueled their perception that the advent of African Americans lowered property values, even though speculators in fact typically commanded excessively high prices on resales, a point apparently not widely understood by fleeing whites but key to those engaged in such speculative activity.[22] It was not until the most intense episodes of the blockbusting era had ended in near total racial changeover in neighborhoods such as Edmondson Village that fair housing advocates were able to document the dynamic of price victimization on both sides of racial change.[23]

The refusal of mainstream realty firms to be involved in racially mixed areas gave blockbusters and attendant real estate speculators a monopoly on the market, which meant that prospective African American home buyers typically had no recourse except to deal with speculators at artificially high prices. Similarly, the shunning of such transactions by mainstream financial institutions afforded these operatives a monopoly in the mortgage arrangements. Speculators financed their operations through loans from large banks that typically did not lend to individual homeowners, certainly not to African Americans, or from federal or state savings and loan institutions, willing to do business with them as white businessmen, thereby only indirectly dealing with African American home buyers.

For speculators the risks sometimes were substantial, but they protected themselves through such arrangements as land installment contracts, lease option contracts, and double mortgages. Land installment contracts, legal under Maryland statutes, provided a mechanism to prospective home buyers that enabled them to acquire housing without initial downpayment or closing charges. However, such contracts did not involve the immediate transfer of title and provided little of the protection afforded buyers under conventional mortgages. In Baltimore during this period, African American families hoping for eventual home ownership frequently had little option except to accept such terms. A 1955 survey by the Maryland Commission on Interracial Problems and Relations found that over half of the sample (53 percent) were purchasing their homes through these means rather than through regular financing. In 95 percent of the cases of contract sales, the arrangement was with a white firm or individual. Expressing the concern that such evidence suggested that "the ownership financial status of the majority of this group is highly tentative," the commission identified a number of factors as possibly responsible, citing "high level demand for housing by non-whites; shortage of rental housing of better quality; relocation requiring families to discover new residences; difficulty in getting regular financing through established institutions; and sudden accessibility of housing of somewhat better quality through release by white families moving to county and peripheral areas."[24]

As part of the blockbusting process, speculators widely applied the land installment contract to their benefit in ways that often left prospective buyers vulnerable. Payments usually were required on a weekly basis, and any failure to meet installment deadlines placed tenants at the mercy of the seller, who was free to declare default on the contract. Sometimes aspiring African American owners had difficulty finding out how much their installment payments had accumulated, especially since subsequent house repairs often were added to the amount due. Only after the seller had covered the costs of his markup (any improvement costs and the desired profit) through such payments would the potential buyer be offered a chance for a conventional mortgage, arranged through the speculator.

Lease option ("buy-like-rent") contracts resembled the land installment version but with even less protection because the agreement was merely verbal and unrecorded. Tenants often believed that their "rent" payments were accumulating equity, whereas in fact the speculator was under no legal obligation to apply them to the eventual settlement, even if the tenant subsequently was offered an option to buy and exercised that option. Lease options provided so little protection to tenants and so little restraint upon sellers that a Maryland state delegate from Baltimore, Wally Orlinsky, sought to have them outlawed in 1969, asserting sarcastically that they were so "obscene" that "they were a beauty to behold"; indeed, he said, "A lease option is not recorded and it has no efficacy whatsoever."[25]

Whether initially employing land installment or lease option contracts, speculators who eventually arranged permanent financing for prospective homebuyers often sought to underwrite the transaction with first and second mortgages, usually secured through building and loan institutions with which they conducted the bulk of their business activities. In these arrangements, the first mortgage covered the outlay for the original purchase (made at or below market value), thereby protecting the investment for the financial institution. The second mortgage covered the markup, an amount that usually represented clear profit for the operative and provided capital for new speculative acquisitions. In 1971, *Sun* writer James Dilts, who was investigating charges raised by fair housing advocates, chronicled a typical financing procedure used by speculators:

The flow of money is as follows: the speculator borrows money on a short-term basis from a large bank. He buys houses from white families cheaply in a changing neighborhood and resells them after substantial markups to black families. He takes the families to a friendly savings and loan association where the families obtain a mortgage loan. This money goes to the speculator. After taking a relatively small profit, he uses it to repay his bank loan. However, at the same time, he secures second mortgages from the families. These second mortgages are generally for several thousand dollars and, when combined with the first mortgage, represent a debt substantially in excess of the values of the houses. The second mortgages represent almost clear profit to the speculator. He uses them in turn as collateral for more bank loans, to buy more houses, and the cycle continues.[26]

These procedures were carefully crafted to assure quick turnovers and replacement capital for further speculative investment. Under such circumstances, there were indeed instances where new tenants lacked the standard economic means to meet the demands of their new housing, since there is little evidence that the interests of prospective tenants were carefully considered. However, the fact of the matter was that the process artificially drove prices far above the market value for comparable housing in other parts of the urban area. Therefore, even those African Americans who would have been able to meet the financial requirements under ordinary conditions were instead forced to bear the added burden of the excessive costs and insecurity of these extraordinary arrangements.

Between 1950 and 1970 the scale of residential racial change, unleashed by various social and economic forces but heightened by blockbusting and speculative real estate activity, rewrote the racial geography of the city in dramatic fashion. (See map 1.) Speculators whose primary investments previously had been in marginal properties—commercial and residential—now rapidly expanded their activities, establishing themselves as dominant actors in the real estate of racial change and accumulating immense business volume in the process. For all of the abuses and exploitation associated with blockbusting, speculators—whether directly responsible for blockbusting or capitalizing on it—shrewdly identified a need in the housing market and calculatingly moved to fill it. As Stanley Greenberg observed of their role: "They pushed this thing and made money off it, but they filled a niche by providing housing for blacks who needed it." Most episodes of systematic and dramatic racial change across the city resulted from operations conducted on a large scale, not simply from lone agents working on their own. In the extensive northwest section where some of the most widespread residential turnover occurred in Baltimore, for example, five or six principal firms played primary roles.

During this period the East Baltimore ghetto area expanded only modestly, since class (working to middle class) and ethnicity (neighborhoods where Central and East European ethnic identities remained strong) seemed to combine to slow the process of change on that side of the city. On its northeastern fringe episodes of blockbusting occurred along lower Harford Road and The Alameda in the 1950s, and in the 1960s they extended beyond these sections into neighborhoods in the vicinity of Lake Montebello, where some rowhouse developments resembled Edmondson Village in age and social character. On the south side, pockets of African American population had expanded in the 1940s, principally in geographically isolated districts like Cherry Hill and Fairfield. Due north, the more affluent wedge formed by Roland Park, Guilford, and Homeland remained exclusive white preserves.

The preponderant direction of racial change was west and northwest along three principal corridors where considerable suburban development had begun in the county areas beyond the city line. In these sections especially intense blockbusting and speculative activity occurred. Along Park Heights Avenue the change process followed the corridor pioneered only a few decades before by the city's Jewish community. Initially concentrated near the city center on the east, Baltimore's Jews first migrated to the Eutaw Place area on the near northwest, then proceeded to settle along a route extending like a spoke beyond Druid Hill Park into the Lower Park Heights rowhouse area. This section had been developed during the 1920s and 1930s, and in many respects—other than religious identification—it resembled Edmondson Village. In 1960 Lower Park Heights had only 5 percent African American population; in 1970 the percentage was 95 percent. As the center of Jewish population shifted farther to the northwest into suburban areas of the county such as Pikesville and Randallstown, racial changeover in this wedge assumed a classic pattern of succession from Jewish to African American.[27]

A related axis of change occurred in northwest neighborhoods along the Liberty Heights corridor, beginning in older rowhouse areas such as Walbrook near west North Avenue, and then proceeding to such middle- to upper-middle-class neighborhoods as Ashburton, Windsor Hills, Forest Park, and Arlington (the latter three also areas of considerable Jewish residence). In relatively affluent Ashburton and Windsor Hills, notable attempts were made to stem white flight and counter blockbusting with "good neighbor" approaches that promoted acceptance of residential integration. However, aside from the modest success in cooling the rate of racial change in these exceptional areas, blockbusting and white flight proceeded at a rapid rate on the far northwest.[28] By 1960 substantial African American presence had reached the old 1888 city boundary; in the following decade it spread to the current city line.[29]

Blockbusting and Speculation Come to Edmondson Village

While these two corridors were closely intertwined geographically, the Gwynns Falls stream valley separated them from the third route of rapid

A White Community Responds to Change

racial change, which proceeded due west along Edmondson Avenue into the Edmondson Village rowhouse section. There, blockbusting and attendant speculative real estate activity during the period from the mid-1950s through the mid-1960s was as systematic and extensive as in any part of the city. To contemporaries on both sides of the transactions many of the dynamics in Edmondson Village were not fully understood in this period of panic, confusion, and rapid resettlement. In retrospect, however, considerable evidence points to widespread employment of a variety of solicitation methods to induce panic and trigger white flight. Once change was set in motion, these conditions attracted speculative real estate activity on a large scale.

In a section formerly characterized by residential longevity and high home ownership levels, the sudden appearance of outside interests as intermediaries—real estate brokers and investors—provides one indication of the mechanisms involved in neighborhood turnover. To investigate this process, I examined the biannual tax assessments for the ten blocks included in the sample block survey, checking the years 1955 to 1973. Many nonresident parties appear on the lists during this period, including the following sample:

Firms:	Individuals:
Arbor, Inc.	Daniel W. Caplan
Best Realty	Howard W. Cohen
Bob Holding Corp.	Anthony Piccinini
Butler Building Co.	Henry J. Shmidt
Chesco, Inc.	Donald Terry
Crown Enterprises	Henry E. Caplan
Fairfax Investment Corp.	Harold Goldsmith
Lee Realty	Louis Singer
Oak Investment Co.	Albert T. Smith
Rab Corp.	
Rainbow Realty	
Woodhaven Investment Corp.	

(See Appendix B for tables showing the complete record of ownership on selected blocks.)[30]

A check of city directories for 1961 and 1964, key years in terms of the transactions considered here, failed to turn up listings for most of the company names cited above, a curious—and perhaps telling—circumstance, since it suggests that these firms may not have been operating on their own and that they chose not to make their identities readily available to the public. A number of the individuals listed addresses downtown (presumably business locations) or in affluent sections of the metro area outside Edmondson Village, principally in the northern section of the city and the adjacent Baltimore County area of Pikesville.

On block after block essentially the pattern was repeated: stable tenure by long-term residents, the appearance of outside interests on the tax rolls in scattered fashion (with many of the same individual and corporate names showing up repeatedly throughout the area), rapid property turnover on the rest of the block, followed by a mix of new resident ownership and some property retention by nonresident investors. This profile, evident on eight of the ten sample blocks, suggested that, typically, resale rather than long-term investment was the primary goal. On some blocks, however, the prevalence and persistence of outside ownership indicated speculative activity that resulted in longer-term investment, possibly because of oversaturation of purchases and lack of resales.[31] Of course, the survey of tax records can provide no evidence whether any of these individuals or firms might themselves have engaged in the activities defined as blockbusting or whether as investors they instead stepped into the void created by panicked white flight. However, the pattern of concentrated outside investment that emerges from the survey suggests that this indeed was a community under siege.

In the aftermath of the massive scale of racial change that occurred in the Edmondson Village section, the episode became the major focus of public controversy over the role of real estate operators when a civil rights organization, the Activists, specifically challenged the Morris Goldseker Company regarding its involvement there. The Activists asserted that the company had operated under a variety of other names (including Lee Realty; Fairfax Investment Corp.; Best Realty; Arbor, Inc.; Rainbow Realty; Woodhaven Investment Corp.; and others). These Goldseker-affiliated firms, the group claimed, had been party to over one-third of the real estate transfers in census tract 1608 (on the north side of Edmondson Avenue) between 1960 and 1968. Further, they charged that the markups on the transactions represented excessive profits, a process that took advantage of both sellers and buyers.[32] Representatives of the Goldseker Company admitted large-scale business operations in racially changing sections of the city but claimed that the firm had been providing housing to people otherwise denied opportunity, that the variety of names under which it operated was only a legal device for tax purposes, and that the markups had been neither excessive nor exploitative when consideration was given to legitimate operating costs and risks.[33]

Morris Goldseker was one of several real estate entrepreneurs who had built businesses upon the acquisition of properties in low income districts of older parts of the city and who—during the 1950s and 1960s—expanded their operations to a number of working-class or middle-class neighborhoods that previously had been considered white-only. Purchasing houses in a systematic manner, these brokers then sold or rented them to African Americans. Whether anticipating or taking advantage of the unprecedented growth of the real estate market, they chose to operate on the back side of white flight rather than on its suburban frontier. As in the case of Edmondson Village, the charge frequently was made that they—or those closely associated with them—contributed mightily to the process.

To Morris Goldseker's defenders, he represented an American success story, one of a number of remarkable tales spun by the generation of East European Jewish immigrants who settled in the United States at the turn of the century and applied their energies and talents to finding niches within the system of American capitalism. The Polish-born Goldseker, who arrived in Baltimore alone at age fourteen and never married, began working in real estate in the 1920s, eventually starting his own business, which concentrated upon the purchase of old properties at depressed prices in declining sections of the city. The Great Depression, a calamity for so many, proved a boon to Goldseker, who positioned himself to make expanded acquisitions at rock bottom prices. Profits in a speculative business with high risks came through rents or through improvements and resale. By most accounts, rental or sale clients were among the city's low income residents, though whether Goldseker was a slumlord exploiting less advantaged tenants or a pioneer providing a service to those otherwise left out of the city's housing market has always been a subject of controversy.[34] There is general agreement, however, that Goldseker's proven success opened access to financial sources that provided credit for further operations and positioned him to be a significant player in the fluid real estate market following World War II. By the 1960s the firm had become what his nephew and business associate, Sheldon Goldseker, claimed was "one of the largest and most respectable real estate firms in the city of Baltimore."[35]

The charges and countercharges in the Activists-Goldseker controversy will be discussed more fully in chapter 5 in relation to the circumstances confronting new African American settlers.[36] Suffice it to say here that the eventual public controversy over the Edmondson Village case illustrated the degree to which it came to epitomize in a particularly intense fashion the complex dynamics of the era's rapid racial change process: blockbusters to stir panic, white residents vulnerable because of their own racial prejudices, African Americans in desperate need of improved housing, and speculative real estate firms as beneficiaries.

White Perceptions of Initial African American Settlement

According to the testimony of interviewees, Edmondson Village residents felt insulated from the social and racial diversity of older urban areas even as symptoms of widespread change began to appear across the Gywnns Falls stream valley in nearby sections of west Baltimore. Residents shared a belief, both literal and metaphorical, that the bridge would not be crossed. Agnes Malone remembered prevailing white sentiment: "People had said they'll never cross the Edmondson Avenue bridge."[37] Madge Cooper recalled similar sentiment: "The bridge on Edmondson Avenue was supposed to save Edmondson Village; they were not going to come across that bridge."[38] And Ann Morgan agreed regarding feeling at the time: "They were to the bridge, and everybody said they'll never cross the bridge."[39]

When change did occur, the bridge crossed was not along Edmondson Avenue, often thought of as the main access from the city to the rowhouse neighborhood, but in the southeastern corner of the area at Baltimore Street. (See map 2.) It was as if the moat had been breached by a rear gate. Ann Morgan recalled: "We always said they came the back way, you know; they came Hilton Street and Gwynn Avenue—they came that way, instead of coming over the bridge and our way. But people had foolish ideas; they said they'd never move opposite Western Cemetery, because black people didn't like to live opposite the cemetery. You know, people had all those dumb ideas." Marilyn Simkins pictured the process similarly: "It started down around the junior high school; it seemed to come the back way, so to speak—up Caton Avenue, and then across Edmondson—to Denison Street, Edgewood Street, and on up."[40]

Once African American presence was established in the southeastern corner, the change that ensued was perceived as rapid and inexorable. Alice Hughes recalled the feeling of white residents: "When the [African American] people started moving into the neighborhood, they did come in, literally, block by block. I can recall when they came across the Hilton Street bridge everybody was very upset; they said, 'Oh my God, they're over the bridge now; our street will be next.'"[41] Agnes Malone remembered the path of racial change similarly: "They came up Poplar Grove Street to Edmondson Avenue and Ellicott Driveway, which is just at the beginning of the bridge. And then gradually it began coming in Denison

Street and back around Hilton, Culver, and that area, and eventually along Gelston Drive." Other recollections reinforce the perception of the change as relentless and overwhelming, once the bridge crossing was breached. Vera Johnson said, "It was a creeping thing from Monroe Street. . . . It kept crawling and crawling. We all said, 'Come on, now, it will never get past Poplar Grove Street. It will never come across the bridge, never.' And that's how we lived; we convinced ourselves of all that. But then it started to creep across the bridge, and they all moved because everybody got so frightened. This was the initial beginning of the breaking up of neighborhoods."[42] Marilyn Simkins heard people refer to "the incoming change" as "the Black Wave"; the result, she said, was "The Exodus—that was the white people leaving." Whether a "black wave" or something that was "creeping" and "crawling," the result indeed was a white "exodus."

The words chosen by the interviewees in their retrospection reflect the insulated culture of a white community that could not entertain the possibility that African American presence meant anything other than invasion. In the first place, as a relatively recent suburban rowhouse development, built and settled in the context of a rigid dual housing market, the Edmondson Village rowhouse district had never had any African American residents. "You just didn't see black people in the neighborhood, except women who came in to do day work or delivery men, or something like that. They just didn't live in the area then," Marilyn Simkins observed. Agnes Malone's family employed a part-time domestic: "Some of the women had cleaning ladies who used to come in every week or every other week; in fact, my mother did after my brother was born—and after a while she became just like one of the family. Mom could go out shopping and just leave her there to do whatever she had to do—she used to come twice a week to iron and clean. She lived on Mount Street, down Edmondson Avenue, farther." Or, as Joe Slovensky noted about his own experience growing up in the area: "You know, there's a joke on 'Happy Days' or somewhere that back in the fifties we didn't have black people. I never had a black person in any of my classes until I was fourteen years old. . . . So I never really had any dealings; I just didn't know how to deal with it."[43]

Interviewees testify that most whites could not entertain the possibility of residential integration. Marilyn Simkins reflected: "A good portion of the people just felt that they weren't going to live with blacks." Madge Cooper interpreted her parents' attitudes: "Remember that they had never in any way had dealings with black people. . . . They may have met them, like daddy, who knew men who worked at the dairy—but not in his capacity, probably on the janitorial side. My parents, yes, I guess they were prejudiced. They felt that they had a certain place, and they belonged there. And they didn't feel that they were equal to them in any way." Agnes Malone's assessment of her parents' views was similar: "They [her parents and their generation] were very prejudiced then, and I found after I got out and started working for the ———— company that kids get their prejudice from home." Joe Slovensky spoke of the reason for his mother's decision to move: "I know a black person moved next to us, and that was it." Both in their sense of insulation and in their racial prejudice, Edmondson Village residents certainly were not very different from whites elsewhere during the period.

The settlement of African Americans in the neighborhood seemed bound up with complex social, cultural, and economic mechanisms which white residents felt were beyond their control. Whether the issue was school desegregation, decreed by a distant Supreme Court and implemented by a city school board, or the activity of blockbusting real estate agents, who represented shadowy but powerful financial and property powerbrokers, their home neighborhood was being assaulted by elements of change that appeared at once new and relentless. Restrictive covenants had not been widely used in this neighborhood, so the Supreme Court decision in 1948, which ruled their enforcement by state power unconstitutional, had little direct consequence for Edmondson Village residents. However, changes in school policy impinged more directly, signaling unsettling challenges to the traditional pattern that had kept neighborhood institutions white-only, a topic to be addressed more fully later in this chapter.

These legal assaults on the edifice of institutionalized segregation may have had less impact on white apprehension than the dawning awareness that the invisible boundaries, which had held areas of African American residency in check so systematically in the silent conspiracy of residential segregation, were rapidly crumbling. Wheras normal financial and real estate forces always had seemed so effective in maintaining the dual housing market, now they appeared in different guise, either as impotent and ineffective or, worse, as conspirators in overturning the status quo. Around the year 1955 the sudden wave of newspaper references to instances of blockbusting in various parts of the city confirmed rumors that powerful forces of neighborhood change were underway. Whether Edmondson Village residents were aware of the specific tactics of blockbusters, these reports came from urban areas familiar to many of them, and they began to create uneasiness.

The experience and observation of Edmondson Village residents led them to the conclusion that once racial change began, racial succession was inevitable. This article of faith squared with their real life experience, and they accepted it as social reality. Many had come to the Edmondson area from inner city neighborhoods where such change had been the reason for their relocation—they had seen it once and knew its telltale signs. Christine Wallace recalled that the people who bought her mother's house in 1945 only to confront a racially changing neighborhood ten years later had moved from closer to the city's center: "We felt so sorry for the [couple] who bought my mother's house because they were both so elderly. . . . And they had moved from the home where they had lived all their life [on Appleton Street], on the account of the colored people moving in."[44] Residents could observe the process of racial turnover and resegregation clearly etched in the changing racial demographics of the past decade along the Edmondson Avenue corridor many of them traveled each day. Neighborhoods where experience gave reason to expect anything else were distinct exceptions. In more affluent Windsor Hills and Ashburton, located just across the Gwynns Falls Park ravine to the north, active neighborhood associations valiantly urged calm and the acceptance of gradual integration from the mid-1950s, but their example apparently made little impression in popular perceptions of the irreversibility of racial changeover once African American settlement began.

Finally, Edmondson Village residents believed that racial change meant inevitable decline in the socioeconomic status of neighborhoods. Christine Wallace recounted: "My uncle lived on Dukeland, before you get to Poplar Grove Street, and he had colored people on both sides of him, and he said he liked the colored people better than he did his white neighbors. But they, too, eventually moved, because it seems like when they move in, the neighborhood starts to go down; they don't keep the houses up as well as the white people do." Not only did the prospect of neighborhood decline threaten them socially; its corollary was that property values inevitably would fall. That likelihood frightened a predominantly home-owning populace whose financial resources were adequate but not extensive and whose most substantial investment—and resulting equity—was bound up in their houses.

All of these considerations combined to challenge the comfortable and secure suburban ideal that had brought them to Edmondson Village in the first place in their quest for homogeneous neighbors and a satisfying, protected lifestyle. Ironically, blockbusting preyed upon both the social exclusivity and the economic security that served as the basis of this very ideology, simultaneously exploiting their prejudices and economic self-interest. It forced to the foreground recognition that their assumptions about residency depended upon the mechanisms of the dual housing market even as it threatened to unravel the silent conspiracy that maintained residential racial segregation. Residents felt overwhelmed by forces of change beyond their control yet were unwilling or unable to adjust; therefore, they were complicit in the destruction of their own suburban dream, victims and victimizers alike.

White Perceptions of Blockbusting

Interviews with white former residents of Edmondson Village yield vivid descriptions of the blockbusting process. Although the experience there was particularly acute, newspaper accounts suggest similar patterns across the city during the same period.[45] First, real estate operators would try to find a house for sale on an all-white block, often specifically alluding to the prospect of potential racial change in the area and to the threat of lowered property values for those not wise enough to see the handwriting on the wall. As an inducement to sell, the agent typically offered a buying price at or above current market value. Second, having secured the first house by such means, he quickly installed a new African American tenant in the house—renter or buyer, different social class or same social class, these are areas where opinions differed. Third, as soon as the new tenant had taken up residence, if not sooner, the operator moved on down the block, alerting homeowners to the initial sale, warning them of the prospect of increased African American settlement, and offering to buy their houses as well. Those who were among the first to sell might be offered prices above the market value; the next several sales might approximate the actual worth of the house; those who sold later suffered a considerable loss. Typically, for instance, in a neighborhood where the average housing value was ten thousand dollars, the first sale might bring twelve to fifteen thousand dollars, the next sales ten thousand dollars and many of the later transactions as little as five thousand dollars (these figures actually closely approximate the Edmondson experience, as noted below). Eventually prices rebounded, but few stayed long enough to learn the lesson.

Several examples will illustrate the pattern. Alice Hughes, whose family moved in 1962, told me:

> I recall that about 1960 Goldseker came into the neighborhood, and he [presumably an agent of the Morris Goldseker Company] went door to door, literally, offering people a large sum of money for their houses—I would say the sum was fifteen thousand dollars—at least that's what I heard offered on my street. Those people who moved immediately got that; those people who waited till the neighborhood

was "broken," as they called it, got half that—they got six thousand dollars for their houses. My own parents got eight thousand or eighty-five hundred dollars when they moved, but they gave it as a trade-in on a house they bought [elsewhere]. What Goldseker was doing was buying a house for fifteen thousand dollars and almost giving it away to get a black family in, and then he would buy a house for six thousand dollars and sell it for fifteen thousand dollars—that's how he made his money on the deal.

Madge Morgenstern described the pattern on Allendale Street in the 1950s: "They [real estate agents] would call and come around. They would say, 'The neighborhood is going to be black. Don't you want to sell your property now while you can get a good price for it?' Those were the tactics they used. I thought it terrible, absolutely awful, and I would resent it when they called or came to the door trying to buy."[46]

Usually the blockbusting transaction was an all-white arrangement, white seller to white agent, but some interviewees described the involvement of African American agents, as in Marilyn Simkins's experience in 1962:

Our house was sold in a very odd way, and it happened to a lot of people, I'm sure. It was a Sunday morning, in September or October, and my mother and I hadn't been to church yet, the beds weren't made and the breakfast dishes were still at the table, and a knock came at the door, and I answered it—my mother was upstairs getting dressed for church—and I went upstairs and said, "Mother, there's a black man at the door; he gave me his business card, and he says he has a family outside that wants to look at our house." And she said she didn't want to show the house because it was a mess . . . but I said it didn't matter; they wanted to look at the house. So she said, "All right." And they decided on the spot that they wanted it. And this happened time and again.

Eunice Clemens recited a similar instance of door-to-door solicitation:

When we sold it was starting to get colored [in 1961]. The people next door to us on both sides moved. And we decided that we should too; it was just my husband and me. . . . Instead of having people come and look at it, a friend of mine from church had a real estate man come. . . . We gave it to the real estate agent, and he said, "Don't let anybody come in unless I call and tell you." So one day Bill and I were going downtown to the theater, and the doorbell rang, and I went to the door, and this colored man said he would like to come through the house, and I said, "I'm sorry, but you have to have permission." So I called the real estate agent, and he said, "You did the right thing."[47]

Whatever the variation, interviewees' reports on the rapid depression of values once panic set in are in agreement. As a *Sun* article in 1955 observed of the pricing games played by blockbusters: "With his first bargain he recoups the premium laid out to bust the block in the first place. From then on it is gravy—sound structures at prices far below going prices elsewhere, far below the cost of reproduction, which he swiftly makes available at as high a rental as the demand will bear."[48] Most interviewees reported that their families lost out in the process. Vera Johnson, for example, said: "On account of staying in the old neighborhood on the Hill too long—those houses were going for about fifteen thousand dollars—we only got eighty-five hundred dollars because we waited too long." Joe Slovensky, whose mother moved from the northwest section of the area as soon as an African American person moved next to her in 1964, reported that she had bought her house for nine thousand dollars in 1951 but, because of the depreciated values caused by blockbusting, sold it for only one thousand dollars more thirteen years later. Marilyn Simkins recounted the sense of economic vulnerability: "The market dropped, and a man who lived across the street from us stayed a year or two after we did, and he only got thirty-five hundred dollars for his house. . . . People sold because they were afraid they would lose their shirt."

On the other hand, the very few who elected to remain through the most acute stages of panic (recall that in all of census tract 1608 only 390 whites remained by 1970, 96 by 1980) frequently saw their housing values return to their previous levels. John Carpenter, for instance, said that the first panicked sale on Normandy, where racial change came late, brought only four thousand dollars: "That was the cheapest that went for any house, because from then on, every house went up in price, and my mother—who was one of the last [whites] to leave [in 1967]—got eleven thousand dollars." Most interviewees agreed with Carpenter's view that in the long run purchase prices eventually moved back to original levels and beyond—but few whites remained long enough to witness the rebound.

White interviewees tend to view African Americans as having been used in the racial turnover process. However, they differ over the class status of the first African Americans to inhabit formerly all white blocks in the Edmondson area. Marilyn Simkins, for example, expressed the opinion that new African American residents were sold houses they could not afford: "Black realtors would bring in black families who wanted to move to the suburbs, so to speak—because Edmondson Village was somewhat of a suburban area; you had a lot of grass and trees—and entice these people into buying a house they couldn't afford. And I know in the case of the people who bought our house, that's exactly what happened. They had the dream of owning their own home, and this sweet-talking guy talked them into something they couldn't afford." Madge Cooper, on the other hand, viewed the first African American tenants quite differently: "They did not use poor families; they really used people who could well afford it and were normally professional people—doctors and teachers were the blockbusters." Similarly, there were conflicting reports and impressions regarding whether the first African American settlers were renters or owners. Madge Morgenstern made a distinction between her experience in the early stages of racial change on Allendale Street, when she felt homes were bought by speculators and rented to "undesirable" people, and her experience nearly ten years later in the latter stages of racial change on Augusta, when she felt the people buying were "a fine class of black people." However, Alice Hughes viewed the process as exactly the reverse, believing that the first settlers were stable, middle-income people, largely home purchasers, the latter of lower socioeconomic status and more difficult to accept.

Clearly, there were instances where blockbusters rented or sold to African Americans who lacked the economic means to afford the costs of the newly acquired housing. In this sense, the scare tactics may have conformed to the contention that blockbusting involved the intentional introduction of new residents who differed not only racially but economically as well. Moreover, it took relatively few such arrangements to achieve the desired result. At the same time, however, the preponderance of African American settlers who found new housing opportunity in Edmondson Village appear not to have differed in terms of socioeconomic status nearly so much as white residents tended to believe. Many were neither "renters" nor "lower class," thereby calling into question the interpretation that the real issue was not race but class. The *real* issue, indeed, was race.

The fact of the matter is that Edmondson Village's white residents were extremely vulnerable, both socially and economically, to the tactics of the blockbuster. Socially, their subscription to the suburban ideal as a haven, their lack of social contact with blacks, and their general prejudice, widely shared at the time, all would have made adaptation questionable under the best of circumstances—and the tactics of the blockbusting process guaranteed, indeed depended in part upon the likelihood, that circumstances were anything but the best.

Economically, the threat was no less real. In American society, if a man's home is not necessarily his castle, one's home nevertheless is one's accumulated equity and—for the broad middle class—one's economic security. Clearly, the development of the Edmondson area by Keelty and the other rowhouse builders had been made possible by mechanisms that facilitated home ownership, and the area attracted settlers willing and able to make this investment. Sometimes, purchase represented a sacrifice, but one that seemed a risk worth taking for the status and security of residence in the new neighborhood. Home ownership equals stability, so the popular belief goes, and the evidence for the statement is widespread enough to give it credibility. But home ownership also represented countless individual decisions to move up and out, countless calculations of the cost of doing so, countless sacrifices, dreams, and aspirations. Blockbusting, therefore, threatened the very foundation upon which Edmondson Village residents had built a satisfying and seemingly secure community lifestyle. David Graff moved to the area as a new clergyman during the latter stages of the racial change process in the mid-1960s. His observation on this point is instructive: "For people, their home is their biggest investment—that's their security blanket. And that's the fear that [racial change] brings . . . because what happens in our [collective] understanding is that if blacks move into the neighborhood, the value will go down." News of even a few instances—like the one cited earlier from the interview with Simkins where houses worth ten thousand dollars were reported to sell for thirty-five hundred dollars—spread like wildfire through the neighborhood and induced panic of major proportions because the threat seemed so clearly devastating to residents' financial well-being.

The socioeconomic uniformity of the area's white residents was a key characteristic of this rowhouse neighborhood, a source of strength and a source of weakness: if one was threatened, all were threatened; if all acted in concert, security would be preserved, but if *any* acted out of self-interest, as inevitably some would, then the stone foundations became foundations of sand. Bonuses for those who sold early, penalties for those who resisted the offers—these were the high risks and high stakes blockbusting introduced into the residential equation. As David Graff saw it: "If somebody offered someone a couple of thousand dollars more than they knew they could get if they put their house on the market, they'd sell it [right away]. There was a lot of fear involved. And it became personal survival over having any integrity for the community."

Could people afford to relocate? As in any fluid neighborhood, some people had been doing so all along, as personal hopes and the prospects of upward mobility dictated, especially when new suburban housing opportunities boomed during the postwar period. Family type and economics played a mixed role in affecting these proclivities. For instance, under ordinary circumstances the group most likely to consider relocation included younger families, even those whose economic resources may have been strained in the process, because they saw such a move as "something for the kids." When the fuel of racial change was added to the equation, this group fled rapidly and en masse, as indicated by the rate of racial redistribution in the public schools. On the other hand, those whose families were older, including some of the earliest settlers, had strong attachments to the neighborhood and were less attracted to resettlement. In David Graff's view:

I think that the people who were left were mainly the older. And they were probably the first ones on the hill when the houses were built. There was a lot of sentimentality. It was home; they were too old to make any transitional moves. There were just too many things like that in their minds they just couldn't handle. And, also, as I talked with them, they weren't totally disturbed by the transition, because they had gotten to know many of their black neighbors. I can still remember when a couple of them did move, the black neighbors coming out and sitting on their porches and crying, because they had really established some close ties and friendships.

In surprisingly short order, however, residents with these long-term attachments were engulfed by the panic and joined the exodus as well. Among both younger and older family types were those with modest economic resources who typically would not have felt they had the economic resources to contemplate a move, especially one likely involving higher housing costs. For this group, the prospect of lower sale prices was especially threatening. Nevertheless, many proceeded to relocate who could not necessarily afford to do so but who felt they had no other choice. The mechanisms of panic peddlers preyed upon white vulnerability and made a clean sweep.

White Responses to Blockbusting

The tactics blockbusters used in the Edmondson Village area were extremely effective. As Agnes Malone described the consequences: "It was gradual—then there was a rush." While the result indeed was mass, collective behavior, the response in fact took a variety of individual forms.

The climate of blockbusting prompted many to act in isolation, keeping their plans secret even from close friends, neighbors, and relatives. In part, the bribe of the blockbusting system encouraged sellers to get out when it was to their greatest advantage. And what people were told by the solicitors and learned quickly through neighborhood communication networks was that the moment of greatest advantage was to be among the first to sell. Yet to do so, especially in a context that people regarded as a close, friendly neighborhood setting, meant betrayal of one's neighbors. No wonder that so many operated in great secrecy, often at the expense of relationships and in spite of statements to the contrary. Agnes Malone recalled: "A lot of people said they would never sell their houses to blacks, and they were the first ones to do it." And Hughes recounted:

There was a feeling of fear; there was a feeling of, get out fast while I still can. There was a feeling of pressure: I can't afford to move, but if I don't move now, I won't be able to move at all, because I won't be able to afford to buy another house. . . . The only thing that people kept secret was whether they were going to be one of the first sellers—everybody would say, well, if I move, I'm not going to sell to blacks, I'm only going to sell to whites—they would tell this to their neighbors, because they didn't want to be thought of as contributing to the problem. But, of course, there wasn't anybody but the blacks who were going to buy the houses, so everybody did sell to blacks in the end.

Vera Johnson, who talked about the particularly close relationships she and her family valued in the neighborhood, recalled the shocking experience regarding her uncle, who lived next door: "If you were depending on a certain number of neighbors to stick it out so you'd have white neighbors, forget it! Even my dear uncle—guess when we found out he was moving? The day the moving van pulled up! This was right next door, and he never told us one word about it." David Graff described what people had told him of their experience: "They didn't tell their neighbors. Because the way it was presented to me was, I'm making this offer to you, but if you don't take this offer, two or three months from now, you'll receive an offer for maybe eight or nine thousand, not fourteen or fifteen. The whole design of the blockbusting system was built on secrecy, privacy, because if words gets out, your neighbor is going to be the one who gets the prize, not you."

Blockbusting produced a new community ethic, with individual families feeling tremendous pressure not to be victimized themselves yet wanting to act with loyalty toward their neighbors. Many were reported to have taken the attitude described by Madge Morgenstern: "I'm not going to be the first one to sell to a black, but I'm sure not going to be the last." Nola Null expressed a similar consideration in her own case: "I said I couldn't sell because the neighbors aren't going to move. I hated to sell, but the neighbors moved two days before I sold mine. The blacks moved right in."[49]

Individuals kept a close eye on the behavior of their neighbors to try to judge what was happening, since open and honest communication broke down—and trust along with it. Nola Null said, "The couple across the street sold their house to a colored family unbeknownst to us. I used

A White Community Responds to Change

to go look out the corner of the curtain to see if any blacks were looking [at houses] because I didn't want to sell."

In some instances, the threat of racial change was reported to have been used as a means of settling old scores, as silent betrayal became overt revenge. Indeed, Madge Cooper believes that the first instance of African American settlement in the southeastern corner where she lived occurred as the result of a neighborhood dispute: "In 1955 the first black family moved in on North Rosedale in the middle of the night. Ironically enough, by a neighborhood argument: . . . there was an argument between two families, and what they would say was, 'O.K., I'll fix you, we'll sell to a black.' And that was actually how that neighborhood [started to change]. And they had a big meeting, and nobody else was going to do anything, and they were going to try to get rid of this person. But somebody else saw how they could make some quick money—and it just happened." John Carpenter recalled a similar instance where neighborhood conflict led to a threat to sell to African Americans as a means of retaliation: "The man up the street, Mr. Jameson, who had been a fireman with the 53 engine company, lived on the alley next door to an old Army guy who was rough as nails. . . . Well, Mr. Jameson and this man, Mr. Penrose, didn't get along. Mr. Penrose said, 'If you don't shut up, I'll sell this house to niggers!' So he did that. Well, then immediately the Archways sold their house. . . . "

While the predominant tendency was for isolated decisions, collective action was sometimes attempted, particularly in the early stages. Often it took the form of urging united resistance to blockbusters' inducements. Neighbors might reassure one another informally that they would not sell to blacks. Sometimes, as Nola Null recounted, the commitments were more formal: "Before I thought about selling, everyone agreed to stay put. . . . One of the men went around with a paper saying we wouldn't sell. . . . I felt that the neighborhood was going to go, but as long as we stayed, it would stop." In some instances, neighborhood associations sought to curb panic and persuade people not to sell. Marilyn Simkins recalled the efforts of William Donald Schaefer, then president of the Allendale-Lyndhurst Association and newly elected councilman from the district (later mayor of Baltimore and governor of Maryland): "I remember William Donald Schaefer . . . coming to the house and talking to my mother and trying to persuade her to stay. At the time he came she had not put the house up for sale; he was there one afternoon and was trying to talk all the neighbors into staying and having faith in the area." Edith Romaine spoke of similar meetings in the northwest section: "When it first happened, they had meetings, and they told the people, 'Don't panic, don't move—if you don't sell your house, they can't move in.' But evidently people panicked—when one got in, that was enough for everybody else—they just started going. They had quite a few meetings."[50]

Aside from the community associations, few local institutions attempted intervention in the process—perhaps one factor that accounted for the degree of panic. However, efforts to intervene to dissuade flight were seldom effective, sometimes perhaps counterproductive. The priest of the local Roman Catholic church in a neighborhood evenly divided between Catholics and Protestants was a person of considerable influence by virtue of his office and a character of considerable stubborn will by virtue of his personality. According to Father John Smith: "Monsignor Vaeth was a very feisty character. . . . He swore that blacks would never move into Edmondson Village. . . . As white people began to move, they said that he would get up in the pulpit and launch into tirades that 'All you dummies want to move; you ought to stay here; this is a good community!' And they said that for about a year and a half, he just went into tirade after tirade—he began to see his whole parish just disintegrating."[51] Calm counsel, angry tirades—neither seemed capable of stemming the tide of panic engendered by blockbusting.

The monsignor's outbursts may have been his personal style, but the response conformed to the general stance of churches in the neighborhood. Insofar as they addressed the issue at all, their tendency, as voluntary organizations, was to reinforce white control, not to encourage adaptation or acceptance of residential integration. In 1965 Christ Edmondson Methodist Church faced a decision about its future because of racial change, only seventeen years after the merger effected when Christ Methodist closed its doors at its former North Avenue location because of racial succession and joined Edmondson Avenue Methodist. Since most of the parishioners of Christ Edmondson already had moved out of Edmondson Village, the congregation considered a vote to close and to sell out to an African American congregation. Only a minority of the membership urged that the church stay open and try to make the adjustment to racial integration. However, the Methodist hierarchy refused to approve the closing of the local congregation; instead, conference authorities assigned a minister to attempt to integrate the congregation. In response, according to the church's historian, William Joynes, "some 92 withdrew their membership" in protest, leaving only a small white remnant committed to the church's continuation on the new basis.[52]

The blockbusters and new African American residents were not the only outside forces impinging upon Edmondson area attitudes during the decade of massive racial change. Locally and nationally, challenges to

A White Community Responds to Change

segregation had become more persistent, and education provided a fulcrum for concern. Indications of limited change, as in the 1952 vote by the Baltimore Board of School Commissioners to permit integration of the specialized program at Baltimore Polytechnic, paled in comparison to the sweeping decision by the Supreme Court in May 1954, that segregated schooling was inherently unequal and therefore unconstitutional. The Baltimore Board of School Commissioners responded to the ruling at its June 3 meeting by voting unanimously to "conform to a non-segregated basis" and announced that an open enrollment plan would be implemented immediately, to take effect for the fall term.[53] That action brought the first few African American students from outside the area to Edmondson Village's Gwynns Falls Park Junior High School in September. Citywide, 3 percent of African American students enrolled in formerly white schools; at Gwynns Falls the number was eight of 2,109.

Though the initial days of Baltimore school integration were calm, near the end of the month demonstrations occurred at several former white elementary and junior high schools. Parents picketed the schools and kept their children home. Most of the schools where the incidents occurred were on the south and west sides of the city in predominantly white, working-class areas adjacent to predominantly African American sections. The westernmost of the school incidents occurred at Gwynns Falls, located on the eastern edge of the Edmondson Village area it generally served, just across the valley from neighborhoods that recently had changed to African American residency.[54] Interviewees who attended the junior high school as students at the time mention the tensions and the protests that occurred there. Madge Cooper recalled:

I remember when the law was passed that the schools were integrated. . . . Parents marched, mostly the mothers. They were very fearful. I think that the biggest fear they had was their children would pick up some of the traits that they saw in the black community that they thought were less than desirable. [They marched] right in front of Gwynns Falls school. . . . That was quite a time—it was very scary; you didn't know what was going to happen; and I guess you didn't know if someone was going to get hurt—that was what you were concerned about—fear for them. And they were pretty vocal—many carried signs. See, there were none [blacks] who were probably living right there then. . . . They had been precluded from coming there before, but now they could.

Marilyn Simkins described consideration of a boycott of classes:

I think I was in eighth grade. . . . I remember the day that it happened. We knew that it . . . would be effective on such and such a day. I had heard rumors that they wouldn't make us stay in school, and some were saying that when the law passes I have to walk out of school. My mother told me under no certain circumstances was I to come home. It was the law, and I was to stay in school, whether I liked it or didn't like it. And I did. And a lot of the kids' mothers came and demonstrated and wrote signs. It wasn't what you would call a large crowd, by today's standards of a demonstration. But a lot of mothers came and picked up their kids from schools. Some of the boys jumped out of the classroom windows. I think they just all got carried away.

According to contemporary newspaper accounts, a lone counterpicket appeared at Gwynns Falls: Clarence Mitchell, Jr., Washington bureau chief of the NAACP, whose son was one of the new African American enrollees, marched outside the school with a placard that read, "I Am an American, Too." The protests by white parents dissipated quickly throughout the city in the face of concerted calls for calm by elected officials and community leaders, buttressed eventually by a tough stand by the police commissioner, who announced that he would use a Maryland law that prohibited interference with schools or children attending school as the legal basis for action against the protesters.[55]

Conditions at Gwynns Falls calmed down, but Kiefer Mitchell, whose father had carried the counterpicket sign, later told *Sun* reporter Eric Siegel that his experience at the junior high had been "a very trying time": "There was hostility on the part of the students and the surrounding neighborhoods. My father had to take me to school for at least six weeks until things settled down.... [Once, on the playground, I was] assaulted by a neighborhood gang of older youths, caught up in the antagonism of integration. Each day I would get totally involved in art.... It was a safe haven as well as a way of exploring my interests.... After the first year, overt hostility was not as apparent.... But neither were steadfast friends forthcoming."[56] From the point of view of a neighborhood white pupil, Marilyn Simkins, the African American students represented "a very small percentage. Three in my immediate homeroom—maybe four in the classroom next to mine, so it was maybe one percent of my graduating class. [The students were] very nice, very quiet; in fact, they were nicer than some of the white kids that went there.... They were nice kids, well-spoken; they stuck to themselves. They were not boisterous or loud, never caused any trouble." Nevertheless, they were a sign of change and of the inability of the community to control it. The fact that the first instances of white flight occurred near the school in the same southeastern corner the same year may not have been unrelated. Shortly after the integration of Gwynns Falls Park Junior High, the early stages of

A White Community Responds to Change

new African American settlement brought resident minority students into the neighborhood's elementary schools for the first time.[57]

Some interviewees feel that school integration served to trigger racial turnover. Marilyn Simkins said, "It was the new integration law. You just didn't go to school with black people; you just didn't live with them. It was foreign to people then. They found it distasteful. Fear. Prejudice. In some cases I know that the families had planned to move. The area had only been an interim move until they could get into a single family dwelling. But a good portion of the people just felt that they weren't going to live with blacks." Whether school integration precipitated white flight or mirrored it, the ensuing rate of racial turnover in the area's public schools was rapid indeed. One white teacher, Eunice Clemens, reported that when she retired in 1959 she had only two African American children in her elementary school classroom (at Lyndhurst Elementary, in tract 1608); a year later, when she went back as a substitute teacher, nearly the whole class was African American. A new school (Rock Glen) opened on the far western edge of the city in 1962, providing some west-side whites an alternative at the junior high level to rapidly resegregating Gywnns Falls.[58] The changing complexion of Gwynns Falls Park Junior High and the Edmondson area's other public schools was not unique in the city of Baltimore: a 1963 study reported that every one of the nine all-white schools to integrate in 1954 was exclusively African American seven years later.[59] This general citywide pattern of resegregation led civil rights advocates to charge in 1963 that the school board's open enrollment plan had not served to achieve meaningful integration and that the system instead perpetuated discrimination.[60]

In response to blockbusting and residential racial change, instances of community collective action usually took the form of resistance to integration. Few interviewees recall active consideration of racial inclusion as a conceivable or viable option. No doubt some of those who did not move immediately may have stayed because of a willingness to try to make racial accommodation work. However, the rate and speed of change led most to conclude that such prospects were dim. Similarly, few recall explicit instances where those who counseled restraint explicitly did so in the context of urging acceptance of racial integration. One African American pioneer remembered a white neighbor who did actively encourage other whites to accept African Americans as neighbors: "An attorney—Goldberg—used to live on Linnard Street, and he used to always have meetings around in different people's houses—and we were one, so we got to go around. And he wanted to know why was it that when blacks move in a neighborhood, the whites moved out. And he would say how nice the blacks had their homes fixed, because he had visited a lot of the people around here."[61] But such instances are scarce in the interview record, and there is little indication that integration was given much of a chance.

Race relations among two groups under such stress did little to improve its prospects. White and African American interviewees cite some instances of efforts at friendly neighborly relations on a one-to-one basis. However, unpleasant encounters stand out in people's memories on both sides of the racial change experience and certainly influenced attitudes. There is no way to put the nature, quantity, or validity of such instances in any objective context, but their impact must be taken seriously, because in a racially charged atmosphere, incidents perceived as intergroup conflict take on heightened significance.[62]

African American interviewees report some instances of harassment, primarily by teenagers in the early stages of the pioneering period of residential settlement. Their experience will be discussed more fully in chapter 5.

In the case of whites, incidents of African American behavior often confirmed negative stereotypes and convinced them that the social and cultural divide between themselves and their new African American neighbors was unacceptable. Frequently, such episodes were cited by interviewees as the last straw in their family's eventual decision to move, as if in a context already fraught with stress, these events served as triggers. Vera Johnson explained:

My uncle moved out [from next door]; so he sold to blacks. The people who lived in it were nice. The people on the other side you couldn't live with, and the people across the street who moved in were out dancing on the roof of their cars and on the street at two o'clock in the morning. Mortimers up the street told us they had little kids on the second floor roller skating. So it just got to the place we couldn't get to sleep. So after a while my father made the decision [to move] because of two things. The little boy next door (about four or five) opened the screen door; he came in with the hose—it was on—and he was squirting the hallway. Then Daddy had a Pontiac. . . . These kids came down the street, walked over the hood, over the roof, down over the trunk like it was a pavement. So my father said, "That did it; we gotta move!"

Madge Morgenstern explained that her family decided to move when the African American boy living next door broke into their home. Alice Hughes, who felt that the later African American settlers were more "aggressive, quite pushy, and full of hate toward the whites," reported on her own experiences:

A White Community Responds to Change

The last time I ever went to the sub shop, I went down there by myself one evening, I just wanted to bring home a sub, and it was eight blocks away and this was probably nine o'clock at night, and there were probably six to eight black boys in the store, and they started messing around in the store, saying all kinds of insulting things, and when I left the store, they followed me, and I literally ran for my life. I ran as fast as I could for eight blocks, and they chased me, right to my door. That was the last time—that was the turning point for me. That told me, hey, . . . there really is something to be afraid of here. I can recall as the neighborhood started to go, it went very fast. I remember hearing of many people who were beaten up, badly enough to be hospitalized, on the way home from school. One of my friends reported having someone shoot a gun through the window into his kitchen—the bullet went into the wall just above his head. My uncle couldn't open his windows because people were throwing rotten vegetables at him. Little children weren't allowed to go out in their backyards any more, because black children would come in and beat them. Old people were being harassed, pushed down in the street. And so, between the people's own natural antipathy, through their own prejudice, to live with the blacks, and the over-aggressive behavior of the blacks, it is easy to see why the neighborhood changed as fast as it did.

Such incidents played a role in the decision by Edith Romaine's family to move:

I do recall one Christmas Eve I had some people over, and they left, I guess it was about 11:30, and I was sitting in the dining room, wrapping some last minute Christmas gifts, and my mother walked in from the kitchen, and she got to about right here, and she started screaming. And evidently what had happened was that there was a black guy who was standing up on the outside rail, looking in the glass, and she was frightened. And we went in the kitchen and called the police. What had happened was that there was a peeping tom. . . . They caught him . . . so, they got him on our front porch, and they wanted me to go down and identify him. Well, he was drunk, and he lived on Linnard Street. It just got to the point where everybody was afraid. Nothing really happened, [but] my mother was never right after that. . . . It just frightened her. . . . She tried to stick it out.

While such occurrences may not have been widespread, nor necessarily representative, clearly they added powerful fuel to an emotional fire already stoked by apprehension. And it was the folklore of racial change every bit as much as its reality that fanned those flames. When a popular young merchant, Tommy Creutzer, was shot in his Edmondson Avenue store by African American assailants, leaving him crippled, area white residents needed little further confirmation that their worst fears about integration had come true.

As noted earlier, white recollection of new African American settlers make distinctions among them, especially between those they considered to be more stable and more likely to be middle class in income and social values and those considered more transient, with lower income, and with values that clashed with those of a middle-class neighborhood. Frequently, they express sympathy for the former, viewing them as victims, like themselves, and acknowledging that they may have been motivated by the same quest for improved housing and neighborhood amenities that brought the whites themselves to the neighborhood. Often, however, the sympathy is in the context of an opinion that they, like whites, were victimized both by blockbusting and by the in-migration of an unstable social element within the African American community that was believed to accompany blockbusting. Thus, white sympathy for this group affirms one segment of African American pioneers even as it serves to rationalize white flight. John Carpenter, for instance, observed: "I feel sorry for a lot of the black people who first moved in down there around our church. They had good jobs; lot of them were school teachers and so forth; and they're in a vicious circle, too, because, like the Greens, right behind the church, right next door to the Greens the kids are kicking the place apart—the kids kick the spindles out [of the porch railings], and so forth." Vera Johnson expressed the view that some African American settlers had genuinely hoped for integrated residency so were disappointed when blockbusting continued to produce white flight and racial resegregation:

We got the impression that the black folk coming in wanted it the other way around. They didn't want to live with all black folk; they wanted to be in an integrated neighborhood. Just to show you what I tried to tell you is truth, we had a black police officer who moved into the Stephens's house where we used to play ball. He came up to us and said, "I was thrilled to move into this neighborhood, but I can't wait to get out. I can't get any sleep. The kids get in the alley and scream. I don't know what it is about black children, but they can't play without screaming." So he was going to move.

Some former white residents insist that the issue was class, not race, making the distinctions cited above and using them as an explanation for their—or the white community's—actions. Explaining that blockbusters had been unscrupulous in placing African Americans as renters in housing bought up in the early stages of blockbusting on Allendale, for example, Madge Morgenstern insisted, "I mean, it wasn't that they were black—if they were undesirable and white and don't take care of their property—undesirable is undesirable."

Sometimes, white interviewees said this distinction had been used at the time to try to curb racial fears and stem the tide of panic, by emphasizing that the issue might be more class than race and that by welcoming the "right kind" of African American neighbors, community socioeconomic decline might be averted. John Carpenter made this point about an incident on Rokeby Road, in the westernmost section, one of the last areas to experience racial change: "There was a hillbilly, white hillbilly, family moved in, and the man stood out front on the porch every Friday evening and collected money from the men who came to take his wife upstairs; and the kids were just running around on the front yard in their bare feet in cold weather—they were running a house of prostitution. And all the white neighbors would come down and stand opposite and laugh, and thought this was a big joke. But two black school teachers—a husband and wife—moved into one of the houses, and they all sold their houses!"

Blockbusting and white flight produced such rapid change that whites felt engulfed by the large numbers of African American newcomers who had wrested their turf from them. Edith Romaine said, "It was just that there were too many of them. You felt like *you* were out of place." Madge Cooper expressed similar feelings: "The numbers increased—and that was another thing; they felt overrun. A one-on-one situation you can probably deal with better than a two-on-one. And they were the minority then, and I don't think they liked being the minority."

Interpreting the process as a loss of residential turf, fleeing whites took with them feelings of bitterness and resentment. A very satisfying residential environment suddenly had been uprooted by forces they neither understood nor could control. In their collective action they provided dramatic proof of the power of blockbusting to prey upon their own fears regarding race.

The Demographics of a White Community That Succumbed to Blockbusting

The rowhouse community that received African American pioneer settlers in 1955 was one that seemed at the peak of its golden period—its new housing now completed, the shopping center in place, other community amenities bursting at the seams in the wake of postwar population growth and general prosperity. But was it also a community that had become golden in terms of its age profile, as the original settlers from the 1920s and 1930s, so many of whom had found stable roots in this rowhouse version of the suburban ideal, brought up their families and now approached their late middle age and senior years? And were young families moving on to newer suburban housing and schools in the county beyond, either leaving the community to establish new roots or bypassing it altogether on their way outward? Similarly, did other signs of socioeconomic status—income, occupation, home ownership, etc.—suggest patterns of stability or change that might be a clue to the community's relative well-being and help to account for the response to the challenge of race?

The census years are not the most useful indicators, since the period of change roughly corresponds to two mid-decade points—1955 and 1965. Nevertheless, a close look at the 1950 census can provide a portrait of the community prior to change for both census tracts, while the 1960 census affords a profile of one census tract in the midst of change (2007), the second about to change (1608).[63]

The community's age profile showed remarkable continuity from 1930 through 1950. While the 1940 census at the close of the Depression decade recorded a smaller percentage of young children than in 1930, the 1950 census reflected the Edmondson area's modest version of the baby boom. In the latter year, however, the percentage of those in the age group of young parents (age twenty-five to forty-four) had not grown proportionally, a possible harbinger of the loss of young families. At the same time, an increase in older age categories suggested a maturing population, though their numbers were in proportion to overall population growth. Therefore, in the half decade or more immediately prior to the first instances of racial change, there were few marked shifts in the area's age demographics.

It is clear, however, that the onset of racial change drastically altered this pattern. Less than five years after initial integration in tract 2007, the 1960 white profile revealed a striking percentage (and real) loss of the area's twenty-five to forty-four-year-olds and the proportional increase of those over forty-five. Taken together with the fact that white population actually declined by 57 percent, reflecting shrinkages in nearly *all* age categories, these early changes were significant indicators of how white flight and white avoidance converged to alter the age profile of the white community.[64] In 1960 north of Edmondson Avenue (in tract 1608)—where the racial line was virtually intact but where massive change was imminent—substantial alteration in the white age profile had begun to occur as well. Again, the absence of young family-forming adults (age twenty-five to forty-four) was the significant feature of the altered profile.

In terms of occupational status, tract 2007 displayed little change between 1940 and 1950, and even in 1960 the remaining whites represented an occupational profile that had changed only modestly. As one index, for instance, white-collar occupations stood at 50 percent in 1940,

A White Community Responds to Change

52 percent in 1950, and 45 percent in 1960.[65] Similarly, tract 1608 experienced relative stability in occupational status between 1950 and 1960, just prior to the advent of racial change. White-collar percentages there had been 65 percent in 1940; in 1950 they were 61 percent and in 1960, 57 percent.[66] Therefore, while census reports suggest modest changes in occupational level among white residents, they provide little indication of a substantial shift on the eve of racial change, which might be symptomatic of fundamental alteration in the area's socioeconomic status.

The relationship of income and housing value may provide further insight on this question, however, especially when the two tracts are compared. In tract 2007 (below Edmondson Avenue) white income in 1950 stood at $3,717, 32 percent ahead of the citywide figure; by 1960 it had risen to slightly more than $4,940, but that figure was only 6 percent above the city median. This relative decline in the income of remaining white residents in this tract suggested either a general drop in financial resources, or, more likely, that those with higher incomes had been among the first to flee. In contrast, in tract 1608 (north of Edmondson Avenue) during the period 1950 to 1960, median family income ($4,054 in 1950 and $6,239 in 1960) continued to exceed the city level substantially, the percentage advantage dipping only slightly from 44 percent in 1950 to 33 percent in 1960. These figures suggested that on the eve of racial change income medians in this tract roughly kept pace with the citywide rate of income growth and that no significant exodus of those with higher incomes had yet occurred.

Housing values, which had skyrocketed during the decade of the 1940s (by more than 150 percent in both census tracts, 145 percent in the city as a whole), leveled off in the two tracts during the 1950s. Median values in 2007 rose a modest 4 percent to eighty-six hundred dollars; in 1608 they even declined 5 percent to eighty-seven hundred dollars.[67] At the same time, citywide values continued to rise (by 26 percent) to nine thousand dollars, and metro (SMSA) values exceeded those for the city by an additional eighteen hundred dollars.

Taken together, income and housing values pose something of a puzzle, the former suggesting a neighborhood where income roughly kept pace with metro area trends, the latter indicating relative stability—or stagnancy—even as the metropolitan region experienced a substantial rise. Two observations seem justified: first, that some of Edmondson Village's white population likely could afford to live in other parts of the region on the basis of their incomes; but, second, that they were decreasingly likely to receive equity from their housing that would provide the means to improve their housing status with purchases elsewhere. Clearly Edmondson Village's white residents were being caught in an economic and social vise—between housing values in relative decline, making it an inopportune time to consider selling and moving, and the prospect of racial change, which led many to feel they had no choice but to relocate.

The census figures on housing values also help to put the oral reports on the prices offered by blockbusting speculators in perspective. When interviewees mention later panic sale offers on the order of thirty-five hundred to six thousand dollars, these represent prices startlingly short of the two tracts' approximate eight to nine thousand dollars median values in 1960. On the other hand, early overtures reported to have been in the neighborhood of twelve to fifteen thousand dollars represented tempting bait to a community whose housing values had been flat and which had begun to experience depreciation in a relative sense. Since housing costs in newer suburban areas beyond the city line were considerably higher, the bonus paid by the blockbuster to early sellers might provide the means necessary to make the outward move. Moreover, such offers were even more persuasive when residents began to contemplate how low they might become in the latter stages of the blockbusting process.

A strong force for stability throughout the Edmondson area's history had been its high home ownership rate, and there is little indication that this ceased to be the case even as the period of racial change approached. In 1950, 72 percent were homeowners in 2007 and 73 percent in 1608. In 1960 home ownership among whites in 2007 held steady at 74 percent, while in 1608 it had declined only slightly to 65 percent. Ironically, at the same time that Edmondson residents were tied to their homes through ownership (and various other social and personal ties as well), it was home ownership that also left them feeling very vulnerable.

Finally, had residential mobility increased in the area in advance of racial change? Here the ten-year census periods present particular difficulties in determining an answer. In-migration had been very strong in the postwar period, as new housing was added to fill up the remaining parcels of land. Nevertheless, in 1950 less than two persons in ten had moved into the area as a whole during the preceding year, a rate almost identical to that for the city generally (17 percent in 1608; 12 percent in 2007; 16 percent in the city as a whole). In 1960, when the census looked instead at the previous five years, more than six of every ten whites in both census tracts had lived in the same house longer than five years (62 percent for 1608 and 66 percent for whites remaining in 2007), evidence of much greater residential stability than either the rest of the city (54 percent) or the metropolitan area (51 percent for the SMSA). Such relative residential permanence usually would be interpreted as a sign of community well-being. In retrospect, was it an indication of socioeconomic stagnancy for the community?

The census data tells only part of the story, however; the sample block survey provides the basis for a closer examination of mobility patterns, based on close analysis of ten sample blocks. A distinction must be drawn, of course, between the patterns of mobility on settled blocks (for which rates of population change might be considered typical of the neighborhood) and on newly developed blocks (where virtually all residents would be newcomers). As noted previously, population growth due to new housing development continued into the 1950s, accounting for a sizable percentage of the continuing in-migration of white residents. Those moving into new housing on sample blocks along Flowerton Road and Wildwood Parkway, for example, replicated the social character of other white residents both in terms of occupational profile and their prior residence in older sections of Baltimore's western and southwestern sectors. A greater sprinkling of East European and Italian names indicated the out-migration of later ethnic groups from the changing city.

Once blocks were settled in the Edmondson area, rates of in-migration and out-migration remained low, a pattern evident during the Depression, World War II, and into the early postwar period. On sample blocks in the survey, 77 percent of the households in 1940 had the same resident as five years previous, and in 1950 the percentage held firm at 81 percent. During the decade of the 1950s, in advance of racial change, white in-migration and out-migration continued at essentially the same steady, low rate. In 1960 the proportion of whites who had lived in the same residence five years earlier was still 80 percent on blocks not yet experiencing racial change. However, out-migration, which in the past had usually been to other parts of the city, now was almost entirely directed westward into Baltimore County.

Some studies of racial succession have argued that white avoidance may be more significant than white flight as an explanation for racial turnover. However, for Edmondson Village the evidence strongly suggests that whites continued to seek settlement right up to the moment of racial change. Another model of racial succession has argued for a filtering process, contending that the patterns of in-migration and out-migration may lead to a gradual socioeconomic alteration in the complexion of a neighborhood's make-up.[68] Common to both lines of analysis often is an assumption of incipient decline in the socioeconomic status of white residents. While the data on Edmondson Village may not be conclusive regarding whether there was some slight shift in the socioeconomic standing of new white settlers, clearly any process of gradual, long-term change was short-circuited by the rapidity of the racial change process that blockbusting precipitated.

As late as 1956 all ten of the sample blocks were still entirely white in their racial composition. By 1961 racial change had occurred in the three blocks on the south side of Edmondson Avenue (Denison Street, Normandy Avenue, Hilton Street), but none in blocks on the north side, except for Grantley Street, which had one African American household. In 1964 racial residential change on southside blocks was almost total; on the north side, eleven of fourteen Grantley Street households now were African American, but on other northern blocks African American residency was slight and scattered.[69] However, by 1970, 102 of the 108 households in the sample were African American.

White Perceptions in Retrospect[70]

Clearly whites were bewildered by a process that was so rapid and seemingly inexorable that it overwhelmed them. Blockbusting introduced into what had appeared to them to be a secure and stable social world an atmosphere of such panic proportions that confusion combined with traditional racial prejudice to overrule calm and reason. No wonder that retrospective memories of the process suggest a wide range of opinion about the social character of the pioneering African American residents as these two populations literally passed in the night. Many moved so abruptly as to have virtually no direct contact with their new neighbors. Some experienced unfortunate episodes—like incidents of harassment—or heard enough rumors of such behavior to form very negative opinions. Others recall much more positive encounters but felt they had no choice but to bow to the inevitable.

The interview accounts, generally, reflect perceptions that incoming African American settlers represented people of substantially differing socioeconomic status whose presence signaled a significant break with the community's past social identity, an end to the dream of rowhouse suburbia. No doubt at the root of many such feelings was the sense that in a racially divided society, differing cultural styles themselves represented radical discontinuity. But frequently the objection was couched in terms of social class rather than race. In the prevailing retrospective interpretation,

A White Community Responds to Change

socioeconomic homogeneity and residential stability were supplanted by socioeconomic heterogeneity and residential instability, thereby threatening the sense of closeness and security that had been hallmarks of the rowhouse suburb. Many who fled must have harbored similar views at the time, no doubt heightened by the traumatic sense of crisis that blockbusting induced.

The tendency for former white residents to frame recollections in terms of this fault line of discontinuity undoubtedly is colored to some degree by nostalgia for the earlier period, compared to the sense of loss, frustration, or bitterness the era of change engendered. Moreover, for the earlier period their knowledge is direct, first-hand, the impression of the insider; for the latter it typically is more brief, distant, the impression of the outsider. While likely subject to distortions—magnified by the lapse of time—these interpretations bear analysis because such perceptions surely were at the heart of the individual and collective decisions that led to "the exodus." Since people *act* on the basis of what they believe to be true, whether it is objectively the case or not, their perceptions have a social reality that must be taken into account in any effort to understand a social scene as intense and complex as rapid racial change. Federal census tract data and the sample block survey provide retrospective evidence to test some of the salient factors that may have undergirded such perceptions and to place them in a perspective not available to residents at the time. These factors will be commented on only briefly here for the purposes of comparison, since they are treated more thoroughly in the separate chapters on each period in the community's history.

Did residential stability and longevity differ substantially for the prior white community and the succeeding pioneer African American community?[71] On one hand, both community profiles suggested striking degrees of stability, especially if one discounts the absolute discontinuity represented by the short period of near total population turnover. In both eras, in-migrants tended to be young, married adults, already with young children or anticipating children, who shared in common the beginning stages of family formation. Both groups displayed exceptional residential permanence, suggesting either a high degree of satisfaction with housing, neighbors, and neighborhood, or, at least, a calculation that the housing package was the best of available options. The cycle of young couples moving in and beginning new families, which for white residents characterized both the 1920s and the late 1940s and early 1950s, was repeated by young African American families in the early stages of racial change who gave the area its third era of rejuvenation—this time with a different hue.

As each successive group of in-migrants remained in place and matured, residential longevity eventually contributed subtly to change because it produced a gradually aging neighborhood.

While the appearance of stability had a sound basis, the fact of the matter was that the community had always absorbed substantial rates of change, as well. Population growth had been the order of the day for the rowhouse community since its inception in the 1920s during successive waves of new building development up until the late 1940s and early 1950s. And while the sample block survey confirms perceptions of residential longevity, it also makes clear that steady rates of in-migration and out-migration always characterized the area. Although the degree of change had been substantial throughout the first four decades of community experience, the perception prevailed that those moving in and those moving out closely resembled one another in social character, so that the neighborhood's identity seemed constant. Significantly, however, population and migration patterns following the period of massive racial change were not appreciably different. After the initial phase of population change and growth, the area reached its all-time population high in 1970 with 21,500, then actually declined for the first time in its history, in 1980 dipping below the 18,000 mark initially reached in the late 1950s. Moreover, both the census and the block figures indicate levels of residential stability closely matching the earlier levels once racial change occurred. The low rate of out-migration in later years may have been attributable, at least in part, to the lack of housing opportunity for African Americans in the suburban wedge beyond, where new housing was concentrated.

High rates of home ownership undergirded the sense of stability in the rowhouse community from its initial development. This factor, evident in the census and sample block survey data, was frequently cited by interviewees, who noted its desirability as a token of the stake in the community that homeowners were expected to have. Home ownership also appears to have been interpreted as community protection, assuring that only a certain type of person would move in—a perception that proved essentially true in socioeconomic terms. Even after the period of racial change, however, high home ownership rates remained a significant characteristic of the neighborhood, remarkably so, given the destabilizing circumstances under which African Americans gained access to Edmondson Village housing.[72] While this accomplishment might be claimed by speculators to refute the charge that their practices were exploitative, it more likely is testament to the resilience of the new African American settlers and to their resourcefulness in finding ways to sustain the costs of their much-needed housing gains.

Residents from the two periods also had a great deal in common in terms of shared place of origin and prior urban experience, since in both cases they were relocating to the greater socioeconomic homogeneity of the rowhouse suburb from more heterogeneous urban neighborhoods. Most white settlers had come from older sections of the city, principally on the west side, during periods when these areas were experiencing housing pressures in part related to the significant population increase of African Americans and lower-income whites. In contrast to the changing racial and socioeconomic mix of their former neighborhoods, they found a rowhouse community consisting of people who seemed just like them. New African American settlers represented absolute discontinuity with this social definition as far as race was concerned, of course, but in some other respects their experience paralleled the patterns of their white predecessors. They also were not newcomers to the city, nor had they or their families been part of the wartime migration from rural Southern areas to Northern and border state cities. Typically, most had moved from neighborhoods on Baltimore's west side, which had become overcrowded as the result of these demographic dynamics. Like the whites before them, they were following a common path to residence in a neighborhood whose social characteristics were more narrowly differentiated along social lines. But they were doing so as part of a population surge that produced housing needs even more dramatic than those of the earlier migration. Many of them by their own accounts were seeking a greater degree of neighborhood social homogeneity than had prevailed in the more socially and economically heterogeneous ghetto neighborhoods from which they had come. For most, the desire for improved housing and community circumstances took precedence over explicit preferences for residential integration. However, those who intentionally sought an integrated setting, in part because they believed it would serve as a hedge against the socioeconomic decline that often occurred when race rather than class determined neighborhood social character, found their hopes dashed when white flight left a community as rigidly segregated as it had been in the past.

General economic status represented an important area of perceived discontinuity, especially in interpretations that argued that differences in class were more critical than differences in race per se in accounting for white concern about racial change. In terms of household income, from its early settlement this rowhouse community consistently and rather uniformly registered somewhat higher than the city or regional median. As racial change occurred, African American pioneer households had incomes closely approximating the figure for their white neighbors who remained, though white incomes in sections not yet affected by change were somewhat higher. Significantly, household income stood considerably higher than the African American median for the city as a whole, while approximating the metropolitan area figure. Over time, however, the income level of the community began to erode considerably, something that had not happened in the earlier era.[73]

The occupational base from which white households generated incomes above the median level had always been a white-collar/blue-collar mix, with few at either the top or the bottom of the occupational hierarchy. The sample block survey reveals this occupational profile to have been quite stable, even as older residents died or moved away and newer residents moved in, almost as if house type dictated work type, though the reverse more likely would have been the case. Interviewees also recall few adult women having been engaged in the paid labor force during the community's formative decades. Their steady entrance by 1940 and 1950 was notable as a source of additional household income, though they were concentrated in clerical jobs, technically white-collar but typically lower in pay.

As racial change occurred, the occupational profile of the new pioneer group shifted in some important ways, though not as greatly as white perceptions might have suggested. Indeed, block-by-block comparisons from the sample block survey show a striking degree of continuity in workforce makeup even as racial identification changed rapidly. But pioneer households often had to adopt different economic strategies to generate comparable income levels and to afford the costs of life in the new community.[74] In part, this circumstance stemmed from important differences in the character of the African American workforce, highly conditioned by historic structures controlling access to types of jobs. For instance, overall there was a notable tilt toward greater dependence upon blue-collar positions than had been the case in the past, especially pronounced in a comparison of the jobs held by white and African American men. As a result, comparable income levels had to be generated from an occupational base somewhat more concentrated in less skilled job categories, which returned lower pay. Further, African American families placed greater reliance upon women in the paid labor force, a pattern long employed out of necessity within the African American community.[75] In the case of Edmondson Village's young two-parent families, women in the workforce usually represented a second adult earner, a strategy whose importance for economic support in the new neighborhood was underscored by a higher participation rate than was the case for African American women citywide. Still, compared to Edmondson Village's white women workers, African American women were less likely to gain access to coveted clerical jobs, and their job distribution was more broadly divided among clerical, service, manufacturing, and domestic service work categories.

These contrasting economic strategies make judgments about comparative class status for the prior white and succeeding African American communities in Edmondson Village complicated, and they may have contributed in part to conflicting perceptions at the time. There is little doubt that the profile of the new settlers represented some decline in typical indices of socioeconomic status regarding occupation. Even if those African Americans who relocated to new housing opportunity in rowhouse suburbs like Edmondson Village were, with some exceptions, somewhat more advantaged in socioeconomic terms than the urban African American community as a whole, their ranks nevertheless were considerably thinner than was the case for whites of similar status. Under ordinary circumstances the likelihood was that African American settlers might represent greater degrees of socioeconomic heterogeneity, and the extraordinary circumstances of blockbusting and white flight made this likelihood considerably greater. Nevertheless, differing styles in household strategies for economic support may have made these contrasts seem greater in perception than they were in fact.

For white Edmondson residents of the first forty years, consistency in occupational profile appeared to translate into a notable sense of economic security and well-being. Such continuity did not suggest dramatic upward mobility, but, when change did occur, it typically meant modest improvement in status, creating expectations that contributed greatly to the general sense of community economic well-being and stability. Could members of the successor African American community harbor the same sense of stability and optimism about economic status that had characterized the white community's earlier years? Here the data is too recent and limited to be conclusive, but interviews with African American respondents suggest an attitude less hopeful about the prospect for security, less sanguine about the opportunity for advancement. African American workers in Edmondson Village, as elsewhere, have been more likely to be locked into increasingly outmoded, less rewarding, and less remunerative job categories. Similarly, they have been less likely to benefit from important increases in such traditionally white-collar sectors as professional and technical work or upper- and middle-level management. Over time, the occupational profile in Edmondson Village has become less balanced than was the case for the pioneering generation, a decline calling into question whether the neighborhood's economic foundation will continue in the future to exhibit the same kind of resilience that it had in the past, considerations to be developed in the next chapter.

The point of these comparisons is not that the social character of the pioneering African American settlers was identical to that of previous white residents but rather that it did not differ as much as white residents may have assumed.[76] A number of the factors that had produced a sense of homogeneity and stability in the former period were replicated, or at least approximated, by the pioneering group. Yet, when African Americans began to move into the area, race—more than class—dictated the response of white residents, governing their decision to flee under circumstances that preyed upon their racial fears and prejudice. The ideal of the rowhouse suburb embodied in Edmondson Village had seemed to promise a degree of social homogeneity on exclusively white terms, and they refused to expand it to be inclusive racially. Ironically, the missed opportunity to redefine this conception cost them the very turf and territory they sought to protect. Over time, it also produced a more heterogeneous African American succession community, one that faced greater challenges than had ever been the case in the formative years.

Indeed, the environment of the white rowhouse suburb bred an insulated social world, one that apparently felt both stable and secure to its inhabitants yet was ill-adapted to the challenge of social change and therefore ultimately illusory. A setting that seemed permanent, close, and satisfying proved extremely fragile, succumbing to near total change in a matter of a few years. White residents had little prior experience with African Americans, and even under normal conditions they were unwilling to entertain the option of accepting them as neighbors. But conditions were far from normal. Blockbusting not only preyed upon their racial prejudices but magnified them because of the implicit economic threat that fanned the flames of panic. Unwilling or unable to modify their views, not disposed toward overt resistance (despite some incidents of harassment on both sides of the color line), and overwhelmed by forces they felt were beyond their control, white residents pursued the only option they felt they knew: flight.

As Marilyn Simkins sought to explain the thinking of white residents at the time, she offered this insight: "They saw a very secure world changing very drastically, and they couldn't accept it. This was distasteful, and in some respects, it was forced down their throats, and they felt they had no other choice, I guess." Reflecting on this time of social trauma, Madge Morgenstern offered a similar interpretation: "We were just not in the habit of living close to (or next door to) . . . black people. It was somewhat of a shock—culture shock, I guess—to be doing it."

Response to Blockbusting

Edmondson Village whites may have been wrong in important respects about their new neighbors. And insofar as their own racial attitudes were a powerful motivation for their flight, they—like whites in numerous similar settings elsewhere—had only themselves to blame for the sense of loss and exploitation they felt in abruptly fleeing the settled and friendly environs of their neighborhood home. Clearly, there were other choices available to them as modes of response, both individual and collective; nevertheless, they were right in their perception that blockbusting unleashed forces beyond their control. Indeed, at the time few had any very systematic sense of just how complex those networks of responsibility were. While the blockbuster might be the visible agent of such forces, the web of economic, social, and political structures that undergirded the dual housing market and created the loophole that blockbusters exploited was tightly woven into the fabric of a segregated society. White residents may not have grasped such connections fully; what they did know was that they felt powerless to prevent what was happening to them. Since most were as unwilling to entertain the possibility of integration as the system was to permit it, their individual actions assumed collective proportions that contributed to the demise of their community as they had defined it.

Moreover, it was hard to argue with their intuitive sense and informed observation that racial change seldom meant integration but, rather, the inevitability of racial succession and resegregation. They had witnessed the process in urban neighborhoods many of them had inhabited in the past, and they could see its results quite clearly on the west side along the Edmondson Avenue corridor. Despite some important efforts at an alternative response, such as those in nearby Windsor Hills and Ashburton, the inevitability of racial succession and resegregation constituted a norm so ingrained in their observation and experience that it served as an article of faith. Many no doubt shared the sentiment of Nola Null that the advent of African American settlers meant that "the neighborhood was going to go." Right as such perceptions may have been from the point of view of historical realism, ironically, they assured that the prophecy would be self-fulfilling.

Clearly, blockbusting manipulated whites' fears, triggering unprecedented social panic. Just as clearly, it exploited the cracks in the dual housing system, seizing the economic advantage to be gained by violating the silent conspiracy. In its wake African Americans gained desperately needed new housing opportunities—but at a considerable economic and social cost.

5
African American Pioneers

> Everything that is down now was up then.
> —Elizabeth Jones

African American pioneer Elizabeth Jones speaks about the current condition of the nearby park playground in her Edmondson Village neighborhood, but in a sense she speaks symbolically about a larger and extremely complex set of circumstances that have circumscribed the African American suburban quest for middle-class status and security in the American urban experience.

Race and racial fears have had powerful explanatory force in American society, an assertion nowhere more dramatically demonstrated than in the scale and speed of racial change that rewrote the demographic maps of American cities during the three decades following the Second World War. Intensified African American housing needs had been thwarted by legal, real estate, and financial practices that combined with private patterns of prejudice and discrimination to weave a dense web of institutional and structural racism. Ironically, the impasse was broken by blockbusters and real estate speculators, who operated outside the pale of the real estate and financial establishment. Feeding upon white racial fears to induce panic, these agents took advantage of legitimate African American aspirations to make a considerable profit in the process. Whites sold low to blockbusting real estate speculators rather than take the risk of waiting to see what happened to neighborhoods they always had known as "white-only." African Americans bought high for the privilege of residency in more desirable outer city and suburban neighborhoods, in spite of the fact that they often had to do so on the basis of risky financial arrangements. The speed and scale of racial turnover in areas where speculative activity was especially concentrated proved to be a double-edged sword for the new settlers, creating new opportunity even as it left distinctive burdens for individual households and for the succession African American community as a whole.

In the case of Edmondson Village, African American pioneers in many respects mirrored the social character and aspirations of their fleeing neighbors, contrary to the perceptions of many whites. Leaving congested urban enclaves behind and seeking to benefit from the improved housing opportunities and neighborhood amenities of a more suburban-style rowhouse neighborhood, new settlers perhaps resembled earlier residents in general socioeconomic terms more than they differed from them. Indeed, despite the traumatic circumstances under which racial change occurred, the community created by African American pioneers in Edmondson Village achieved remarkable degrees of well-being, judged by such conventional measures as rates of home ownership and residential permanence.[1]

Yet, the African American suburban quest in racial succession settings like Edmondson Village inevitably took a different form than it had for the new settlers' white predecessors. Blockbusting sowed seeds of community instability that made the African American experience of second-wave suburbanization a fundamentally different phenomenon. Many paid exploitative prices, frequently on the basis of financing arranged by speculators to protect their own interests while leaving buyers vulnerable to high interest rates and uncertain finance mechanisms. Moreover, as second-wave settlement, African American suburbanization in such settings meant used rather than new housing. In the Edmondson Village area, most pioneers gained sound residences, but some—especially those built in the initial phase of development during the interwar decades—would require increasing maintenance and repair costs. Faced with these substantial economic burdens, families were forced to develop new strategies to afford their newly acquired lifestyles. Rapid resegregation produced a period of instability, uncertainty, and disorganization that contrasted with the sense of stability, security, and satisfaction that had characterized the white community's suburbanizing experience. Moreover, public and commercial services were strained and showed signs of deterioration just when new demands produced greater needs.

African American pioneers could not assume the same degree of social class homogeneity in their new setting that the prior white residents had taken for granted. Ideologically, such exclusivity ran against the grain of equal rights for individuals eager to reap the initial gains in housing, employment, and education that the civil rights revolution had begun to usher in. Socially, African American pioneers represented a thin socioeconomic group, a factor that worked against traditional conceptions of suburban homogeneity in at least two respects. First, their own financial resources and status were relatively modest, yet they faced higher costs and greater

African American Pioneers

challenges than had been the case for their predecessors. Secondly, they constituted a small vanguard of a larger African American populace, few of whom had gained access to improved socioeconomic status. As new living space expanded to absorb the housing needs of the first wave of pioneers, the ranks of potential successors with comparable resources were diminished proportionally. When to these factors were added the volatility, instability, and exploitation of the blockbusting process and its persistent legacy, the odds for ambivalence and frustration for African American pioneers' aspirations in the new community context were high, indeed.

Herein lay the dilemma thwarting the hopes of a suburban African American middle class: thin both in terms of resources and numbers, the new settlers confronted a fragile balance between change and stability. That tenuous position illustrated the particular vulnerability of these African American pioneers' middle-class quest in a secondhand suburb.[2]

The Impact of Blockbusting and Speculation

In the late 1960s and early 1970s, well after nearly total racial resegregation had occurred in Edmondson Village, the community became the symbolic focus of a public controversy regarding the role of third parties in the racial change process in Baltimore. An interracial fair housing coalition, the Activists, charged that pioneer home buyers had been victimized by excessive profiteering, using the case as a platform for a broader campaign against real estate and finance practices that, the group contended, exploited and defrauded African Americans.

The Activists, an outgrowth of a CORE committee established in the early 1960s, was a coalition of African American and white civil rights advocates, including Protestant and Roman Catholic clergy. Leadership for the group was provided by its chairman, Sampson Green, an African American attorney and member of the Maryland State Human Relations Commission, and its housing committee chairman, John J. Martinez, a white Jesuit teacher at St. Bernardine's Roman Catholic School. When the organization began to focus upon the issue of speculation in racially changing neighborhoods, it was instrumental in the founding of community associations in Edmondson Village on the west side and Montebello on the northeast, the two neighborhoods that became the targets for much of its subsequent activity. A Washington *Post* reporter covering events in Baltimore noted that the group's strategy closely resembled the approach evolved by a similar coalition in Chicago, the Contract Buyers League: research, organization, picketing, economic pressure, and court suits. The

Figure 19. Six pickets were arrested by police during a demonstration against the Morris Goldseker Company in front of its downtown offices on Franklin Street, August 9, 1969. The photographer was Walter M. McCardell of the Baltimore *Sun*. (Baltimore *Sun*)

Activists and their community association partners first dramatized their protest against speculation in racially changing neighborhoods in the summer of 1969 when they began picketing the Mulberry Street office of the Morris Goldseker Company, shouting "Stop the exploiting!" The downtown protests launched what became a three-year campaign, with Goldseker the symbolic center of the controversy.[3] (See figure 19.)

In September 1970, the Activists released a mimeographed study, "Communities Under Siege," which made use of Lusk reports on metropolitan real estate transactions for the years from 1960 to 1968 to document the differential between purchase and sale prices in Edmondson Village compared to a similar but racially stable rowhouse area in northeast Baltimore. The report concluded that the average markup for all sales in the former (census tract 1608) had been double the increase in the latter (54 percent compared to 26 percent). The difference between what might have been fair market prices and the inflated prices that African American homebuyers had been forced to pay the Activists labeled "The Black Tax." Calling the pricing differential in Edmondson Village exploitative, the group concluded its comparison with the contention that "the dollar in the hands of white man buys more than the dollar in the hands of the black man."[4]

The Activists went farther in "Communities Under Siege" to name names, identifying the Morris Goldseker Company as having been involved in over one-third of the transactions in Edmondson Village's census tract 1608 during the period 1960 to 1968. Their documentation of the markups for houses bought and sold by Goldseker companies showed differentials of 69 percent (compared to real estate company markups of 34 percent in the comparison neighborhood); when the creation or increase in ground rent costs was included, the markup reached 80 percent (compared to 38 percent). They also contended that the company operated through such a variety of other front names (Lee Realty, Eagle Corporation, Woodhaven Investment Company, D & E Realty, etc.) that sellers and buyers often did not know they were doing business with Goldseker.[5]

In 1971 the Activists continued to detail the relationship between real estate firms especially involved in racially changing neighborhoods and the finance institutions with whom they did business. Reports released that year focused specifically upon one bank (Jefferson Federal Savings and Loan), the preponderance of whose loans had gone directly to Goldseker Company transactions (70 percent between 1964 and 1969), and more generally upon the pattern of loans by savings and loans associations and by commercial banks, which indirectly contributed to speculative real estate activity by favoring investors over individual home buyers. The reports spelled out the case against land installment contracts, lease option ("buy-like-rent") contracts, and double mortgages as devices for protecting both speculator and finance institution. They asserted that there often was collusion between the latter two parties, further disadvantaging the interests of the customer.[6]

The Activists justified targeting Goldseker throughout the fair housing campaign because they contended that the company was the largest in the city involved in speculative practices in racially changing neighborhoods. However, Sampson Green subsequently insisted that the protests had not been aimed only at Goldseker. Instead, he was quoted as saying, they were "'directed at the whole exploitative operation' of banks that redlined black areas of the city and the 'political structure' that was insensitive to the problems of black families desiring to purchase homes, which made it possible for individual speculators to profit."[7]

In rebuttal to the Activists' campaign, representatives of the Morris Goldseker Company claimed that the firm had not been engaged in blockbusting (a specific charge the Activists themselves avoided making), insisting that its agents had not solicited properties for sale because they had not needed to do so, since the firm simply was filling a vacuum. Meeting the Activists' charges regarding pricing practices head-on, they asserted that the average markup represented reasonable profit when one took into account the risks involved and deducted the company's legitimate costs. Indeed, a statement by the firm calculated its estimated profit as only 18.17 percent. (The Activists had focused on overall price differential; their calculation of profit was 31 percent, so considerable discrepancy remained between the two versions.) Moreover, Goldseker spokespersons defended the use of land installment contracts and buy-like-rent arrangements as a benefit to buyers who had no other access to securing mortgages. And they contended that the number of companies under which the firm operated was purely a device for tax purposes. In an indignant tone, Sheldon Goldseker defended his uncle's firm, claiming that the company had made it possible for people trapped in a ghetto environment to have "the opportunity to become proud homeowners in good houses in decent neighborhoods." "We were," he insisted, "the first liberals. We were the first pioneers. . . . We were supplying a need. We stepped into the market when people couldn't get financing but could make payments. We did it when people were somewhere in the inner city. And we did [it] without blockbusting."[8]

The Activists made their charges against the Morris Goldseker Company the subject of a civil suit, which brought even more public attention to the issue. However, the trial that was to test these charges and countercharges proved inconclusive when the plaintiffs withdrew their suit in 1972. The Activists contended that financial considerations forced them to cancel the proceedings when they were unable to afford the costs of an expert witness who could conduct an independent study of market value to verify their contentions that the housing prices had been excessive. Representatives of the Goldseker Company claimed complete vindication and insisted that the withdrawal proved the suit had no merit.[9]

The heat and light of the controversy between the Activists and the Goldseker Company posed the issues regarding speculative real estate activity associated with racial change in sharp focus. Their specific charges regarded neither solicitation practices nor the possible victimization of white sellers, both subjects of much of the early public discourse on the subject. Instead, their analysis drew attention primarily to the impact upon the succession African American community under such circumstances and to the burdens, financial and otherwise, that had been placed upon individual homebuyers. In their view, the challenges facing racial pioneers in Edmondson Village were formidable: "No statistics . . . can ever document the strains which the real estate and financial industries of the city created in the neighborhoods mentioned in this report. Hidden behind these statistics are parents who have to work two and three jobs together to pay the housing bills, children who must suffer from the absence of their parents and in overcrowded schools, deteriorating properties which cannot be improved because the necessary money is already sunk into the overpriced market."[10] In a 1975 statement Parren Mitchell, the African American civil rights activist who by that date represented the district in Congress, described his view of blockbusting's impact upon the Edmondson Village community: "Our schools could not handle the increase; our city services were strained to the breaking point; our people began to wonder if they themselves were creating another slum. . . . Money was literally carted out of 16-08 for redistribution in the more affluent areas of the city and the suburbs." Nevertheless, Mitchell insisted, in the face of such adversity a viable community had come into existence: "In spite of all these odds against them, far from creating or accepting the slum that was a distinct possibility, my constituents summoned forth their strength and integrity to such an extent that 16-08 is a viable neighborhood today."[11]

Edmondson Village and the Climate of Civil Rights

The issues the Activists raised regarding Edmondson Village signified an important transition in the civil rights climate that had been evolving in tandem with the massive reconfiguration of the racial geography of American cities. The long, slow process of organizing and protest against racial segregation and discrimination had borne fruit at the local and national level in the postwar period, culminating in substantial legislative and policy gains in the 1950s and 1960s. In important ways Edmondson Village's new settlers were beneficiaries of many of those accomplishments. Yet, often the gains proved more symbolic than real, ineffectual in implementation or frustrated by countervailing forces. Ironically, it had not been civil rights, in any direct way at least, that had brought expanded housing opportunity for the community's newcomers but real estate operators, whose methods and motives were now being contested as fraudulent and exploitative. In the aftermath of massive racial change and resegregation, the community faced substantial challenges, both from within and from without. As the agenda of the civil rights movement nationally shifted from integration and tolerance to equity and justice, the case of Edmondson Village pioneers illustrated both the dreams and frustrations of an era of change.

When African Americans first settled in the Edmondson Village area in 1955, Baltimore's civil rights movement was gaining momentum.[12] Initially led by a large and vital NAACP branch, augmented by an increasingly active chapter of CORE, local efforts targeted public accommodations and employment. Astute political alliances helped elect Republican Theodore McKeldin, who as mayor of the city and governor of the state proved to be a valuable ally, opening public jobs, supporting civil rights legislation, and pressuring business and civic leadership to be more responsive to African American concerns. In the late 1950s downtown Baltimore department stores, theaters, and hotels finally yielded to demands for equal treatment. A state public accommodations bill, supported by McKeldin's gubernatorial successor, failed in 1962 but passed a year later. Parallel momentum at the federal level led to passage of the Civil Rights Act in 1964 and the Voting Rights Act in 1965. At the height of the debate over these issues, national media attention focused briefly on Gwynn Oak Amusement Park a short distance from Edmondson Village in Baltimore County, where prominent out-of-town figures (especially religious leaders) joined local protesters in a successful challenge to the discriminatory policies of this privately-owned entertainment facility.[13]

Breakthroughs in employment in the public sector came in part as a result of African American political support for McKeldin, who as mayor opened municipal jobs such as police, librarians, and nurses in the 1940s. As governor, McKeldin ended the practice of separate racial listings for state employment in 1956. At the federal level, the Truman administration took tentative but significant executive action toward eliminating segregation in the armed services and establishing fair employment practices in federal agencies. Relocation of the national headquarters of the Social Security Administration to the Baltimore area on a permanent basis in the 1950s expanded federal job opportunities for African Americans locally. The new main complex, which opened in 1960 in the Woodlawn section of Baltimore County several miles northwest of Edmondson Village, afforded convenient commuting distance for west side residents. In the private sphere, ending barriers came even more slowly. One of the area's largest employers, Bethlehem Steel, long had hired a substantial African American work contingent at its Sparrows Point complex, but advancement was tracked separately from whites. In 1941 African American support for the union (SWOC) was considered crucial in a decisive contract vote at the steel plant. Union commitment to equal opportunity seemed slow to translate into company policy, but by 1950 advancement to more skilled and supervisory positions was becoming a possibility for African American workers. Progress in the public and private sector required continual prodding; in the 1960s the local organization of CORE mounted campaigns against the Social Security Administration and Bethlehem Steel to push for greater job access and fairer employment practices.[14] Edmondson Village's new settlers were among those African Americans who benefited from these employment gains, many of them working in the government sector and for some of the area's larger corporations where opportunities had begun to open up in the 1950s and 1960s. Though they had experienced the greater employment access that made it possible for them to seek new residential space, they nevertheless faced the persistent limitations upon advancement and mobility that increasingly frustrated the civil rights movement as it confronted the gap between legislative mandates and economic realities.

Maryland politics illustrated just how controversial the issue of fair housing could be in this border state, with its distinctive mixture of urban and rural, liberal and conservative, native and ethnic, African American and white. It became a major subject of controversy in the gubernatorial race in 1966, in which the position of the Republican candidate and eventual winner, Spiro Agnew, seemed more moderate than that of Democrat George Mahoney, who campaigned on the slogan, "A Man's Home Is His Castle." Fair housing legislation was enacted in 1967, only to be defeated subsequently by state voters in referendum. Passage of the federal Fair Housing Act of 1968 made the state action moot. The new national legislation addressed issues that had been at the heart of the Edmondson Village story; forbidden were discrimination in house sales and rentals, blockbusting and steering, and unfair lending practices.

The hard-fought, hard-won gains of the civil rights movement seemed to culminate with passage of the Fair Housing Act. However, both nationally and locally, frustration and conflict increasingly became the dominant note, as victories seemed more symbolic than real, and as deeper problems of discrimination, injustice, and economic disadvantage persisted. In response, the rhetoric of the civil rights movement took a decided turn from integration and nonviolence to separation and confrontation. Locally, membership in the Baltimore branch of the NAACP began to decline precipitously, and CORE became distinctly more militant.[15] Frustration erupted into violence, first in the simmering racial climate of Cambridge on Maryland's Eastern Shore in 1967 (site of H. Rap Brown's famous "Burn, baby, burn" speech), and then in Baltimore (and across the nation) in April 1968, following the assassination of Martin Luther King, Jr. Baltimore's disorders began on Saturday evening, April 6, and escalated rapidly, prompting deployment of fifty-seven hundred Maryland National Guardsmen, assisted eventually by five thousand federal troops. Before the disturbances ended there had been six deaths, six hundred injuries, eleven hundred businesses damaged by fire, and fifty-six hundred arrests. By the third day, Monday, April 8, a large section of west Baltimore east of Edmondson Village had become a "no-man's land," and that afternoon episodes of violence spread to more distant neighborhoods previously unaffected. According to the *Sun*, a "thieving mob roamed out to the Edmondson Village Shopping Center," where looters shattered the windows of three stores; that evening "hundreds of Negroes" gathered on Edmondson Avenue, and eight to ten corner stores were ransacked, though none was set on fire. The following day, Tuesday, the traumatic episode had run its course. In a tense incident that vividly illustrated the impasse the civil rights movement had reached by the late 1960s, Governor Agnew lashed out at African American leaders for what he considered to be their betrayal in not controlling the violence, even though many of them had been on the streets trying desperately to do just that.[16]

When some Edmondson Village residents participated in the Activists' picketing against Goldseker in the summer of 1969 and three hundred joined the Edmondson Village Association as part of the coalition's fair housing campaign, they were giving voice to frustrated hopes in their own quest for the promises of an era of change.[17]

The Social Character of a New Community

A community born through the agency of blockbusting, particularly on the scale experienced in the Edmondson Village area, faced great odds. So did its pioneer settlers. Saddled with high housing costs, subject to shaky finance mechanisms, their economic burdens would be heavier, their economic status more insecure than had been the case for whites who preceded them. The social costs might likely be high as well. A larger, younger population would produce new strains upon public and private services, historically not as responsive to the needs of African American neighborhoods as to white areas. And African American pioneers were the vanguard of a larger, poorer social group still confined to a racially restrictive residential ghetto. No wonder that the Activists, not to mention fleeing whites, would question whether the end result of racial turnover through exploitative speculative activity would be slum creation.

Demographic evidence suggests a more complex picture, however. On the one hand, the socioeconomic status and stability of the pioneer group belied the frequently voiced anecdotal impression that many, even most, new settlers differed profoundly in these respects from whites they replaced. On the other hand, the economic resources of the new settlers were indeed stretched relatively thin, their prospects for improving their status, even holding their own, somewhat dimmer than had been the case for their predecessors. Moreover, as the cost of housing cooled from its artificially manipulated heat, the gates of neighborhood settlement were opened to a broader African American populace. Socioeconomic succession may not have been inevitable when racial succession occurred, but in the wake of acute forms of blockbusting and white flight, its specter was unmistakably present.

The destabilizing effects of blockbusting and white flight might be expected to show up chiefly in low home ownership rates and unstable residential patterns.[18] However, in both respects the experience of African American pioneers seemed to contradict the expectation. In 1960 home ownership rates for the first African American settlers actually exceeded the very high rate for whites, 84 percent to 73 percent, at a time when African American home ownership in the city was only 34 percent. This extremely high figure in part suggested that the primary avenue for African American entry into the neighborhood was through purchase arrangements rather than rentals. Ten years later, in 1970, when the two census tracts had become overwhelmingly African American, the overall home ownership rate in the Edmondson area (58 percent) exceeded the figures for whites citywide and for the metropolitan area (SMSA) as a whole (54 and 56 percent, respectively). Moreover, it compared with a city African American home ownership rate of 30 percent, which actually had declined during the ten years.[19] By 1980 it is no longer possible to isolate the pioneer group in the census data; however, home ownership rates of 64 percent in Edmondson Village not only surpassed the metropolitan average of 60 percent but nearly doubled the rate for African Americans citywide (34 percent). Therefore, in spite of the highly tenuous conditions under which many African Americans owned their homes initially—land contracts and lease options, for example—home ownership rates in the neighborhood remained consistently at a surprisingly high level.[20]

Residential stability in the period after racial change represented a second area of contradiction to the expectation of potential transiency. Of course, the census figures show very high rates of in-migration as racial change progressed from the mid-1950s onward.[21] In 1970 the earliest pioneers had been engulfed by a larger population stream, as four in every ten of the area's residents had moved in during the past five years.[22] Yet in 1980 those who had relocated to the area prior to 1970 represented a substantial 40 percent of the area's population, and 72 percent of all residents in 1980 had lived in the same house in 1975.[23]

While the census figures only provide aggregate data on residential stability, the sample block survey permits some observations about specific individual households over time.[24] Comparison of residential patterns on five study blocks that had become predominantly African American by 1964 with their 1970 and 1980 profiles reveals a high degree of continuity once blocks were settled by new African American residents. On one sample block, listed by the Activists as having Goldseker-related sales in 1962 (houses were purchased for seven to eight thousand dollars and sold for $12,800 to 13,000),[25] all eleven African American householders in 1964 had moved there during the three years since 1961, and three whites remained. Of the eleven newcomers, ten were still there in 1970, and seven in 1980. Moreover, between 1964 and 1970 seven of those who remained in residence maintained their home ownership status, one gained it, and one lost it; ten years later only one original homeowner was missing, and an additional pioneer resident had gained home ownership status.

Four additional sample blocks were among those that changed racially in the period after 1964. The Activists identified Goldseker-affiliated real estate activities on or near each of the four. Despite clear indication of profiteering on house sales to new African American residents in these latter stages of the racial change process (on one nearby block, for instance, houses were bought for $6,825, sold for $12,475),[26] the pattern of residency on the four sample blocks between 1970 and 1980 was relatively stable: forty-one (of fifty-four) were second or third householders in 1970; ten years later thirty-six were in those same categories.

As these examples from the sample blocks testify, however, the price of home ownership and residential stability was high. In 1960 the first African American homeowning settlers in tract 2007 inhabited houses valued at a steep ninety-eight hundred dollars when compared to the tract median of eighty-six hundred dollars. That amount was one indication of the cost of blockbusting and speculation, what the Activists later termed the "black tax." It represented an inflated figure that placed more economic pressure upon new African American residents than upon their fellow white neighbors and stood in advance of the median for African American homeowners in other parts of the city (the African American city median for owners was eighty-two hundred dollars). Ten years later, in 1970, values in Edmondson Village were 12 percent higher than those for African American homeowners citywide. However, by 1980 median housing values in Edmondson Village (ranging from $21,500 to $28,100) more closely approximated the African American citywide figures ($24,600) and were lower than the total city median ($28,700). The relative decline in housing values seemed confirmation of the inflated prices associated with the blockbusting era, testifying to the consequences of overvaluation for those early settlers who had paid the high prices, because it reduced their equity investment. Simultaneously, of course, leveling housing values opened the area to new settlement at less cost.[27]

The trends in housing values may partly account for the degree of residential stability for homeowners, providing a clue to the ambiguous status of many Edmondson pioneer settlers, whose persistence in the community in part reflected their lack of options for subsequent physical mobility. In 1970, Edmondson area African American residents would have faced economic difficulty, not to mention social resistance, in finding desirable housing elsewhere, since the median value for owner-occupied housing in the metropolitan area exceeded the tract 1608 sum by nearly 45 percent (the 1608 median was $10,500; the SMSA, $15,200). Ten years later the relative decline of Edmondson area housing values contrasted with a metropolitan area median now more than double the Edmondson valuation.[28] By this point many Edmondson residents may have felt they had little choice but to remain where they were, even if resistance to African American residency was beginning to break down to a small degree in the suburban counties nearby. In a highly mobile society, residential stability might indicate entrapment and limited choices for a group finding opportunities for social mobility restricted as well.[29]

Income figures provide substantiation of the new group's median position as well as its vulnerability. They also point unmistakably to a relative decline over time, no doubt a function both of pioneers' inability to improve their status and of the more modest means available to later settlers. Throughout the period Edmondson Village's African American residents earned income in advance of African Americans citywide, and their relative position remained close to the metropolitan median. New African American settlers in 1960 registered an annual household income closely approximating the households of whites who remained ($4,881 compared to $4,940 for the tract as a whole) but an amount 45 percent in advance of African Americans from all parts of the city. Ten years later, in 1970, median income in the predominantly African American Edmondson area exceeded the citywide African American figure by 47 percent but fell short of the metropolitan median by 6 percent.[30] By 1980 Edmondson Village income still stood at roughly the same relative position; in that year it was approximately 59 percent ahead of the citywide African American median, and 6 percent below the metropolitan median.[31]

Employment for new African American residents was concentrated in governmental and corporate sectors where opportunity had increased in the period during and after World War II. Leading employers included the U.S. government (especially Social Security, the Post Office, and the Armed Forces), Bethlehem Steel, Westinghouse, Baltimore Gas and Electric, Baltimore Transit, the Baltimore City Public Schools, and area hospitals. Many were located downtown, but some—like Bethlehem Steel, Martin Marietta, and Edgewood Arsenal—were on the east side of the metropolitan area, where housing opportunities for African Americans continued to be even more limited than on the west.[32]

While the household income of initial African American settlers was only marginally lower than the level for neighborhood white residents, the occupational profile reflected a distinct decline in the proportion of white-collar jobs relative to blue-collar positions. In 1960 among whites remaining in census tract 2007 the white-collar/blue-collar ratio stood at two to three, while for new African American workers it was two to seven. Similarly, a comparison between predominantly white tract 1608 in 1960 and the same tract ten years later in 1970, when it was almost entirely African American, shows over half of the former to have been in white-collar positions, while only one-third of the latter were so engaged.

New African American residents were less likely to be in professional, technical, and managerial capacities, in sales, or in positions as craftsmen (skilled trades) or foremen, more likely to be manufacturing or transportation operatives, service workers, or laborers. Along gender lines, several important distinctions stand out. While only slightly more than one-fourth of white males had been employed as operatives or laborers, almost half of all African American male employees worked in these categories.[33] White women in the area's paid labor force had been almost exclusively in clerical occupations, while African American women were heavily concentrated in three categories: clerical, manufacturing, and service. Still, African American women in clerical positions accounted for a sizable percentage of the white-collar positions held by new householders as a whole, a factor that underscored the relative exclusion of pioneer males from the white-collar sector.[34] Indeed, the occupational distribution of African American settlers throughout the period did not substantially vary from the general pattern for African Americans citywide, even though median income was somewhat higher, suggesting the occupational base from which Edmondson residents generated a higher income was not substantially broader.

New African American residents maintained their economic status in part as a product of a significantly high percentage of females in the labor force. In 1960, for instance, 48 percent of Edmondson's African American adult women (in tract 2007) worked in positions outside the home, compared to only 33 percent of white women in the same neighborhood and to 44 percent for African American women in the city as a whole. This percentage increased to 62 in 1970 for Edmondson's African American female population (44 percent SMSA; 51 percent African American city) and stood at 61 in 1980 (52 percent SMSA; 53 percent African American city), as the community's women continued to play a greater role as breadwinners than did their African American peers across the city and other women in the metropolitan area as a whole.[35]

Finally, age, family structure and size, and housing density all are significant considerations in the socioeconomic profile of the new neighborhood, bearing on the issue of neighborhood well-being and stability. In 1960 the median age for the first African American residents was approximately twenty-three years; by 1980 it was close to thirty. Perhaps more revealing, only 9 percent of the 1960 pioneer cohort had been forty-five years of age or over, while in 1980, 29 percent of the total were in that age category.[36] The earliest African American pioneers overwhelmingly constituted young husband-wife families; in 1960 eleven of twelve African American households included a married couple; in 1970 seven of ten were so composed; and in 1980 six of ten.[37] These changes over time were partly a function of aging and mortality, but they also were partly a function of changing social patterns. Households with female heads were fewer than the African American citywide percentage throughout the period, though they continued to increase, reaching a substantial one-third of all Edmondson households in 1980.[38] While Edmondson female household heads earned incomes approximating those for their peers metrowide and substantially more than other African American household heads in Baltimore City, their incomes were still considerably less than the median for all households.[39]

In the early period of African American settlement, youthful families contributed to a housing density that not only surpassed that of whites who preceded them but African American household size across the city as a whole.[40] But population increase and greater housing density generally were not accommodated by the subdivision of existing housing units, a typical strategy in areas characterized by larger, older housing and more impoverished new residents. In 1960, 76 percent of Edmondson Village households resided in single structures; after ten years of racial change the percentage was 75 percent; and in 1980, 82 percent.

Both the census and sample block survey suggest that the new African American community weathered the period of blockbusting and racial change to emerge with considerable resilience and stability. The potentially destabilizing consequences of white flight, speculative housing activity, and massive in-migration did not produce the rapid degree of socioeconomic decline many had predicted. Indeed, the home ownership rates achieved by African American pioneers and the degree of residential stability were surprising, given the nature of the blockbusting process.

Yet, the toll of blockbusting had been enormously high, not only producing short-term instability but weighting new residents with a heavy financial burden as the price of their effort to improve their residential circumstances. Coping strategies, such as high female participation in the paid labor force, provided some measure of the cost of the quest for middle-class status. However, even the high degree of residential persistence, which helped to provide a new semblance of stability, suggested not only commitment to the community but limited opportunities for physical mobility, which mirrored limited opportunities for social mobility. As the pioneer generation aged, its members leaving the labor force to live on the restricted means of fixed retirement incomes and other sources of assistance, familial and governmental, more recent settlers frequently lacked income and occupational status comparable to those of the pioneers at the time of their initial move. These twin phenomena—an aging pioneer populace and the arrival of new settlers—contributed to the relative socioeconomic decline for the community as a whole over time.

The neighborhood's demographics during the period of African American pioneer settlement present a picture of a new community resembling its predecessor in important respects yet with a greater degree of socioeconomic diversity and unmistakable signs of relative decline. The product of complex racial politics and urban dynamics, second-wave suburbanization took on a very different and distinctive cast.

The Experience of African American Pioneers

The ambivalence evident in the demographic record is reflected in the experiences and attitudes expressed in interviews with selected residents from Edmondson Village's pioneering group, providing a key to the perceived social reality of life in the new community. The interviews reflect the hopes and aspirations of African American pioneers but also the dilemmas and frustrations of community-building in an area that underwent such rapid racial change and resettlement.

Seeking improved housing, neighborhood conditions, and urban services, African American pioneers repeated the suburban quest of the middle-income white settlers who had preceded them in Edmondson Village's rowhouses. Yet, while previous white in-migrants had been welcomed into a developing area that was experiencing continuing growth, expansion of public and private community services, and relative security, these new settlers were greeted with resistance and faced enormous new challenges. Some fifteen to twenty-five years after their move to Edmondson Village, African American pioneer interviewees speak of the community experience with a mixture of pride and frustration. This ambivalence is evident, for instance, in their attitudes toward such issues as white flight, the nature and legacy of real estate practices that accompanied the racial change process, the role of public and commercial institutions, and the problems posed by newcomers who may not share their socioeconomic status or values. Their testimony illustrates the particular vulnerability of their suburban dream.

The pioneers interviewed were among the first African American residents to move into particular blocks during the racial change period, the earliest who located in the first section of African American residency in 1956, the latest in the last phases of racial change in 1968. To the interviewees, Edmondson Village afforded a promise of the suburban dream: improved housing opportunity, greater space, and a more secure neighborhood setting. Annie Green—hers was the second African American family on the block in 1961—recounts: "When I moved into the neighborhood, I said, 'Gee, it's so nice and clean'—it was just a perfect place, I thought, and convenient, everything. I walked around the neighborhood and saw all the beautiful houses, and Edmondson Village [the shopping center] was so nice, and I just couldn't believe it—it seemed that it was just like a little colonial town."[41] Elizabeth Jones and her husband moved to Wildwood Parkway when the threat of the East-West expressway forced her family to relocate in 1968: "We used to ride through this neighborhood when it was about half and half; I was just impressed with this neighborhood. It was something we could afford, and it wasn't too far out. . . . After the expressway pushed us out, we picked up and moved, and this looked like one of the better neighborhoods, and Wildwood at the time was very pretty."[42]

Upward social mobility clearly was part of that dream for many of the interviewees. Asked why a large number had settled on the west side of the city when some of their major employers were on Baltimore's east side, Horace Green replied: "It's hard for many blacks to feel that they are moving up in the world and live in east Baltimore—it's amazing; but if you live in northwest Baltimore, you figure you are moving up."[43]

The area's middle-class attributes clearly were attractive to aspiring African American settlers. Whether residential integration per se was part of that aspiration is less clear. Annie Green maintains that blockbusters sometimes held out the prospect of an integrated neighborhood as an attraction to potential African American buyers: "They'd say, 'O.K., you're moving into a nice clean neighborhood; you're coming up to a white neighborhood, integrated neighborhood.'" Some express the view that white retention might have assured that community services and amenities would not have been neglected, confirming their common-sense evaluation that African American neighborhoods do not get the same consideration as neighborhoods with substantial white presence. Ensuing white flight quickly dispelled whatever hopes African American pioneers may have harbored along these lines, however.

African American interviewees in retrospect, at least, reflect considerable realism about what happened. For example, Margaret Dawkins and her husband decided against buying a house offered them by a real estate agent when they realized, "we would have broke the block if we had gone in there," noting with both pride and irony, "we weren't that desperate for a house."[44] Instead, they moved into a residence in a block where African American settlement already had occurred.

Whether African American pioneers' suburban dream implied the degree of social homogeneity and class exclusiveness that often had accompanied the white suburban experience is also difficult to determine. Many of the settlers migrated from older sections of Baltimore's central city, areas almost totally African American but with considerable social class diversity. Indeed, all but one of the pioneer interviewees followed this route.[45] In this sense, they were repeating the odyssey of social class differentiation that had characterized white suburbanization. Of course, socially homogeneous neighborhoods had not really been an option for them in the past, given the realities of the dual housing market. A few testified that they had experienced earlier phases of rapid racial succession, as in the case of Mary Slade, who had moved into an east Baltimore neighborhood in 1954 only to see an area that had been in good condition quickly "go kaput" as whites fled ("they ran like it was the plague") and large homes were subdivided for poorer African American settlers.[46]

Unmistakably, the prospects in the new neighborhood pointed to a greater degree of social class differentiation than had been the case in their previous experience. Narrow social distinction ran against the grain of an equal rights ideology that justified their own right to move, and none of the interviewees explicitly argued for social class exclusivity. However, some did regret that ordinary economic considerations had been waived by speculators willing to sign virtually anyone to a contract sale, regardless of ability to pay. In their view, these practices created a great degree of instability in the short run and contributed to eventual decline in the long term. As Mary Slade put it: "A lot of people want home ownership, but they don't realize the expense that's entailed; and unfortunately speculators don't care whether people are able to take care of the house or not; if they can get their down payment from you, the house is yours. . . . When you're black, anybody else who is black can move in beside you, because they [the speculators] take you as being equal." Similarly, Annie Green observed: "When the houses were booming, they made it so easy for people—just come on in, and you don't have to have any money down, and you pay as you go."

Family opportunity, often a corollary of the suburban ideal, played a prominent role in pioneer settlers' explanation of their move to the new area. Virtually all of the interviewees brought young families with them, and many cited opportunities for their children as an important reason for their desire to move into the area. Slade, for example, recounted: "I had four kids, and I always followed them through school even though I worked for [the federal government] for twenty-some years. I worked an evening shift for seven or eight years because I could get the kids off in the morning and do whatever I had to do to get dinner ready, so that when father came home in the evening, he could see that they were fed, and eventually I had an aunt who came in to live with me, and so she took care of things then." Indeed, the cost of such opportunity frequently required two adult salaries; in all but one instance among the interviewee group both husband and wife were employed.

Their general assessment of real estate practices in the racial change process betrayed considerable ambivalence. Frequently critical of the exploitative practices that often accompanied blockbusting, they also noted that institutional racism had closed off other avenues to housing opportunity. Annie and Horace Green, for instance, were among those who felt that real estate speculators had a destabilizing effect, especially when settlers purchased through land contracts: "Most of them came, and bought, and either had problems keeping the house, or—I don't think that too many sold—I think they had problems keeping their houses—like foreclosures. Then, too, I think a lot of those people lost their homes through these contract sales. . . . Goldseker was one that had a lot of those houses with contract sales, and you never got to own them." Blockbusters, they said, often held out a false hope to prospective African American purchasers to justify the high housing prices being asked: "In a lot of cases, people could have gotten soaked. . . . What the realtors were saying then was, 'Yes, you get up in Edmondson Village because that's an integrated neighborhood'—they weren't telling the truth, knowing that it was going to turn over because of blockbusting—there was a lot of that going on at the time. So I think they gave people the wrong information. But that was a sales pitch, in order for the person to buy."

On the other hand, a number of interviewees were less critical of the role played by real estate interests. Elizabeth Jones, for example, observed that she had heard of some blockbusting tactics—"little games," she called them—and she believed that there had been some profiteering—"realtors had a little field day," as she put it. Nevertheless, she felt African Americans had limited choices if they wanted the housing: "When you've been down and out, you know they're having a field day, but that's what you want, and you're going to pay that. It's a dream you want to come true, so you will pay that." And even though "buy-like-rent" contracts had involved risks: "I didn't have any problem with that; it was better to have something to hold onto if you really like it instead of staying somewhere and paying a lot for rent; with an option to buy, eventually it would be theirs."

Similarly, the Goldseker name draws mixed reactions from the pioneers. While the Greens were critical of Goldseker's role, some, like Mary Slade, believe that Goldseker may have served a necessary function in breaking the dual market and expanding African American housing opportunities: "When we came in here, it was stated, nobody would show me a house beyond Hilton Street—because black folks weren't going to move up there: 'We're not going to have them in the Village'; 'They're not going beyond the bridge.' Maybe that was Goldseker's problem; he made sure that some black folks went beyond the bridge!" Her view is shared by others who note that without white prejudice Goldseker's peculiar role would have been unnecessary.

African American pioneers similarly have mixed feelings about the actions of whites who fled the neighborhood. Few tell stories of overt hostility or resistance. Some even have a tendency to view the whites as victims, too. For example, a number mentioned white neighbors who put their houses up for sale, only to say at some later point that they regretted having done so once they got to know their new African American neighbors. Mary Slade remembered: "My next door neighbor said, 'Had I known you, Mrs. Slade, I'd never have put my house up for sale.'" Annie Green had a similar experience: "We had a neighbor here next door to us, one of the last ones to leave, and as a matter of fact, almost sold her house for nothing in order to get out, but when she did sell it, she regretted the fact that she had. She said to me, 'You know, I'm sorry that I sold it. If I had known I had such good neighbors as you and the lady next door, . . . that you all were as nice as you are, I wouldn't have moved.'" Slade also remembered how some whites in her section put up "This House Is Not For Sale" signs in an effort to resist the approaches of blockbusting agents but to little avail. Janice Watkins recounted the efforts of a white resident to stem the tide of white flight, telling others "how nice blacks had their homes fixed."[47]

Such accounts may function to rationalize the harsh reality of rejection—if only whites had *really* gotten to know us, they would have realized we were really just like them. But many speak of the changeover as so rapid that there was hardly any occasion for contact, even if any had been desired, and most speak with some bitterness of the prejudiced rejection they felt. One interviewee told her story: "We were the only colored family that lived there [on the block], but after we got in there, nothing but signs went up—'For Sale.' Almost every house put a sign up. And, of course, they didn't all sell, but quite a few moved away." Another told of her experience: "When I moved to the 500 block of Denison Street, there were just three [African American] families, and the next two years all the whites had scooted out." Or, as Margaret Johnson expressed her feelings (in the statement cited previously in chapter 1): "They [whites] were friendly, but they were prejudiced; they didn't want to live where colored people did. . . . They don't have to say it. . . . They didn't tell you [why they moved]; they just moved!"[48]

Often the feelings expressed about white flight were somewhat more indirect, stressing its negative impact on community stability. Annie Green, for instance, recounted:

When we first moved to the neighborhood, it was more white—we were just about the second black family on this block. . . . We could see the changes, because when we moved, there were so many sale signs all around, and it did make a difference in the neighborhood, because there was a change, and you had to get yourself adjusted to the people who were moving in, and you couldn't really know the ones who were moving out, because they were leaving so fast, so we were really going through that transitional stage. People were moving in and out overnight;

you really didn't know who your neighbors were. It was a very difficult period, because when we moved, we thought maybe the neighborhood would be stabilized; it just wasn't.

Asked why she felt the change was so rapid, Green continued: "Because the blacks were moving in, and the whites did not want to be integrated. It was as simple as that. . . . See, it was a threat to the whites—but they didn't stay here long enough to realize what kind of people we are, the people moving in. They were ready to give up and run away. . . . They saw black people come, and they took off." Any possible thoughts of integrated residency quickly vanished, and in their wake many questions about the prospects for the new community remained.

African American pioneers met resistance from existing institutions as whites acted from an assumed position of power to try to maintain hegemony in "their" neighborhood, making institutional adjustment difficult. Early experiences with many of the churches, for example, were negative, and these rebuffs cut deeply into the pride of African American pioneers. When the Greens asked the white minister of the Methodist church in the same block as their new home about the time of Sunday School for their children, he suggested an African American Baptist church outside the neighborhood. Similarly, African American parishioners report initial rejection and discourtesy when they sought to attend Roman Catholic St. Bernardine's. As Father John Smith recounted: "One lady told me that she went to communion, and someone in the bench said, 'They even go to communion!'"[49]

Some previously white churches simply folded their tents when the white membership aged and the number who returned on Sundays dwindled; some made a belated effort to adjust their policies and minister to the new African American community, but few successfully made the transition from white to African American control. One exception tends to confirm the rule: St. Bernardine's virtually died as a white church before being reborn as a predominantly African American institution. The change came not because of the internal dynamics of the parish as much as because of a policy decision at the archdiocesan level. In 1975, well after the racial transition period, the Baltimore Archdiocese sent a young pastoral team—one white, one African American—to St. Bernardine's with the express charge to develop a new African American constituency. A new style of worship and of community outreach developed. African American parishioner Roberta Warren described the change as "night and day; dead and alive."[50] Other than this case of belated, but effective, institutional adjustment, new African American-controlled religious institutions were slow to develop to fill the void in the early years; more recently, several African American congregations have mounted sizable building efforts as signs of growing church memberships and resources.

The transition at the school door was more abrupt, illustrating a difference between voluntary and public institutions. In its 1954 decision on desegregation the Baltimore Board of School Commissioners relied upon an open enrollment plan. While the board's action represented a positive institutional response to the Supreme Court's mandate to end segregation, the plan nevertheless was a gradualist step rooted in voluntary choice. As noted in chapter 4, the entry of the first African American students into Gwynns Falls Park Junior High School was met by a partial boycott of classes, part of a series of outbreaks at schools on the south and west sides of the city, though public calm was quickly restored. These initial junior high school students came from outside the immediate neighborhood, but the first African American settlement in the nearby southeastern corner of the Edmondson area soon brought new resident African American children into the neighborhood's educational institutions at the elementary level as well. Area schools experienced rapid racial turnover, so fast that Eunice Clemens, a white teacher, reported that the composition of her elementary school classroom changed from only two African American children in 1959 to an almost entirely African American class the following year.[51]

Not only was the racial complexion of the schools transformed dramatically, but younger African American residents with substantially more children quickly meant severely overcrowded school facilities. Enlarged class size and a perceived decline in school services continued to concern African American pioneer parents as much as resegregated schools. Two new elementary schools built in the late 1950s and early 1960s temporarily eased the pressure, but dissatisfaction with schools stood out as a sore spot in many of the interviews.[52]

Neighborhood frustration with the schools and with the effects of resegregation were echoed at the citywide level as well. In 1963 parents and community leaders brought considerable pressure to bear upon the school board for policies that continued to disadvantage African American students, 80 percent of whom were in schools 90 percent or more African American and a substantial number of whom were taught by part-time instructors.[53] By the 1970s officials were acknowledging that the series of policies employed to implement desegregation had not assured equal educational opportunity or improved racial balance, though prospects for the latter goal continued to be undermined by changing housing patterns and by resistance to regional solutions.[54]

Nowhere was the impact of the community's changed demographics and its new sense of powerlessness more evident than in commercial services, most notably the decline of the Edmondson Village Shopping Center. Though in its early years the shopping center was as much a white preserve as the prestigious downtown stores, by the time African American pioneers moved into the area most overt discrimination against African American shoppers had been abandoned. When African American pioneers began to patronize the Village, it was in its heyday. Roberta Warren told me: "When I first moved here, I shopped at Edmondson Village for most everything. It was like heaven." A racially changing neighborhood, exploding white suburbanization beyond—the two factors combined to doom the center and its service to the community. In 1956 a second major department store, Hecht's, opened across the street, but in 1958 the newer, larger Westview Shopping Center was built near the circumferential beltway two miles farther west. When Hochschild's, the first department store in Edmondson Village, closed in 1974 (Hecht's closed five years later—only twenty-three years after it was built), it simply confirmed a common perception of dramatic decline in the condition of the shopping center.[55]

In 1967 the Edmondson Village Shopping Center was acquired by Honolulu Limited, owned by Baltimore-born billionaire Harry Weinberg, formerly a Baltimorean and then a resident of Hawaii. Weinberg's firm also owned large sections of the old downtown retail district around Howard Street as well as several other marginal shopping centers on the city's periphery. According to newspaper accounts, Weinberg had a reputation for buying up "distressed properties" and permitting them to deteriorate, a reputation earned over a long history of purchasing commodities at moments of decline—whether Depression-era housing, failing rapid transit companies, or retail districts after their prime—then holding them for long-term investment. This posture greatly frustrated Baltimore City officials and community leaders interested in property improvement and redevelopment, whether on the large scale required for downtown revitalization in the city's declining central core or on the smaller scale for upkeep and renewal of neighborhood shopping centers.[56]

Why did the shopping center decline? Some pioneers blamed merchants, who, they felt, drastically cut back on the quality of merchandise and the level of service when the clientele became increasingly African

Figure 20. Despite "Acres and Acres of Parking," the Edmondson Village shopping Center parking lot stood nearly deserted, many shop windows boarded up in this December 1979 photo. In 1987 a local developer leased the center from its absentee owner, announcing plans to renovate the shops and attract new businesses. (Photo by David Lavin)

American. Similarly, considerable community concern targeted neglect by an absentee landlord whose investment strategies appeared to preclude improvement. Others noted such economic factors as the decreased buying power of the new residents combined with new competition in the suburbs. And some pointed fingers at elements of the African American community itself. Asked what made the Village change, for instance, senior citizens at the Rodman Center replied: "The people that hang out up there. They have a lot of ruffians up there; they have a lot of dope addicts; they have a little bit of everything; when you come out of the bank, the younger people take your money—they do everything. People are scared to go up there."

The vandalism and looting that erupted in the Village during the urban rioting in 1968 following the assassination of Martin Luther King, Jr., occurred as part of a broader social crisis, and it is difficult to determine the extent to which local residents joined outsiders as participants in these actions. Nevertheless, it may be significant that in this episode the role of the Edmondson Village Shopping Center had been transformed from community center to community target. In Elizabeth Jones's view, the riots sounded a death knell to the few merchants still remaining, leading to even more closures.

If the Edmondson Village Shopping Center served as a fitting symbol for the golden era of white settlement, its deterioration—and the frustration African American residents feel as a result—epitomized the later period. Whether the decline of the shopping center was the consequence of larger social and commercial consumer patterns, changing community demographics, individual and corporate investment policies, failure of local governmental intervention, or such antisocial behavior as vandalism and muggings, its transformation to a community problem rather than community asset illustrated the strong sense of powerlessness that many African American pioneers expressed in the interviews. (See figure 20.)

Recent years have witnessed a more hopeful prospect for the center. In 1987 a local Baltimore firm, JHP Realty (headed by developer Jack Pechter), succeeded in securing a lease for the shopping complex and announced plans to undertake major renovations, a welcome sign for the community and for those concerned about the impact of Weinberg properties throughout the city. (The nature and significance of this development and the irony of the legacy of Weinberg, who died in 1990, are considered in chapter 6.)

Finally, social class appears to be an unresolved issue for many of the pioneer settlers. A number explicitly link their own prospects for mobility to gains of the civil rights revolution, literally viewing themselves as "pioneers" in that movement, and there is considerable discomfort in addressing issues of class diversity or succession because of these sensitivities. Yet, early settlers attribute part of the difficulty encountered in the initial stages of their neighborhood experience to the minority of new residents attracted by the blockbusting process who lacked the economic means to make it in the new setting. Moreover, as the first generation has remained rooted, aging in the process of residential longevity, pioneers sometimes express bewilderment at the nature of newer, "younger" residents whose socioeconomic status and values they perceive to be different from their own. Roberta Warren, for instance, speaks of her feelings about contrasts between pioneers and subsequent settlers. For the early African American residents, she says, "It was more like a family affair. In this area in the morning the families would begin sweeping the back alley, and sweep down as far as they could go. They would take up the trash, wash down the middle of the alley. . . . It was just the people on that side of the block. And we kept it clean. . . . Some of the older blacks have moved out, and we have younger blacks here now. They could step over trash all day long." When asked what she thought made the difference, she replied, "I don't know! Some will cut the grass. But in the old days, younger people would get out and cut the grass." Some tend to point the finger at "renters," often correlating them with younger settlers, contending that they seem to have less interest in keeping up their homes and yards. Margaret Dawkins noted that her block "was really very stable, so most of the people who are there now are the people who originally bought those houses"; however, she feels, "if they're renters, they're different. You see some things happening that you didn't see before." Annie and Horace Green live on a block that has had a great deal of stability among the pioneer generation. Yet, in recent years there has been deterioration in the condition of some houses and yards, changes that they attributed to "renters": "I think why it changed a lot was because there weren't as many homeowners. Because once you have something of your own, you take pride in it; but if somebody is just renting, it doesn't matter to them how well it looks as long as they pay their rent, and the landlord will just rent it, not screen people, put anybody in." Elizabeth Jones believes that the perception that newcomers are contributing to neighborhood deterioration has been particularly troubling to African American pioneers who struggled financially to pay off mortgages only to feel that the community has changed in the meantime: "I have talked recently with some older community members who have felt 'down in the dumps.' They had just paid for their homes and here came a big change, and they kind of got disgusted." Nevertheless, when pressed for a further explanation of the change, Jones resists collective analysis, instead identifying problems as attributable to "a few rotten apples."

"Renters," "young people," "a few rotten apples"—such terms crop up in the interviews with African American pioneers as they seek to put their fingers on subtle but significant challenges to community cohesion and well-being. All hint at but tend to skirt issues of class in the context of race, as recent years clearly have witnessed the broadening of the socioeconomic definition of the community evident in the demographic data discussed earlier. Mary Slade pointed to this uneasy balance in a predominantly African American neighborhood at the socioeconomic mid-point when she talked about a community that had the appearance of middle-class status yet in fact embodied a wider range of socioeconomic status and need: "It's a misnomer that all the people that live in zone 29 [the area's zip code, 21229] have a lot of money or are above the poverty line—maybe they were initially, but as the neighborhood changed rapidly, we had people from all strata, and it presented a problem, because they had green grass in the front and green grass out back, and you usually thought of those folks as having a little bit of money, but we have people who

Figure 21. Young residents in the Lyndhurst section of Edmondson Village pose outside the recreation building which neighborhood residents repainted as part of a campaign to pressure the city government to permit them to reopen it to serve the needs of the community. (Photo by the author)

receive food stamps . . . and it's necessary for them to do so in order to survive." "Green grass" and "food stamps"—these are among the anomalies of the neighborhood that African American pioneers settled in their effort to find a more satisfactory residential environment and where many still reside. While pioneers are outspoken champions of equal rights and embrace a vision of community allowing for considerably more socioeconomic diversity than has been typical in first-wave suburbanization, they nevertheless express the ambivalent mixture of hope and frustration at the heart of the African American suburban experience. (See figure 21.)

Secondhand Suburbanization on Balance

West Baltimore's Edmondson Village case epitomizes the dilemmas confronting African American pioneers in the wake of systematic blockbusting and rapid white flight. Initial resistance from individuals and institutions; the decline of services, public and private; the difficult process of developing new community institutions; gradual socioeconomic change—all cloud the picture of relative residential stability, a high level of home ownership, and improved housing opportunities in the experience of the interviewees. Moving out to Edmondson Village under circumstances of blockbusting and white flight has brought measures of both satisfaction and frustration, as if the lines between stability and security, on the one hand, and stagnancy and deterioration, on the other, have been fine indeed in the experience of African American pioneers. The black tax has had its social as well as financial dimensions.

No social processes have been more important in shaping the twentieth-century history of American cities than suburbanization and racial change. Yet, the link between the two has been too little acknowledged or understood. In the case of the Edmondson area, the early period of development served the needs of an expanding, upwardly mobile white populace, offering not only the explicit promise of new housing but the implicit promise of social class differentiation that has been an integral part of the American suburban experience. The blockbusting era opened up desperately needed housing opportunities for middle-income African Americans, but the exploitative cost of their new housing gains placed economic strains upon individual families, while an array of challenges confronted the new community collectively. Moreover, the sheer rapidity and scale with which new housing opportunities became available quickly thinned the ranks of those who shared the economic status of most early settlers yet concentrated new settlement within particular confines. Over time, some who retraced the pioneers' odyssey to Edmondson Village were more likely to have marginal social and economic resources—the "younger people," "renters," and "rotten apples." Therefore, the thinness of a African American middle-income group and the dynamics of a dual housing market have made the process of second-wave suburbanization a very different experience for African American pioneers than for their white predecessors in instances of massive racial change. While the former might harbor the illusion, if not always the reality, of social class differentiation, African American successors—not necessarily seeking white neighbors or social class exclusion—nevertheless have struggled for measures of residential stability and satisfaction in a changed neighborhood within a context of considerable stress and uncertainty. Only seventy years after the rowhouse community's initial development, Edmondson Village's African American pioneers today have a somewhat tenuous hold on an African American middle-class quest in these secondhand suburbs.

6
The Legacy of Blockbusting

> Edmondson Village is one of Baltimore's larger townhouse communities, an area which has surmounted tremendous odds to offer some of the western section's most affordable housing.
> —Baltimore *News-American*, 1984

> People are afraid. A lot of people today still do not accept integration. But I don't know where they are going to go to get away from it. You can't; it's part of everyday living. . . . There will always be those who will knock themselves out to get away from all of it. But it's got to stop someplace—I hope it does.
> —Marilyn Simkins

> Today you don't see too many signs going up, crosses burned, craziness. When you move in, it's just another neighborhood. I'm not saying there are no problems; there will always will be problems. There are also problems black among blacks—don't put it all on racial prejudice. But people have accepted it.
> —Elizabeth Jones

This study ends in 1980, twenty-five years after the first African American pioneers moved into Edmondson Village. Of course, the saga of the community and its inhabitants, past and present, is an ever-evolving one. Its meaning is tested daily in the unfolding demographics of the metropolitan region and within the boundaries of the Edmondson Village area itself. Have there been more Edmondson Village-type experiences of manipulated massive racial change, and are there likely to be in the future? Has there been social learning as a result of such traumatic episodes? And what has been the legacy of the wave of urban racial change it epitomized? The record is not always easy to measure or interpret, but the general patterns deserve comment in conclusion.

First, episodes of racial change on the massive scale of Edmondson Village have cooled considerably during the past two decades. While the reasons are many, they are somewhat difficult to document. The slowdown of the economy in the 1980s may have had as much effect as any other single factor in reducing the readiness to move, both for African

Americans and for whites—though the point has been made that at the peak of blockbusting in Edmondson Village whites sold in panic almost without regard to the economic consequences. The dramatic expansion of the housing pool available to potential African American movers as the result of the opening of large sections such as Edmondson Village temporarily absorbed the demand for middle-income housing, though hardly provided the range of options available to whites with comparable socioeconomic status. Revised institutional practices governing real estate and financial practices mandated by such actions as the 1968 Fair Housing Act and comparable reforms at the state and municipal level corrected some of the most egregious of the discriminatory policies and practices, which at once undergirded the dual housing market and provided the crevice for blockbusters to manipulate the racial demographics of housing. The general patterns of institutional segregation, however, have remained remarkably resistant to change. And at an individual and collective level, it may well be that the changing national social climate and the specific lessons of episodes such as Edmondson Village have had their effect in changing attitudes and behavior. In 1982 a local newspaper article by political scientist Robert D. Loevy could note with emphasis, "for almost three out of every four Baltimore [City] citizens, neighborhood [racial] change simply was not a part of their lives during the decade of the 1970s"—a statement that spoke volumes in its implications regarding the urban norm in the previous decade.[1]

Second, the exodus from cities such as Baltimore to the suburbs may have slowed down, but the general pattern persists. Indeed, in the 1970s those leaving residences in Baltimore City for the surrounding suburban counties—for whatever reason—actually outnumbered the out-migrants of the 1960s. In the case of the Baltimore metropolitan region this apparent increase was in part a function of jurisdictional boundaries and the location of suburban development. In the 1960s moves to new housing often could be made to areas of recent development within the city limits, but in the 1970s new suburbanization became concentrated almost exclusively in the surrounding county ring. Significantly, however, while white out-migration from the city remained strong during the 1970s, for the first time African American out-migrants outnumbered African American in-migrants, and African Americans therefore constituted a substantial minority of the total exodus from the city's limits. Noting that these trends represented a serious loss to the city of a generally middle-class population, both white and African American, the Baltimore *Sun* in a 1983 article perceptively gauged the likely consequences: "As middle-class residents leave a city, taxes may go up, services may decline, and fewer middle-class children attend the public schools."[2] When the United States Civil Rights Commission conducted hearings in Baltimore in 1970, Commission Chairman Theodore Hesburgh concluded the lengthy sessions with an expression of concern that the city and the surrounding county areas were becoming "two separate worlds in existence and the gulf that widens [between] them produces growing hostility and fear."[3] In 1986, *Baltimore 2000*, a systematic review of socioeconomic trends in the metropolitan area, reached much the same conclusion.[4]

Third, the segregation of existing housing and the resegregation of racially mixed neighborhoods have continued to constitute the prevalent residential pattern in the metropolitan region as a whole, despite some indications of greater degrees of integration than in the recent past. The 1980 federal census offered some moderately hopeful news on this score. A Johns Hopkins University study that used the census to examine racial patterns at the neighborhood level found a modest increase in the number of Baltimore City neighborhoods that had remained integrated without experiencing sizable racial change as well as in the total number of neighborhoods with a white percentage in the 30 to 70 percent range. However, the preponderance of the city's neighborhoods were clearly divided between those mostly African American and those mostly white.[5]

Moreover, the substantial increase in adjacent Baltimore County's African American population during the decades of the 1970s and 1980s was primarily concentrated—some might say channeled—along a single corridor, Liberty Road. Racial change in northwest Baltimore City along Liberty Heights Avenue had paralleled the experience of the western corridor and Edmondson Village, with many of the same dynamics, including blockbusting and massive white flight, and during roughly the same period, one difference being the concentration of predominantly Jewish population in some northwest sections of the city and adjacent county. In the late 1960s and early 1970s African American residency leap-frogged the city boundary, with substantial turnover occurring in Baltimore County along the Liberty Road corridor approximately five miles to the general Randallstown area.[6] This section, which in 1980 accounted for half of the African American population of a county only 8.2 percent African American, represented a clear example of a racial spillover pattern rather than even dispersion into a large metropolitan jurisdiction with widely ranging housing levels and costs. In 1990, when the African American percentage in the county as a whole had grown to 12.4 percent, the Liberty Road corridor continued to account for half of the enlarged percentage.[7]

The Legacy of Blockbusting

By contrast, along the western corridor racial change proceeded at a much slower pace after the mid-1960s. Rowhouse and detached house neighborhoods between Edmondson Village and the city limits to the west had substantial African American percentages by 1980 but sufficient white presence to be considered integrated, perhaps stably so. Comparable Baltimore County neighborhoods along the northern side of the Route 40 corridor west to the beltway represented varying degrees of integration, though south of Route 40 county neighborhoods remained almost exclusively white. The 1980s witnessed persistence of these patterns, with steady increases in African American percentages in the city neighborhoods west of Edmondson Village and in the Baltimore County neighborhoods north of Route 40 to the beltway but very little African American presence on the south side of Route 40. During the same decades the general suburban Catonsville area of Baltimore County experienced only a slight increase in its African American populace, which stood at 9 percent in 1980 and 10 percent in 1990.[8]

In racially mixed sections on the west side, the demographic pattern often suggested two relatively distinct population profiles: among whites a preponderance of older adults with a smaller number of young adults, either in pre-family or starter-family stages, while among African Americans a preponderance of households made up of relatively young to middle-aged adults and their children. The pace of racial change in these communities has been relatively slow; panic has been much less evident among whites, and—unlike in Edmondson Village—there has been some opportunity for extended neighborly interaction. It certainly is too early to judge whether integration is truly being given a chance.[9] Nevertheless, if the destabilizing climate of the Edmondson Village experience can be avoided, the prospects for community well-being is likely to be enhanced for all.

White Attitudes and the Trauma of Change

Edmondson Village's white expatriates dispersed along the natural corridors of suburban migration westward, some to nearby neighborhoods, others throughout Baltimore County's general Catonsville area and beyond to Howard County. Many friendship and family networks persist, and people often encounter old neighbors on visits to regional shopping centers, churches, or social organizations. The experience of uprooting lingers as an unhealed wound, the source of mixed feelings of nostalgia, bewilderment, bitterness, and social learning. Some believe they have found new suburban havens that provide the social homogeneity and insulation Edmondson Village afforded for a while. But others view life in their new neighborhoods differently as a consequence of the Edmondson Village experience.

Interviews with white former residents of varying ages inevitably evoke considerable nostalgia for the old neighborhood and the lifestyle that accompanied it. Qualities of closeness, neighborliness, commonality, and security bubble forth unprompted in such discussions. For example, Marilyn Simkins, who was a teenager in the 1950s, offered this summation of her experience: "Personally, I would be satisfied if I still lived there, if things had stayed the way they were. It wasn't exactly what you would call paradise, but it was a nice neighborhood." Nola Null, whose brother worked for the Keelty Company and who herself settled on the Hill in the 1930s as an adult, expressed similar feelings: "I was proud to think that I lived in that neighborhood and had a nice village [the shopping center] like that. . . . I felt that I had bought in a nice section—security, a job, everything there you needed. I was proud to tell people in different parts of the city that I lived there and that Edmondson Village was my home."[10]

Retrospective nostalgia is common in oral history interviews, frequently masking considerable degrees of ambivalence and contradiction, part of a normal inclination to put the best face on past experience and to romanticize the earlier life-cycle stages of childhood or family formation. While it often takes the tone of affirmation and lament for a lost time and place, in the case of Edmondson Village it assumes a distinctive note in the remorse for a place that still exists but where there no longer are any ties of kin or friendship because the break was so abrupt and so total.

This sense of relatively recently lost turf is nowhere more evident than in the phenomenon of a series of reunions, conducted by large networks of people who grew up in Edmondson Village from the late 1940s through the early 1960s—broadly speaking the period of 1950s teen culture—and consider themselves the "Village crowd." The first reunion, held in 1973 at a fire hall in a distant suburban location, attracted nearly two hundred people who revelled in fifties music and photos screened by an opaque projector. Building on this success, the organizers planned the "25th Anniversary of the Village Crowd" for 1979, an event that drew some 350 to 400 people. Defined as primarily for those then between their early thirties and midforties, the event prompted interchanges in which participants placed themselves by age and social peer group. Illustrative was the following conversation, related by Joe Slovensky, one of the organizers: "This one guy I was talking to said, 'Joe Slovensky, I don't remember you,' and I said, 'Well how old are you?' He said, 'Forty-four,' and I said, 'Oh, you're one of the boys from the Arundel,' and he said, 'Yeah, yeah,' and I said, 'We didn't go up there, man; you guys were too old for us; we used to hang down at Whalen's.' I used to just go to the Arundel, get an orange sherbet and leave. Yes, we were afraid of that place. That was where the bigger boys were."[11] Edith Romaine, another event planner, described the evening's activities: "We cut out paper letters, and we had the names of all the places we used to hang out: like the Varsity, Champs; we had drapes, squares, ponytails, blue suede shoes, hula hoops—things like that. . . . About an hour later, I turned around, and everyone was just standing in the middle of the floor [talking]. . . . They were going around taking a poll; they wanted one every year."[12] The most recent reunion—held in 1990—again attracted a capacity crowd.

Such events have not been unusual as the aging of the postwar teen generation has produced national waves of fifties revival. But in the context of Edmondson Village, the reunions seem to take on special significance, because at the heart of nostalgic memories is the omnipresent sense that something more was lost from the neighborhood experience than the innocence associated with growing up and that that something had to do with race.

Some white former residents return periodically to see their former houses and the neighborhood, but frequently they speak of feeling depressed by the changes they see, especially by signs of deterioration. Simkins, for example, said wistfully: "It's just not taken care of anymore. I've driven through the area since I've moved out, and it depressed me so, I don't go back anymore." Voiced concerns about upkeep or signs of structural aging certainly may mask deeper unexpressed concerns about social and cultural changes as well. Indeed, change of any kind seems upsetting to memories of this past, interrupted by collective trauma. Joe Slovensky suddenly exclaimed: "I took David [his son] up where I played baseball—up on the Wildwood diamond—and they had changed the whole diamond around! It ain't the same way it was when I was there. They used to have it facing toward the woods; it's around the other way now!" The "they" seems to represent a whole array of individuals and forces, somehow responsible for forced change. But former residents do find themselves drawn back, as if a part of themselves was left behind in the uprooting. Slovensky described the return trip a friend had recounted to him: "This friend of mine came from Georgia. He brought his children—his son is sixteen— and I guess where they live, people are always coming and going. He drove his son through [Edmondson Village] that weekend and took pictures. His father owned a liquor store on Edmondson Avenue, down from the Edgewood movie, and they lived upstairs. He said his son can't imagine—he's not used to the way that we lived—and he feels he's missing so much—the closeness—whereas where they are now I'm sure they have friends, but it's so transient—people always moving." When asked how his friend's son reacted, Slovensky replied "I don't think it really did anything for the boy."

Racial change of the type and magnitude that occurred in Edmondson Village between 1955 and 1965 indeed represented a pivotal social and cultural moment, a major challenge to the suburban dream of homogeneity and exclusivity for a group of new rowhouse suburbanites. Bound up with that version of the dream was an interwoven lifestyle, status, and sense of security that had seemed insulated from the factors of diversity and change at work in a dynamic metropolis. Yet, inherent in white rowhouse suburbia were the seeds of its own demise: its unwillingness to adapt to new definitions of community and its consequent vulnerability to the manipulation and exploitation that ultimately befell it. Baltimore *Sun* columnist Michael Olesker, reflecting on his own very similar neighborhood in the northwest section of the city, where the experience of racial change was virtually the same ("It happened in my old neighborhood in 1962"), has written perceptively: "The white families of the early '60s were in transition not only between neighborhoods, but between lifestyles. This neighborhood was our first framework of middle-class security. Too bad we didn't hang around long enough to look in the mirror. We might have seen the faces of our new neighbors reflected in the framework."[13]

Many former Edmondson Village residents now reside in westside suburban neighborhoods. Some, particularly in sections along the Route 40 corridor, have already experienced recent African American settlement. Others live in neighborhoods characterized by racial homogeneity but where they recognize that minority residency is not out of the question. What is their response to the prospect of African American settlement, and how do they feel their communities will respond? Has the social learning of the Edmondson Village experience taught greater resistance, the necessity of flight, or accommodation and acceptance? As they express their own attitudes and seek to interpret the feelings of other former residents of Edmondson Village, interviewees acknowledge that resistance and flight continue to characterize much suburban white behavior. In their reflection, however, there sometimes is another note, one that suggests that the

The Legacy of Blockbusting

social learning associated with the Edmondson Village experience may have led to greater willingness to accept new forms of community. Ann Morgan, who resettled in a rowhouse neighborhood across the county line in the 1950s, recalls how the ripple effects of the Edmondson Village panic initially produced some reverberations there but believes that recent African American settlement has been accepted without the earlier fears:

> Well, we've been here about thirty years, and about twenty-five years ago a girl up on Channing Road said, "I'm not staying in this neighborhood because it will change. And I'm going to get out while I can get my money, because all of that property is going down." And she moved twenty-five years ago—for that reason. And it's only been in the last few years that we've had any blacks in the neighborhood. And it doesn't bother anybody. They keep their places nice. In fact, this old friend of mine that lived on Denison [in Edmondson Village] now lives back on Channing. She has a young black couple next door to her, and she says that they're better than the white people who were there before. She says the whites were terrible and didn't take care of their house, and this couple do, and they're very nice. She doesn't see them that often—they both work—but she says they're very nice to her.[14]

David Graff, who believes that the slowing of racial turnover in westside rowhouse neighborhoods may be as much due to economic realities as changed attitudes, nevertheless thinks that people in these communities do not feel as threatened as did whites in Edmondson Village: "These are people who have lived in Edmondson Heights—in those areas, grew up as kids, and it's almost like in Little Italy; they're buying into their own community that they grew up in. They're well aware of those changes. But they're saying, 'If I'm going to move anywhere, [it's here]. I know this community, and I feel more comfortable buying into this community.' "[15] Marilyn Simkins, whose family relocated to the Catonsville area of the county, says that her neighborhood is now receiving its first African American and Asian American settlers. Asked whether she felt that white flight would occur again in the way it did in Edmondson Village, she offered the view that she, at least, had come to the realization that people are mistaken in thinking they can find a place where they can escape: "You can't; it's part of your everyday living." And then she added, "It's got to stop someplace—I hope it does."

Institutional Impact and Community Well-Being

Whether white attitudes and behavior have changed substantially during the past several decades—as a result of specific episodes such as Edmondson Village and broad developments in American culture as a whole—questions of community stability in general and the character of neighborhoods relative to race and racial integration have always depended to a great extent on institutional factors as well. White prejudices and fears may have made the residents of Keelty's hill fertile ground for manipulation. However, the systematic application of blockbusting tactics and speculative real estate practices, the formal and informal mechanisms of a dual housing market, and the absence of either a commitment or will to prohibit and regulate such practices from both the public governmental and private business sectors combined with residents' proclivities to light the fuse and produce the explosion. In recent years much greater attention has been paid to institutional factors in the attempt to understand the persistence and impact of segregated housing patterns.[16]

Title VIII of the federal Fair Housing Act of 1968, passed just a few years after racial turnover was virtually complete in Edmondson Village, explicitly banned discrimination in the sale or rental of housing. Included in Title VIII was a prohibition against blockbusting, declaring it unlawful "for profit, to induce or attempt to induce any person to sell or rent any dwelling by representations regarding the entry or prospective entry into the neighborhood of a person or persons of a particular race, color, religion, or national origin." The act also sought to guarantee open access to the real estate market, forbidding steering—the process of directing members of racial, ethnic, or religious groups only into neighborhoods in which members of the same group already live. Discrimination in multiple listings or other services related to the rental or sale of property was forbidden. Further, Title VIII made discrimination in housing loans illegal. Enforcement authority rests with the Department of Justice, while implementation procedures and regulations have been the responsibility of the Department of Housing and Urban Development. Critics have faulted both federal departments for failing to use the authority and power of the act to develop affirmative federal housing policies and programs effectively to challenge the institutional roots of the dual housing market.[17]

Current Maryland law, the most recent version of the Maryland Real Estate Brokers Act having been approved in 1982, has a specific subsection (16.608) prohibiting blockbusting, defined in language that echoes the federal Title VIII. The subsection stipulates that brokers must not state that the entry of members of different social groups might result in "(i) the lowering of property values; (ii) change in the racial, religious, or ethnic character of the block, neighborhood, or area; (iii) an increase in

The Legacy of Blockbusting

criminal or antisocial behavior in the area; or (iv) a decline in the quality of schools serving the area." A separate subsection (16.609) prohibits the solicitation of residential properties to sell or lease, if the purpose is to change the racial composition of the neighborhood. Specifically banned for such intent are door-to-door or telephone solicitation and the mass distribution of circulars. Subsections directed to particular jurisdictions prohibit steering practices in Baltimore City (16.525) and mass solicitation in Baltimore County (16.527). Further, the Real Estate Commission may declare an urban neighborhood a real estate conservation area if there is evidence that the racial stability of the area is threatened by the volume of transactions (16.522).[18]

The systematic real estate and finance tactics applied in Edmondson Village to manipulate racial change appear not to have been repeated in their exact form on the west side. In the late 1960s and early 1970s the specific charge of blockbusting was heard on the northwest along the Liberty Road corridor where the speed and scale of racial change resembled the slightly earlier Edmondson Village pattern. More recently, however, the primary concern has been about real estate activity that may be more subtle. For instance, in the view of community activists committed to fair housing practices, steering continues to be a serious problem, contributing to the perpetuation of the dual housing system. Since steering employs the guise of the free market system, it is often difficult to detect and prove. However, real estate spokespersons often contend that the absence of documented and prosecuted complaints confirms the industry's contention that people steer themselves.[19]

When the Activists challenged blockbusting in Edmondson Village, their focus was primarily upon its destabilizing consequences and upon the exploitation of African American buyers. Not only did they document exceptionally high markups in sale prices, but they faulted shaky finance and loan mechanisms such as the land contract and lease option, which provided little protection for buyers and seemed designed to induce default. African Americans had no alternatives other than these arrangements, because they had been systematically closed out of the normal house mortgage loan process. As Samuel Brown, a key member of the Activists, explained what the group's objectives had been in 1968:

> Prior to our dealing with that problem there were two markets in the Baltimore metropolitan area: there was a black market and a white market. The white real estate market belonged to the legitimate real estate firms; they were financed by VA and FHA issuance of mortgages to the buyers. Then there was the black market.

That market was 85 to 90 percent land contracts, lease options—absolutely no regulation, and totally taking as much as the market would bear. At the same time you had the blockbusting syndrome, making housing available for exploitative purposes, and the white flight, white fright syndrome—so they were getting the houses from the whites for below market value and selling them to the black people for anywhere from 50 percent to double on the lease option or land contract.[20]

After a prolonged process of organization, protest, and litigation, the actions and publicity generated by the Edmondson Village example did benefit African Americans by opening conventional avenues for housing mortgages and educating potential homebuyers. In the view of the same interviewee:

There were a lot of silent understandings within the housing industry. But we opened up the financial institutions so black people could go in and purchase houses with regular FHA and VA financing. We also educated the black community regarding how houses should be bought. Most black people thought that this was a perfectly honest, legitimate way to obtain a home—the lease option or land contract. But most of the working-class people never received title to their home that they were attempting to purchase. For one reason or another the land contract was canceled or the lease option was canceled. They were that loaded [against the buyer] that almost at the will of the seller, the buyer almost had to violate the contract—they were that loaded. We broke that method of transfer up.

Lease options and land contracts did become outmoded mechanisms for housing purchases and conventional loans became much more widely available; however, the patterns that undergird the dual housing market remain deeply entrenched. As recently as 1987 a study of Baltimore area mortgage lending patterns found that the flow of credit from area financial institutions reflected disparity along racial lines. It concluded that the greatest number of mortgages continued to go to suburban and gentrifying areas and that banks avoided loans to low- and moderate-income African American families. These findings led Baltimore *Sun* columnist Garland Thompson to muse despairingly on their implications for perpetuating neighborhood racial segregation: "The neighborhood, that great meeting place expected to break down society's divisions, continues to be a fortress, proof against incursions of darker 'others.'"[21]

Other kinds of institutional decisions have had indirect impact on the stability of Edmondson Village and other urban neighborhoods, whether intended or unintended. The East-West Expressway, planning for which had begun in the 1940s with twin justifications of improved transportation and slum removal, created uncertainty and instability for the section east of Edmondson Village. When site clearance finally got underway in the late 1960s along a one-mile corridor formed by Franklin and Mulberry Streets (eventually designated I-170), housing shortages occurred as a sizable low-income African American populace numbering some nineteen thousand was displaced and forced to seek new shelter.[22] The rippling effect was felt by neighborhoods to the west and northwest, including Edmondson Village, even though the neighborhood was over a mile from the highway's abrupt terminus. In the view of Edmondson Village pioneer Mary Slade, the displacement contributed to a new period of instability in the recently racially changed Edmondson Village community. She said that the expressway "impacted because people had to go someplace, and they had to go whether they could afford it or not. So I understand that a lot of them came into zone 29 [a large portion of which included the Edmondson Village area], and a lot of them went up to Park Heights [to the northwest].... People just *had* to go someplace, and *had* to do the best they could under the circumstances. And it made it rough—for them, and also for the people they had to live near."[23] Further completion of the interstate route through nearby Gwynns Falls and Leakin Parks was vehemently opposed by a citywide coalition of environmentalists and community activists, but supported by a number of Edmondson Village pioneer political leaders. Their position was partly motivated by promises that the project would include substantial funds for recreational facilities adjacent to their neighborhood, an indication of the tough political choices forced upon a community where city resources were increasingly in short supply.

The institutional aftermath of the Edmondson Village experience takes on special irony in the unfolding of the Goldseker story. Morris Goldseker died in 1973. According to the terms of his will, the Goldseker Foundation was established three years later. Following the organization of the foundation, the Morris Goldseker Company served primarily a real estate management function; in 1985 the company disposed of its remaining properties and closed its doors as a business. In that year assets of the foundation were listed as approximately $26 to $27 million. According to the foundation's director, Morris Goldseker's will specified that grants be used for projects in the Baltimore area, especially for the disadvantaged. The will further stipulated that grants could be awarded only to nonsectarian organizations that did not discriminate on the basis of race or religion. Between 1976 and 1985 the foundation conferred grants in the amount of $7 million. In July, 1989 it combined with the Baltimore Community Foundation; during the 1989 fiscal year the enlarged philanthropy conferred $1,556,768 in grants to thirty-four nonprofit organizations for programs in categories of community affairs, education, health, human services, and neighborhood development.[24]

Not surprisingly, the Goldseker legacy still draws the mixed response the living Goldseker received. Sheldon Goldseker, named as one of the trustees of the foundation, always has argued that his uncle was very much misunderstood. In his view his uncle's firm early established a viable business selling houses to low- and moderate-income people, many of whom could not afford conventional mortgages. At the time of the suit brought by the Activists he vehemently denied that the company had been directly involved in blockbusting and that the profits in Edmondson Village (and elsewhere) were inappropriate. He continued to stress that the charges brought by the Activists and community organizations had not been proven in court. In his view, the establishment of the foundation was consistent with his uncle's life-long concern for the disadvantaged and his record of civic generosity, hitherto little known because many gifts had been made in anonymity. While even Sheldon Goldseker admitted that his uncle "was always an enigma," a 1978 *Sun* article could find many among Baltimore's leading corporate officials ready to praise Goldseker and to stress the consistency between his career and his bequest.[25]

Those involved in the protest against the Morris Goldseker Company, on the other hand, found the establishment of the foundation a shocking surprise, an action they had difficulty reconciling with their view of the role the company had played. For example, one prominent Baltimore African American politician involved in the actions against the company in the late 1960s was quoted by the *Sun* in 1978 as saying: "In every confrontation I had with Morris Goldseker, he certainly was not sensitive to the problems people had. He was a very hard-nosed businessman. He didn't demonstrate any sensitivity at all." Although Goldseker's bequest equally surprised another protest participant, he told the reporter that the Activists had targeted the Goldseker Company not as an attack upon its head personally or upon his firm more than others but to dramatize the systematic problems African Americans faced regarding fair treatment in housing: "His being the target was incidental. The protests were directed at the whole exploitative operation of banks that redlined black areas of the city and the political structure that was insensitive to the problems of black families desiring to purchase homes, which made it possible for individual speculators to profit."[26] Interviews with Edmondson Village residents found views on Goldseker's establishment of the philanthropic organization ranging from skepticism about possible motivations to ex-

The Legacy of Blockbusting

pressions of considerable appreciation for the foundation's grants to projects serving the needs of Baltimore's urban population.

Recently, another player in the Edmondson Village story has also entered the ranks of Baltimore's major philanthropies. Harry Weinberg, for a number of years the absentee owner of the Edmondson Village Shopping Center along with a great number of other Baltimore area properties including substantial holdings in the old, decaying downtown shopping district along Howard Street, died in 1990. Long the target of neighborhood and municipal complaints for the deteriorated condition of his properties, Weinberg left a bequest to establish the Harry and Jeanette Weinberg Foundation with $900 million in assets, a figure that made it the twelfth largest foundation in the country, dwarfing most other Baltimore area charities, including Goldseker's. Half of the approximately $45 million specified for annual grants is required to be distributed to projects in the Baltimore area, especially for institutions and programs aiding the poor.[27]

Of the entire institutional legacy relating to the Edmondson Village experience, the philanthropic bequests of two of the story's main players may be the most startling reminder of the complexity of the circumstances involved in racial change and its aftermath.

African American Experience and the Challenge of Community

Just as major earthquakes produce enormous upheavals, then successive after-shocks, so the Edmondson Village experience of systematic blockbusting and massive racial change prompted both immediate and long-lasting consequences for the community and its new generations of African American residents. As recently as 1984 the Baltimore *News-American* began a routine review of area housing for its real estate section with the statement that Edmondson Village had "surmounted tremendous odds to offer some of the western section's most affordable housing," without anywhere in the article specifically mentioning what those odds were or suggesting that they were related to racial change—as if everyone knew or as if it was something one did not talk about in an article playing up the reasonable cost of available housing.[28]

As chapter 5 has suggested, the process of racial change and its aftermath was extremely destabilizing to the community. African American pioneers and later arrivals found new housing opportunities and the amenities of the new community satisfying in many respects, typically viewing both housing and neighborhood as improvements from conditions in their places of prior residency. Nevertheless, the flight of new neighbors, the instability that accompanied the change process, and the uneven record of public and private sector performance all combined to frustrate their aspirations in the new setting.

Even for those with adequate economic resources, the financial burdens and risky loan arrangements associated with this episode of blockbusting placed a heavy burden. And for those whose status was more marginal, the process was considerably more problematic, a condition that contributed to housing turnover and to early signs of physical blight or deterioration as what had been sound housing now began to show its age when it could not be kept up. While the neighborhood absorbed a number of new residents with comparatively more marginal status, it simultaneously held on to a sizable proportion of an economically secure middle-income group of residents for whom Edmondson Village continued to represent a desirable residential opportunity, especially when other options were limited by patterns of segregation and discrimination.

After the unnatural succession of the early racial change decade, recent years have given evidence of more normal urban patterns of what social scientists have called natural succession or filtering, the product of the gradual aging of a neighborhood and the expansion of housing opportunities in the outer city and in selected areas of nearby Baltimore and Howard Counties.[29] No longer the new frontier of African American housing expansion, Edmondson Village today may be more of a half-way house, still a desirable alternative for African Americans able to make the move out from the problems of inner city neighborhoods but less attractive for an expanding African American middle class. Indeed, gains in housing opportunity over the past two decades have produced patterns of African American suburbanization not unlike earlier white out-migration trends, raising concerns about a fundamental shift in the demographics of urban African American communities, formerly characterized by a greater degree of socioeconomic heterogeneity than their white counterparts, but now following a similar pattern, which separates along class lines. At the same time, deep-seated structural inequalities have been compounded by social and economic trends in the 1980s to place further limits on opportunities for a sizable proportion of the African American urban poor. In a division that some observers have called the separation of an African American middle class from an African American underclass, Edmondson Village is a borderland.[30]

The thinness of an African American middle class is demonstrated in both the earlier and more recent periods of African American experience in Edmondson Village. In the early stages, many African American pioneers were of modestly middle-class status, resembling the socioeconomic profile of whites who fled more than differing from them. However, the rapid flight of whites combined with the lack of new white settlers to create a vacuum—a vacuum that in turn absorbed the pool of middle-income African Americans seeking new residences. Unconventional real estate and finance mechanisms doubtless attracted some newcomers who were unable to pay for the cost of life in the neighborhood. The result of these factors was a community more broadly defined along socioeconomic lines than its predecessor and certainly more so than in instances of typical suburbanization. Over time, this process of social class broadening has continued, especially as residential opportunities for African Americans with middle incomes or above have opened up in outer city and county neighborhoods. Therefore, in more recent years the thinness of an African American middle class, even one that has been gradually expanding, has further reduced the attraction of the Edmondson Village neighborhood for middle-income settlers with upwardly mobile aspirations.

The 1990 census provides recent confirmation of the ambivalent socioeconomic status of this borderland African American community, exhibiting trends indicative of continuity but also of relative decline. During the 1980s Edmondson Village residents maintained high rates of home ownership (68 percent) and residential stability (75 percent residing in the same house as five years before), exceeding both city and metropolitan area levels. The percentage of the area's labor force in white-collar jobs increased slightly (from 38 to 45 percent), though at a smaller rate than the metropolitan region (which rose to 58 percent). However, these white-collar gains were entirely in sales, clerical, and technical categories, not in typically higher paying managerial or professional jobs. Indeed, sales, clerical, and technical workers combined with those in the service sector to account for 56 percent of the Edmondson Village labor force. As in recent decades, the Edmondson area depended upon a high degree of female participation in the labor force (60 percent of women over age sixteen, compared to 61 percent in 1980), a factor that by 1990 had become prevalent for the metropolitan area as a whole (61 percent in 1990; 52 percent in 1980). The rate of unemployment and the percentage of families below the poverty line remained relatively constant at levels that appeared disturbingly high in comparison to the metropolitan figures but were slightly lower than citywide averages. Families below the poverty line represented approximately 15 percent of the total (compared to 22 percent for the city and 10 percent for the metro area), and unemployment stood at roughly 10 percent (compared to 13 and 5 percent, respectively). Perhaps most troubling, household income continued to decline in relative terms; in 1970 and again in 1980 it had lagged approximately 6 percent behind the metropolitan area figure, but in 1990 the gap increased substantially to a figure 28 percent lower (approximately $28,600 compared to $36,550). As housing aged, housing values failed to keep pace with the metropolitan real estate market, a belated echo of the era of inflated prices now reversed in a trend that affected homeowners by reducing equity, threatening security, and limiting options for mobility even as it made purchase for prospective homebuyers more affordable. Housing values in 1990 stood at approximately $42,000 compared to $53,900 for the rest of the city and $100,000 for the entire metropolitan region.[31]

During the 1970s and 1980s the decline and deterioration of the Edmondson Village Shopping Center became a symbol in popular perceptions for an increasingly negative image of the area as a whole, one evident not only in the views of many whites, including former residents, but also in the opinion of many African Americans, residents as well as outsiders. Similarly, the physical deterioration of housing along such main transportation arteries as Edmondson Avenue and Hilton Street increasingly suggested urban blight, though many side streets still displayed standards of upkeep and attractiveness long associated with the suburban rowhouse style of living. Residents expressed major concerns about such public institutions as schools, police protection, and general urban services. Recently, some public and private sector resources have been directed at a community not perceived to be in dire straits yet sometimes recognized as having clear needs. A decade ago local and federal funds were allocated for major renovation of the area's two large apartment complexes, Edmondale and Uplands. In 1985, the Allendale senior housing facility opened, providing the first publicly supported housing for the elderly in an area experiencing substantial aging of its population. The new building punctuated the two-story rowhouse hillside with the area's first high rise. Several imposing, modern churches have been erected by local African American congregations along Edmondson Avenue. And in 1987 a local development firm worked out a lease with the Edmondson Village Shopping Center's absentee ownership to renovate the retail and commercial facility, signaling a degree of commercial revitalization that may help to counter the negative community image it symbolized in recent years. By 1992 the center had been refurbished and many of the

The Legacy of Blockbusting

commercial spaces reoccupied by enterprises offering modestly priced lines of merchandise.

As in many contemporary urban neighborhoods, issues of personal safety and concerns about crime frequently come up in interviews with residents, in the words of aging pioneers—whose generation now represents a sizable percentage of the community—as well as in those of younger residents. Both groups recount incidents of muggings or of house robberies that create uneasiness and apprehension and have led them to take precautions regarding everyday patterns of shopping or going to school. Underscoring their concern about the threat of crime in the area, a study of incidences of violent crimes committed in Baltimore City between January and September 1992 listed substantial sections of the Edmondson Village community in the highest category (more than 150 homicides, rapes, robberies, and assaults), a troubling distinction shared primarily by sections of the city with considerably lower socioeconomic status.[32] Further confirmation of their concerns about physical decay and the deterioration of the quality of life, for example, was the 1988 decision by Baltimore City's Department of Housing and Community Development to designate Edgewood, a section in the older northeastern corner, as one of three outer-city Community Conservation Areas. The districts were described as having a core of stability but experiencing problems related to the maintenance of home ownership and to blighting conditions. In announcing the program, Baltimore's Mayor Kurt Schmoke said, "We intend to make sure our stable and solid neighborhoods continue to make the progress we expect." In a related development, a year later the same section was designated as one of eighteen "drug-free" zones in the city, one of a handful in the city's outer ring.[33]

The pioneer generation exhibited exceptional rates of residential stability, especially given the destabilizing conditions its members had to cope with, and many have remained, strongly committed to the neighborhood. However, the eventual availability of new housing opportunities elsewhere has attracted some residents with sufficient economic resources to consider relocating, especially as African Americans have settled in other communities along the western and northwestern suburban corridors. For example, in 1983 a *Sun* reporter investigating patterns of African American out-migration evident upon the release of the 1980 census, interviewed a family in the Liberty Road corridor of Baltimore County who recently had relocated from Edmondson Village. Raymond and Vivian Sykes had decided that their rowhouse was too small for them and their three children and found more suitable housing in a three-bedroom rancher in a section of the county where African American settlement began in the late 1960s and early 1970s. The husband, a forty-three-year-old fire inspector in nearby Howard County, told the reporter he liked living in the city and had no particular desire to leave, except the need for improved housing.[34]

Interviews with young people, especially those of high school and college age, indicate that many of their patterns of sociability are outside the neighborhood. Like many adults, they commute considerable distances to the outer suburban ring for entertainment and shopping or sometimes to the popular revitalized downtown Inner Harbor area for special occasions. Frequently they express negative feelings about life in the neighborhood that stand in stark contrast to the strongly positive memories of those who were white teenagers in the 1950s and 1960s, even when one filters out the aura of nostalgia in interviews with the latter. And often their aspirations—whether necessarily realistic or not—are eventually to settle as adults in newer suburban areas. A recent interview study with a small sample of Edmondson Village highschool-age young people, all themselves involved in one of the neighborhood's Protestant churches, found their response to be significant both in terms of their upwardly mobile aspirations regarding career and residence and their reservations about their home community. Most said they would prefer to live in outer suburban areas and that they would not want to bring up children in Edmondson Village, citing such reasons as drugs, overcrowding, and poverty.[35] Claudette Newsome, a college student whose family relocated to Edmondson Village from a deteriorating neighborhood on the near northwest side of the city, says her family's experience has not lived up to expectations. While she believes that her parents will stay, she hopes "to get away as fast as I can." Her goals are a career as a medical professional and residence in the redevelopment area near the Inner Harbor. Amanda Franklin, another student, says that she feels vulnerable as a female on the area's streets and expresses the view that there is a great deal of fear in the neighborhood. She is attracted by what she considers to be the more desirable rowhouse areas west of Edmondson Village along the city line. Speaking of parkland near her house, she exclaims, "I hear that people used to picnic there, but I wouldn't."[36]

For some of these interviewees upward and outward mobility may be strong possibilities. They may constitute a new generation of African American pioneers, as their parents before them. They may themselves settle in predominantly African American suburban communities or, indeed, forge new models of residential integration, possibly without the white flight that was so typical in the past. However, for many of Edmondson Village's youth, such a scenario is less likely. The real challenge of community in this aging secondhand suburb will be to maintain a livable and viable setting for an increasingly heterogeneous African American populace.

Beyond Edmondson Village

Embedded in the recent historical experiences of a typical rowhouse neighborhood is the story of twin suburban dreams and the unsettling discontinuity that left its lasting mark on both. Perhaps it is the dream itself that needs serious re-examination in this preponderantly suburban nation. If the suburban dream is valid in its promise of a middle ground between countryside and city, offering security, serenity, and comfort, then it must be available to all who can afford it—without regard to race or ethnicity. This is the principle of fair housing. Its advocates point out that when all communities are open without discrimination, there is no opportunity for pressure to build up to the point of explosion as it did in Edmondson Village and as so often has happened when African American settlement has been channeled into narrow corridors of opportunity. Long-time Baltimore fair housing advocate Alan Hillman put it this way in his explanation of the efforts he and his neighbors have made to promote acceptance of integration in nearby urban neighborhoods and to stem the tide of white flight: "We were city-wide integrationists. If every neighborhood were open, then we wouldn't be feeling this pressure—everybody could take it in stride."[37]

In recent years, some fair housing advocates have become wary of programs to reduce the impact of racial change and assure stable integration in formerly all-white suburban neighborhoods, fearing that such measures may place undue limits on the housing choices of minorities just when opportunities should be increasing. They have argued that efforts to stabilize integration often have good intentions but place the goal of racial balance above the principle of fair housing. Such efforts run hard up against the dilemma that levels of African American presence low enough to assuage white fears and thereby assure "stable integration" are considerably lower than African American preference and needs. They argue that only systematic promotion and enforcement of equal opportunity in *all* communities can provide the basis for resolving the dilemma.[38]

While fair housing rules out discrimination, it does not necessarily address issues of class or other forms of diversity. The power of the suburban dream cannot be denied, but its principal flaw may be the assumed necessity of exclusivity and homogeneity as the price of residential membership. Indeed, class difference, not race, frequently is cited by whites—even those who subscribe to the principle of residential racial integration—as their fundamental concern. Often this assertion is accompanied by the assumption that new African American settlers in predominantly white residential areas must themselves be of a lower class—or serve as harbingers of class change. And African American suburbanites themselves frequently share with their white counterparts this desire for class exclusivity. Though typically more careful to subscribe to an equal rights ideology and generally much more accepting of a wider degree of socioeconomic diversity, African Americans who have found a new and desirable residence in suburban settings may feel threatened by the arrival of newcomers of lower socioeconomic status—"renters," "young people," "a few rotten apples." Edmondson Village pioneer Elizabeth Jones recognizes these crosscutting issues of race and class when she asserts that today African American newcomers to suburban areas may be less likely to meet overt white resistance and white flight than in the past—"you don't see too many signs going up, crosses burned, craziness"—but that socioeconomic status continues to be a barrier, both among whites and among African Americans: "There are also problems black among blacks—don't put it all on racial prejudice."

The American pattern of suburbanization has taken homogeneity as a given, with little questioning of its fundamental assumption. Therefore, as a society we have few models of community designed to be more broadly inclusive—accepting and affirming diversity as a desirable rather than negative condition. However, as we confront the realities and prospects of a post-suburban age in which the luxury of physically separate social space is no longer as feasible as it was in a nation where there always seemed to be a new frontier to be developed, new forms of community may be a necessity—whether they can be worked out in the satisfactions and frustrations of life in neighborhood settings like Edmondson Village or must result from new affirmative institutional initiatives by the public and private sectors.

It is imperative that we understand the link between suburbanization and racial change so dramatically illustrated in the experience of Baltimore's Edmondson Village. The kind of white flight that occurred there, fueled by blockbusting in a context where conditions were ripe for massive panic and rapid racial turnover, epitomized a particularly acute instance of the relationship. However, the experience of Edmondson Village was unique only in degree, not in kind. In various forms the phenomenon

The Legacy of Blockbusting

of rapid racial succession has affected virtually every metropolitan area in this country, and its legacy is still with us. While many of the earlier restrictions on African American settlement have changed in law and practice, and the traumatic scale of racial change that occurred there has been less common in recent years, persistent racial residential segregation and the resegregation of racially changing areas are testimonies to the continuing significance of the connection between race and suburbanization in American society.

Appendix A
Suggested Reading

The Dual Housing Market

For an early statement of the mechanics of the dual housing market, see Charles Abrams, *Forbidden Neighbors* (New York: Harper, 1955). Other analyses of real estate industry and governmental roles in maintaining residential segregation include Rose Helper, *Racial Policies and Practices of Real Estate Brokers* (Minneapolis: Univ. of Minnesota Press, 1969); Calvin Bradford, "Financing Home Ownership: The Federal Role in Neighborhood Decline," *Urban Affairs Quarterly* 14, 3 (March 1979): 313-35; Kenneth T. Jackson, "The Spatial Dimensions of Social Control: Race, Ethnicity, and Government Policy in the United States," in Bruce M. Stave, ed., *Modern Industrial Cities: History, Policy, and Survival* (Beverly Hills, Calif.: Sage, 1981) and "Race, Ethnicity, and Real Estate Appraisal: The Home Owners Loan Corporation and the Federal Housing Administration," *Journal of Urban History* 6 (August 1980): 419-52, versions of which are included in his *Crabgrass Frontier: The Suburbanization of the United States* (New York: Oxford Univ. Press, 1985); and Beth J. Lief and Susan Goering, "The Implementation of the Federal Mandate for Housing," in Gary A. Tobin, ed., *Divided Neighborhoods: Changing Patterns of Racial Segregation* (Newbury Park, Calif.: Sage, 1987). Yale Rabin contends that governmental policies, both national and local, have continued to contribute to residential racial segregation; a recent statement of his case is "The Roots of Segregation in the Eighties," in Tobin, *Divided Neighborhoods*.

The dual housing market has been studied as it functioned in several specific cities. On Boston, two important studies focus on the interaction of real estate and governmental interests in shaping the city's racial geography: Harriet Lee Taggart and Kevin W. Smith, "Redlining: An Assessment of the Evidence of Disinvestment in Metropolitan Boston," *Urban Affairs Quarterly* 17 (September 1981): 91-107; and Hillel Levine and Lawrence Harmon, *The Death of an American Jewish Community: A Tragedy of Good Intentions* (New York: Free Press, 1992). For Chicago, Arnold R. Hirsch argues that politics played a major role in creating what he calls the "second ghetto" in the post-World War II metropolis in *Making the Second Ghetto: Race and Housing in Chicago, 1940-1960* (Cambridge: Cambridge Univ. Press, 1983). On the legal history of the dual housing market in Baltimore, see Garrett Power, "'Apartheid Baltimore Style': The Residential Segregation Ordinances of 1910-1913," *Maryland Law Review* 42, 2 (1983): 289-328 (see especially p. 321).

Appendix A

The Persistence of Residential Racial Segregation

Attempts to calculate indices of racial residential segregation using census data from 1940 through 1980 have found the patterns to be strongly persistent in metropolitan areas. When Karl and Alma Taeuber first developed the index as a tool of analysis, based upon 1940, 1950, and 1960 census data, they discovered rates of 85.2 percent, 87.3 percent, and 86.1 percent for the three periods, respectively. *Negroes in Cities: Residential Segregation and Neighborhood Change* (Chicago: Aldine, 1965), p. 44. Replicating the earlier study for the period 1960 to 1970, Annette Sorensen, Karl Taeuber, and Leslie J. Hollingsworth, Jr., argued for "a distinctive pattern of change," a decline in the index to 81.6 percent. "Indexes of Racial Residential Segregation for 109 Cities in the United States, 1940 to 1970," *Sociological Focus* 8 (April 1975): 125-42 (see especially pp. 125, 131). However, subsequent analysis by Thomas L. Van Valey, Wade Clark Roof, and Jerome E. Wilcox, "Trends in Residential Segregation: 1960-1970," *American Journal of Sociology* 82 (January 1977): 826-44, and by Ann B. Schnare, "Trends in Residential Segregation by Race, 1960-1970," *Journal of Urban Economics* 7 (May 1980): 293-301, attributed the finding of decline primarily to methodological considerations and to the addition of new SMSAs in 1970, concluding that any change during the decade probably was very small.

For the decade of the 1970s, Barrett Lee, comparing 1970 and 1980 census data, found some comfort that racial change in mixed tracts (in twenty-five selected cities) had not proven "inevitable." "Racially Mixed Neighborhoods During the 1970s: Change or Stability?" *Social Science Quarterly* 66 (June 1985): 346-64. In related research, Peter B. Wood and Barrett A. Lee have argued that the model of inevitable resegregation may be time and place specific, primarily descriptive of north central and northeastern cities during the period before 1970. "Is Neighborhood Racial Succession Inevitable? Forty Years of Evidence," *Urban Affairs Quarterly* 26, 4 (June 1991): 610-20 (see p. 618). Karl E. Taeuber's analysis of census data for twenty-five cities for the decade of the 1970s found a slight overall decrease (6 percent) in the index of racial segregation. Cited in Reynolds Farley and Walter R. Allen, *The Color Line and the Quality of Life in America* (New York: Russell Sage Foundation, 1987), pp. 140-43.

However, John Farley's examination of data for St. Louis led him to conclude that there had been little change in the degree of segregation in that metropolitan area for the past forty years. "Metropolitan Housing Segregation in 1980: The St. Louis Case," *Urban Affairs Quarterly* 18 (March 1983): 347-59. Similarly, John R. Logan and Mark Schneider found that the increased rate of African American suburbanization during the 1970s, the greatest growth in northern and urban areas occurring in the inner suburbs adjacent to central cities, was accompanied by well established patterns of racial succession. "Racial Segregation and Racial Change in American Suburbs, 1970-1980," *American Journal of Sociology* 89 (January 1984): 874-88.

Racial Residential Change

The literature of racial residential change is surveyed by Howard Aldrich in "Ecological Succession in Racially Changing Neighborhoods," *Urban Affairs Quarterly*

10 (March 1976): 327-48. James T. Little, Hugh O. Nourse, R. B. Read, and Charles L. Leven, *The Contemporary Neighborhood Succession Process: Lessons in the Dynamic of Decay from the St. Louis Experience* (St. Louis: Institute for Urban and Regional Studies, 1975), provide an instructive analysis of the racial transition process on a metropolitan scale in St. Louis, where the rapidity of residential change approximated the situation on Baltimore's west side. Primarily examining housing values, they analyze the relationship of race to other factors contributing to the socioeconomic decline of neighborhoods.

Morton Grodzins advanced the tipping point concept in *The Metropolitan Area as a Racial Problem* (Pittsburgh: Univ. of Pittsburgh Press, 1958). John Goering summarized the many studies that sought to test the hypothesis in "Neighborhood Tipping and Racial Transition: A Review of the Social Science Evidence," *American Institute of Planners Journal* 44 (January 1978): 68-78; he concluded that there was no social evidence for a "universally applicable" tipping point that triggered white flight (p. 69).

For the argument downplaying the causal role of white flight and emphasizing nonracial factors for the racial changeover of neighborhoods, see Harvey Marshall, "White Movement to the Suburbs: A Comparison of Explanations," *American Sociological Review* 44 (December 1979): 975-94, and W. H. Frey, "Central City White Flight: Racial and Nonracial Causes," *American Sociological Review* 44 (June 1979): 425-48. However, Clarence J. Wurdock, "Neighborhood Racial Transition: A Study of the Role of White Flight," *Urban Affairs Quarterly* 17 (September 1981): 75-89, found evidence in a 1976 Detroit study for a continuing white propensity to flee integrating areas.

For examples of studies placing emphasis upon white avoidance, see Harvey L. Molotch, *Managed Integration: Dilemmas of Doing Good in the City* (Berkeley: Univ. of California Press, 1972), especially chapters 7 and 8; Harold Rose, "The Development of an Urban Subsystem: The Case of the Negro Ghetto," *Annals of the Association of American Geographers* 60 (March 1970): 1-17; Avery M. Guest and James J. Zuiches, "Another Look at Residential Turnover in Urban Neighborhoods," *American Journal of Sociology* 77 (November 1971): 457-67; and Reynolds Farley, Howard Schuman, Suzanne Bianchi, Diane Colsanto, and Shirley Hatchett, "'Chocolate City, Vanilla Suburbs': Will the Trend Toward Racially Separate Communities Continue?" *Social Science Research* 7 (1978): 310-44.

African Americans and Suburbanization

Studies of the experience of African Americans in suburban areas in general have shown patterns of persistent discrimination, racial turnover, and resegregation. See, for example, Harold Rose, *Black Suburbanization: Access to Improved Quality of Life or Maintenance of the Status Quo?* (Cambridge, Mass.: Ballinger, 1976); Farley et al., "'Chocolate City, Vanilla Suburbs'"; Thomas A. Clark, *Blacks in Suburbs: A National Perspective* (New Brunswick, N.J.: Rutgers Univ. Press, 1979); Kathryn P. Nelson, "Recent Suburbanization of Blacks: How Much, Who, and Where," *American Planning Association Journal* 46 (July 1980): 287-300; Robert W. Lake, *The New Suburbanites: Race and Housing in the Suburbs* (New Brunswick, N.J.: Rutgers

Appendix A

Univ. Press, 1981); Logan and Schneider, "Racial Segregation and Racial Change in American Suburbs, 1979-1980"; and Dennis Gale, George Grier, and Eunice Grier, *Black and White Urban-to-Suburban Outmigrants: A Comparative Analysis* (Washington, D.C.: Center for Washington Area Studies [Occasional Paper No. 4], May 1986); George C. Galster, "Black Suburbanization: Has It Changed the Relative Location of Races?" *Urban Affairs Quarterly* 26, 4 (June 1991): 621-28.

Andrew Wiese has chronicled the development of small African American communities on the urban periphery during the period from 1940 to 1960; he argues these settlements sometimes served as precursors of later African American suburbanization. "Driving a Thin Wedge of Suburban Opportunity: Black Suburbanization in the Northern Metropolis, 1940-1960" (Richmond, Va.: paper presented to the Society for American City and Regional Planning History, November 9, 1991), p. 4.

A general bibliographical review is provided in Halford H. Fairchild and Belinda Tucker, "Black Residential Mobility: Trends and Characteristics," *Journal of Social Issues* 38, 3 (1982): 51-74.

Appendix B
Home Ownership Patterns on Selected Blocks, 1955-1973

Table 1.   400 Block of Denison Street

	400	402	404	406	408	410
1955 1957	Finch	Schaum	Albright	Johnson	Germack	LaPaglia
1959	*Preston*	*Wheatley*	**Butler Bldg. Corp**	**Oak Invest. Corp.**	*Johnson*	**Lynn Corp.**
1961						*Gale*
1963 1965				*Chapman*		
1967 1969	*Vaughn*					
1971 1973	NA					

	412	414	416	418	420	422
1955 1957	Hoffman	Leach	Elam	Pryor	Wood **Realty Finance**	Morris
1959 1961	*Putnam*	*Martin*	*Alexander*	**Realty Finance**		
1963 1965	**Best Realty**		*Campbell*			*Viney*
1967 1969		*Strong*				
1971 1973	NA					

	424	426
1955 1957	Harmon	Franklin
1959 1961		*Mitchell*
1963	**Woodhaven Invest. Corp.**	
1965	*Cromartie*	
1967 1969		
1971 1973	NA	

Key:
Resident homeowners, white
Resident homeowners, African American
Non-resident owners, corporation or individual
*Unable to determine race of homeowner
Note: 1971 data is missing; after 1955, new names appear only when property ownership changes.
Source: Tax Assessments for Baltimore City, 1955-73

Appendix B

Table 2. 600 Block of Grantley Street

	600	602	604	606	608
1955 1957	Rollman	Keffer	Collier	Sandall	Durkin
1959 1961					Bob Holding Corp.
1963 1965	Gould	Crown Enterprises	Pettie		
1967 1969					Payton
1971 1973	NA	Brown			

	610	612	614	616	618
1955 1957	Herrera	Harden	McGinnis	VanSant	Kendrick
1959 1961				Fairfax Investment	
1963 1965			Caplan		
1967 1969		Rainbow Realty		Banks	
1971 1973	NA	Singer			Slaughter

	620	622	624	626
1955 1957	Crockett	Helweick	Service	Sansone
1959 1961		Svotelis		
1963 1965	Booker		Blue	Jones
1967 1969				
1971 1973	NA			

Appendix B

Table 3. 3800 Block of Cranston Road

	3800	3802	3804	3806	3808
1955	Durkee	Kimmitt	West Balt. Bap. Church	O'Connor	Vaeth
1957					
1959	Sullivan		Hannon		
1961					
1963		Albert Realty			
1965		*Eddy*	*Rice*	*Fonder*	Embassy Realty
1967	Real Estate Develop.				
1969					
1971	NA				
1973					

	3810	3812	3814	3816	3818
1955	Bossi	Menn	Geisendaffer	Ireland	Seigh
1957					
1959					
1961					
1963					
1965	**Caplan**	*Arons*	*Lewis*	*Davis*	*Lindner*
1967				Nance	
1969					
1971	NA				
1973		**Carmichael**			

Appendix B

Table 4. 601 Block of Augusta Avenue†

	601	603	605	607	609	613
1955 1957	Rinaudo	Egner	Beltz	R. Lee	P. Lee Ward	Mussachio
1959 1961					Cramer	
1963 1965		Gregory* Camper	Shields			
1967				Real Estate Develop.	Carter	Jefferson
1969	Jones					
1971 NA 1973						

† Sampling of block numbers due to length of block

	615	619	621	625	627
1955 1957	R. Lee	Poe	Gorman	Baker	Fox
1959 1961					
1963 1965		McHugh*	R. Lee		Rainbow Realty
1967	Opher	Real Estate Develop.	Comegys	Hamm	Boatwright
1969					
1971 NA 1973					

	631	633	637	639	643
1955 1957	Ritter	Simering	Amos	Berchett	Emmerich
1959 1961			Morris	Mussachio	
1963 1965				Lee Realty	Lee Realty
1967	Glazer	Rainbow Realty	Rainbow Realty	Brown	
1969					
1971 NA 1973	Robinson				

Notes

1. The Trauma of Racial Change

1. Interview with Marilyn Simkins, September 17, 1980.
2. Interview with Margaret Johnson, December 14, 1982.
3. The themes of white flight and racial change along the Edmondson Avenue corridor are explored more briefly in Orser, "Flight to the Suburbs."
4. Garrett Power, "'Apartheid Baltimore Style,'" especially p. 321. See Appendix A, for bibliographical notes on the concept of "The Dual Housing Market."
5. Osofsky, *Harlem*, pp. 7-17, 92-95.
6. S. Olson, *Baltimore*, p. 275.
7. On Chicago, Goodwin, *Oak Park Strategy*, p. 67; McPherson, "'In My Father's House,'" and Rose Helper, *Racial Policies*, p. 35. For historical accounts of the nature and impact of this period of racial change at the metropolitan level in Chicago, see Hirsch, *Making the Second Ghetto*; and Lemann, *Promised Land*. On Washington, D.C., Green, *Secret City*, pp. 322-23; and Grier and Grier, *Equality and Beyond*, pp. 26-30. On dynamics in sections of New York, see Connolly, *Ghetto Grows in Brooklyn*, p. 136; and Rieder, *Canarsie*.
8. Levine and Harmon, *Death of an American Jewish Community*, pp. 5-8; see chapter 4, part D, below, for a discussion of Jewish to African American succession in northwest Baltimore communities.
9. Snow and Leahy, "Making of a Slum-Ghetto."
10. Rieder, *Canarsie*, pp. 1-2, 20-21.
11. Goodwin, *Oak Park Strategy*. In Baltimore good neighbors programs were initiated in several sections, including Ashburton and Windsor Hills and Baltimore Neighborhoods, Inc., was established to promote housing equity and acceptance of integration (see chapter 4).
12. See Appendix A for the scholarly literature on "The Persistence of Residential Racial Segregation."
13. See Appendix A for the scholarly literature on "African Americans and Suburbanization."
14. See Appendix A for a discussion of the scholarly literature on "Racial Residential Change."
15. Erikson, *Everything in Its Path*, p. 131.
16. Useful discussions of the dimensions of community as applied to historical study are provided by Bender, *Community and Social Change in America*, and Conzen, "Community Studies, Urban History, and American Local History"; the

sociological perspective afforded by Hunter in *Symbolic Communities* also has informed my conceptualization (see especially pp. 4, 67). In the mid-1950s Hillery reviewed sociological definitions of community and provided a bibliography in "Definitions of Community."

17. Thernstrom argues strongly for objective criteria for social status in historical study in *Poverty and Progress*, p. 84. As an example of sociological conventions regarding the classification of class in American society, W.L. Warner in his influential formulation identified six categories, estimating that approximately three-fifths of the population were included in two of them, the lower middle and upper lower class designations, which he referred to together as "the common man level." *American Life*, pp. 74-80. For discussion of the concept of class, see Williams, *Key Words*, pp. 51-59.

18. For oral history interview citations, exact dates of the interview sessions have been provided along with the pseudonyms assigned to the interviewees. Scholars interested in verification of the interview material may contact me to examine the transcribed record. Differences between historians and ethnographers regarding oral history conventions are discussed in Di Leonardo, "Oral History as Ethnographic Encounter."

19. Portelli, "Peculiarities of History," p. 99.

20. Orser, "Racial Change in Retrospect," p. 51.

21. Census boundaries for tracts 1608 and 2007 correspond closely with the developing neighborhood's borders and therefore make the census tract data extremely useful. (The tracts bore the designations 16-8 and 20-7 in 1940 and 1950; in 1960 the same tracts were labelled 0016-8 and 0020-7; in 1970 the new designation was 1608 for the former, while the latter was subdivided as 2007.01 and 2007.02; in 1980 1608 was also subdivided, becoming 1608.01 and 1608.02. Throughout, the outer boundaries of the tracts remained the same.) Though Standard Metropolitan Statistical Area (SMSA) tract data for the Baltimore region was only first made available in 1930 (for a limited number of categories), the listings are increasingly detailed from 1940 onward. Boundaries for the tracts are Hilton Street on the east, Gwynns Falls Park on the north, Woodington Road on the west, and Old Frederick Road on the south. Tract 1608 encompasses the area north of Edmondson Avenue, 2007 the area on the south side. (See map 2.) Some of the rowhouse development in the 1940s and 1950s occurred in adjoining tracts just west of this area. The study tracts are located approximately three and a half miles west of the city center.

22. Ten sample blocks with a total of 127 residences were selected to provide a cross section of the households of the neighborhood, taking into account such factors as period of development, cost levels, and geographical distribution. A profile for each household was then developed at ten-year intervals, providing information regarding the name of the household head, that person's occupation, and whether the home was owned or rented; additionally, comparable information was gathered on place of prior residence (five years earlier) and future residence (ten years later). This method made it possible to compile a profile of particular household histories, tracing the tenure of household heads, as well as patterns of in- and out-migration. A major source for the data in the early period was the set

of Baltimore City directories, published by the R.L. Polk Co. annually into the 1930s, then less regularly until 1964. Directory information was supplemented by Baltimore City tax records for home ownership and voting records for place of residence. For later years, telephone directories and door-to-door surveys were also used to provide necessary data on residence and occupation.

There has been an ongoing debate about the merits of city directories as a resource for social history research. See Goldstein, *Patterns of Mobility*; Knights, *Plain People of Boston*, pp. 127-39; and Thernstrom, *Other Bostonians*, pp. 279-88. While tests of their reliability have verified their value for historical demographics, reservations have been raised in terms of their inclusiveness regarding women, racial minorities, and those more transient. Aside from the notable limitation of gender bias, some of the other drawbacks to reliance upon such data are minimized in the present study because most new residents had prior and subsequent settlement in the Baltimore area, the community had high rates of residential stability, and additional means of verification were available for more recent years, when residential turnover and racial exclusion might otherwise have created gaps in the record.

23. On the evolution of the suburban ideal, see Jackson, *Crabgrass Frontier*; Schuyler, *Redefinition of City Form*; Ebner, *Creating Chicago's North Shore*; and Stilgoe, *Borderland*.

24. Waesche, *Crowning the Gravelly Hill*, p. 86.

25. Hayward examines the historical evolution of Baltimore's nineteenth-century rowhouse forms in "Urban Vernacular Architecture in Nineteenth-Century Baltimore." On the history of the Baltimore-style rowhouse, also see Shivers, *Those Placid Rows*.

26. Perin, *Belonging in America*, argues that the quest for socioeconomic homogeneity is at the root of the suburban dream; see especially pp. 62, 66.

27. Fairbanks, *Making Better Citizens*, pp. 36-39, 52-53.

28. Douglass, *Suburban Trend*, pp. 36, 218-24, 236, 312-13.

29. Groves and Muller, "The Evolution of Black Residential Areas in Late Nineteenth-Century Cities"; and Neverdon-Morton, "Black Housing Patterns in Baltimore City."

30. Power, "'Apartheid Baltimore Style.'" In his history of social patterns in Detroit in the late nineteenth and early twentieth centuries, Olivier Zunz has observed that African American migrants to the city, compared to European immigrants, "lived history in reverse," experiencing increasing degrees of residential segregation. *Changing Face of Inequality*, p. 6.

31. *Cost of Living in American Towns*, p. 80.

32. For a general sketch of African American activism in the city, see K. Olson, "Old West Baltimore"; also, Calcott, *Maryland & America*, pp. 145-71.

2. The Making of a Rowhouse Neighborhood

Note: This chapter is a revised version of an article that appeared under the title, "The Making of a Baltimore Rowhouse Community: The Edmondson Avenue

Area, 1915-1945," in the *Maryland Historical Magazine* 80, 3 (Fall 1985): 203-27. The epigraph is from House, "Street Car System and Rapid Transit," 1:557.

1. Warner, *Streetcar Suburbs*, pp. 46, 158. See also, Thernstrom, *Other Bostonians*. From different perspectives, Sennett, *Families Against the City*, and Ryan, *Cradle of the Middle Class*, have argued that nineteenth-century middle-class out-migration to socially differentiated communities represented a retreat from the city to a private world of domesticity.

2. G.W. and W.S. Bromley's *Atlas of the City of Baltimore* (1896 and 1906 editions) show the rural character of the Edmondson section at the turn of the century. A contemporary source with information on some of the gentry families and their estates is Hall, *Baltimore: Its History and People*, 1:106-7, 2:888-89.

3. The preceding profile of the area's ninety-seven residents is based on the manuscript version of the 1910 federal census. United States Department of Commerce, Bureau of the Census, *Thirteenth Census of the United States Taken in 1910* (Baltimore City Wards 16 and 20).

4. Insurance maps issued by the Sanborn Map and Publishing Company in 1914 provide detailed information on the two Edmondson Avenue settlements and the development along Walnut Avenue in Rognel Heights; on the new span, "The New Edmondson Avenue Concrete Bridge," Baltimore *Sun* (November 22, 1908), p. 15; ads in the classified section of the *Sun* announced the sale of new houses along Edmondson Avenue between 1911 and 1914.

5. Ad in the Baltimore *Sun*, October 6, 1912.

6. Title map prepared by E.V. Coonan and Co., surveyors and civil engineers, April 4, 1930, for the James Keelty Co., provided by courtesy of the latter.

7. "James Keelty" [obituary], Baltimore *Evening Sun*, June 15, 1944; interview with Joseph Keelty (younger son of James), October 26, 1982; notes prepared by Mary Ellen Hayward for the Peale Museum exhibit, "Rowhouse: A Baltimore Style of Living"; ads in the *Sun*, April 2, 1911; October 6, 1912; April 2, 1916.

8. *Sun*, October 7, 1917. Another builder advertised an early "daylight house" in a nearby residential area as early as 1914 (*Sun*, October 4, 1914).

9. Two alternatives had been introduced along Edmondson in some of the houses prior to the daylights, both having similar dimensions as the standard rows. One, the duplex, provided light to internal rooms via a long, narrow areaway separating every two houses but with the added expense of exterior side walls. The other, the "areaway" (pronounced "air-y way") house was part of an unbroken row in front, but had a short passageway extending from the rear to provide windows on the side of the kitchens, which they separated, as well as to an inner dining room (below) and bedroom (above).

10. S. Olson, *Baltimore*, p. 302. On the social implications of Baltimore's zoning reform in the 1920s, see Power, "Unwisdom of Allowing City Growth to Work Out Its Own Destiny."

11. In April 1920, for instance, the municipal building permits department noted an historic record number of permits issued, nearly three-fourths of them for brick two-story dwellings. *Sun*, May 2, 1920.

12. Interview with John Carpenter, October 7, 1982.

13. *Sun*, October 7, 1928. The Wildwood homes were viewed as an example of the developer upgrading his product. Interviews with Joseph Keelty and John Carpenter.

14. As one barometer of the nose dive in housing starts, the *Sun*'s real estate section plummeted from eight or more pages in the late 1920s to two or three by 1932 and a mere half page by 1933.

15. Sanborn Co. insurance map (1914) for water lines; sewer connections along Edmondson were first listed in housing ads in the mid-1910s (*Sun*, October 4, 1914; October 1, 1917).

16. Kenneth Morse, "Baltimore Street Car Routes" [typed ms., revised 1960], Maryland Historical Society. For examples of Keelty ads giving directions by streetcar, see the *Sun*, October 7, 1928; October 4, 1931; October 1, 1939. In the early 1920s the double tracks were moved from the south side of Edmondson to the center: subsequently, the avenue was widened and paved, sure signs of the increasing importance of automobile travel. (See Figure 2.) On the history of Baltimore's street railways, see Farrell, *Who Made the Streetcars Go?*

17. *Sun*, January 16, 1932.

18. A unique feature of Maryland's property system permitted title to land and house to be established separately, with the former subject to a ground rent of 6 percent. The net effect was that the initial purchase price could be lowered substantially, a considerable benefit to buyers who might have difficulty raising sufficient funds for the total purchase of house and land. The system also was an advantage to builders, many of whom apparently counted on the ground title (or the rent from it) as their margin of profit. As an example, a typical house purchased from Keelty in 1923 sold for $3,650; the additional land title (purchased by a third party as an investment at a cost of $1,226.30) created an annual ground rent for the new buyer of seventy-two dollars per year. In 1930, seven years later, the buyer had managed to pay off the mortgage on the house; in seven more years he bought the land title as well. Documents relating to the mortgage of their house on West Franklin Street provided by the Robert Lansinger family.

19. Rossi, *Why Families Move*, argues that the primary housing package consideration was housing size, related as it was to family size and needs on the one hand and economic status on the other, though he seems to have neglected social status as a consideration; pp. 17, 144, 225.

20. Kemp's report, *Housing Conditions in Baltimore*, described two alley and two tenement districts, providing documentary photographs to illustrate the findings on urban poverty.

21. Power, "'Apartheid Baltimore Style,'" especially pp. 294-96; 316-17.

22. The 1920-30 growth figure is an estimate; the 1930-40 percentage is based upon federal census data. Population increase or decrease typically masks much higher rates of in- and out-migration. Census figures cited here and subsequently for the two census tracts (1608 and 2007) comprising the Edmondson Avenue section are from the United States Census census report of tract data for the Baltimore Standard Metropolitan Statistical Area (SMSA), 1930, 1940, and 1950. This source hereafter is cited as *U.S. Census*. Figures regarding out-migra-

tion here are from the sample block survey. See chapter 1 for the methodological note regarding the use of census data and the procedures involved in the sample block survey.

23. Sample block survey.

24. *U.S. Census*, 1920, 1930, and 1940. In 1930 adults age twenty-five to forty-four represented 37.5 percent of the population and children through age twenty, 32.4 percent; in 1940, when population figures had grown by nearly two thousand, adults in that age range constituted 38.4 percent, children through age nineteen, 26.1 percent—a comparison suggesting that the Depression decade may have brought both a lower birth rate and a gradual aging trend. In 1940 median household size in the Edmondson area was listed as 3.08 (for tract 1608) and 3.19 (for tract 2007); for the city as a whole it stood at 3.36, and in owner-occupied housing at 3.53. *U.S. Census*, 1930, 1940.

25. *U.S. Census*, 1940, 1950. The discrepancy between rates of home ownership in the sample block survey and the total tract figures suggests that the former was above average on this scale, a factor that must be taken into consideration in judging other findings from the survey.

26. Interview with John Carpenter.

27. Argersinger, *Toward a New Deal in Baltimore*, pp. 7-8, 19, 207; she notes that unemployment hit various social groups disproportionately; for African Americans, for instance, it went as high as 50 percent. For the Edmondson area there is no 1930 tract data to compare on these indices, but in 1940 unemployment in this neighborhood was only 3.75 percent compared to a city rate of 9.95 percent, and home ownership was 63 percent, compared to 39 percent (*U.S. Census*, 1940).

28. Sample block survey. The assertion that the great majority were not newcomers to the city is based on the large number of settlers whose prior residence can be traced through the city directories to city addresses (five years previous) and the comparatively smaller number for whom no data was available, some of whom (but not all) might have migrated from outside the metropolitan area.

29. *U.S. Census*, 1930, 1940.

30. Interview with Madge Cooper, November 4, 1982.

31. Interview with Marilyn Simkins, September 17, 1980.

32. Power, "'Apartheid Baltimore Style,'" pp. 318-19; Helper, *Racial Policies and Practices of Real Estate Brokers*, p. 201. On racially discriminatory policies of federal mortgage agencies, see Jackson, *Crabgrass Frontier*, especially pp. 190-218.

33. On the religious history of the area's congregations as well as the names of early members, see *St. Bernardine's Church Silver Anniversary, 1928-1953* and Joynes, *Thirty-Two Years at Christ Edmondson Methodist Church*. Ward figures for 1920 (when no tract data was available) show the foreign-born population to have been relatively slight on the outer west side of the city as a whole (7.4 percent in wards 16 and 20, when the citywide ratio was 11.5 percent). In the Edmondson Avenue neighborhood, only 5 percent of residents were foreign-born in 1930 and 4 percent in 1940. In 1930 another 17 percent were the offspring of foreign or mixed parentage, a figure that no doubt declined over time (though the 1940 tract data does not include the category). *U.S. Census*, 1920, 1930, 1940.

34. Henretta, "The Study of Social Mobility," and Chudacoff, in "Success and Security," for example, raise important questions about the use of occupational classification in many social mobility studies: 1) the adequacy of occupational classification and ranking systems; 2) the extent to which occupation may correlate with other factors in people's lives (though they concede the often close correlation with income); and 3) the assumptions that are made about occupational status and social mobility, especially the inference that all Americans *want* to be socially mobile and use occupation as a means to achieve that goal.

The present study uses the descriptive categories for occupation and the occupational coding for those categories developed by the U.S. Bureau of the Census. For purposes of standardization, the codebook used is the 1970 version. *1970 Census of Population Alphabetical Index of Industries and Occupation* (Washington, D.C.: G.P.O., 1971). While the Census Bureau's general categories have changed some over the years (as, of course, has the coding system), use of such a standardized system not only provides a generally accepted basis for occupational coding but makes it possible to compare the earlier block data (when no census tract information was available) with comparable later data, as well as to compare the latter data (from 1940 onward) with the tract figures.

35. In their classic early community studies of Middletown, Robert and Helen Lynd observe that "One's job is the watershed down which the rest of one's life tends to flow in Middletown. Who one is, whom one knows, how one lives, what one aspires to be,—these and many other urgent realities of living are patterned for one by what one does to get a living and the amount of living this allows one to buy." *Middletown in Transition*, p. 7; see also, *Middletown*, pp. 22-24.

36. Sample block survey.

37. Sample block survey and *U.S. Census*, 1940. Again, some caution must be used in comparing the sample block data and that from the census, not only because of slight deviation in the former in comparison to the latter but also because the sample block data is based on information regarding household heads only, while the census figures provide data for all workers.

38. The sample block survey is limited to household heads, which city directories usually list as male. Though directories sometimes include a wife's occupation, few in the sample were so indicated. In some cases an unmarried daughter living in her parents' home received a separate notation. Otherwise, women whose occupations were provided were single or widows, though in this neighborhood few widows were employed.

39. Tract data on employment is not available for 1930; in that year census figures for Baltimore as a whole reveal that 27 percent of native white women (age ten and over) were in the paid labor force, compared to 17 percent of foreign-born white women and 51 percent of African American women. In 1940, 30 percent of white women (age fourteen and over) and 47 percent of African American women were engaged in paid labor; for Edmondson area women, 29 percent. *U.S. Census*, 1930, 1940.

40. While the small share of professional and managerial positions paralleled the low ratios for these groups in the city total, laborers and domestics were nearly

absent from the occupational equation. Slightly more oriented toward the crafts than manufacturing (particularly for men), Edmondson's middle-level job profile was striking for its greater prominence in sales and clerical positions, where it surpassed city averages by 18 percent (by 9 percent for males). *U.S. Census*, 1940.

41. Between 1900 and 1920, for example, Baltimore's adult employees expanded by more than half (60 percent, from 217,350 to 347,754), while between 1920 and 1930 the number advanced a modest 4.6 percent (to 362,172) only to fall back 3.8 percent by 1940 (to 348,358), after a decade of economic depression. *U.S. Census*, 1900, 1920, 1930, 1940. In the latter year, however, the figure is for those over age fourteen; previous figures are for those over age ten.

42. In Zunz's terms, a substantial number of them were the corporation's white-collar workers, salaried employees rather than upper or middle-level managers. *Making America Corporate*, pp. 9, 126-27.

43. The percentage of in-migrants (those who had lived elsewhere five years previous) making an occupational change was relatively consistent: in 1920 only 21 percent had done so; in 1930, 19 percent; and in 1940, 17 percent. Sample block survey.

44. Comparison of cohorts of new residents in 1920, 1930, and 1940 over their first ten years in the neighborhood indicate a 28 percent occupational change rate for the 1920 group, and 16 percent for the 1930 group. While missing data on the 1940 group makes any observation quite tentative and the period of consideration must be extended for 16 years (because of the absence of a city directory in 1950), the available data show only one in fourteen making a change. Sample block survey. Compare Goldstein, *Patterns of Mobility 1910-1950*, pp. 190-93.

45. Those who moved out of the neighborhood during this period were much more likely to move to another part of the city (though usually not to the older sections from which many had come) than to proceed into the suburban county. Occupational data is much thinner, but it suggests that movers were no more likely to change occupational category than nonmovers. Sample block survey.

46. Warner viewed the process of streetcar suburbanization in the late nineteenth century as producing a more specialized metropolis, one that physically separated primarily middle-class suburbs from the older, more heterogeneous parts of the city, citing as among the consequent problems of modern life "the discipline of the lives of city dwellers into specialized transportation paths, specialized occupations, specialized home environments, and specialized community relationships" (*Streetcar Suburbs*, p. 3). Wise and Dupree found that by 1925 "the extension of streetcar service had paralleled residential growth patterns to such an extent that 93.8 percent of the total population of Baltimore lived within one-quarter mile, or a five-minute walk, of a streetcar line," though already the auto was becoming a significant factor in the commuter and leisure transportation equation. "The Choice of the Automobile," p. 154.

47. These dimensions of community culture are identified in chapter 1. The present section is based primarily upon oral interviews with approximately fifteen residents of the neighborhood during the period being examined. Only in cases of direct quotation, however, are specific citations provided.

48. Interview with Ann Morgan, March 23, 1981.

49. Hunter, *Symbolic Communities*, contends that names and boundaries (social as well as natural) function as symbols of shared community understanding (p. 67).

50. Interview with Ann Morgan and Christine Wallace, March 23, 1981.

51. Interview with Alice Hughes, October 2, 1980.

52. Not only were men providers; they were, for the most part, husbands and/or fathers; very few adult males were single or unattached. City directories seldom listed a second employed male living in a household on the blocks surveyed; analysis of the 1950 census tract data, slightly after the period considered here, suggests that only 16 percent of males age twenty or older were single.

53. Ryan found precursors of this ideal among the emerging "new" middle class of mid-nineteenth-century Utica, a "cult of true womanhood," which she argues actually narrowed women's sphere (*Cradle of the Middle Class*, p. 189); though the occupational mix of Edmondson's settlers was not so clearly white-collar as Ryan's middle class, they were doubtless seeking to emulate a widely shared aspiration. In the 1920s the Lynds concluded that the absence of business class married women among Muncie's paid workforce was one of the important differences separating that group from its working-class counterparts (*Middletown*, p. 27). Yet, it would seem that in Edmondson Village the line was not quite so clearly drawn in actual practice as in ideology.

54. Again, marriage was the norm: 1950 census tract figures list only 18 percent of all females over twenty years of age as single.

55. Interviews with John Carpenter, Madge Cooper, Ann Morgan, Christine Wallace, and Marilyn Simkins; interviews with Agnes Malone, September 12, 1980, and with Henrietta Latour, September 12, 1980. In response to a question about how important were the churches to the neighborhood, for instance, Marilyn Simkins responded: "Very important; as far as social life, for myself as a teenager, St. Bernardine's was it. . . . That was our social life. St. Bernardine's had a very active CYO, one of the best, if not *the* best in the area. They had a lot to offer kids."

56. In mid-nineteenth-century Utica children of middle-class families deferred marriage and family until they were considered economically established (Ryan, *Cradle of the Middle Class*, p. 179); the Lynds found a growing trend toward early marriage and family responsibilities in Muncie in the 1920s (*Middletown*, p. 111), but a renewed tendency for the middle class to defer during the Depression years (*Middletown in Transition*, p. 150). In the Edmondson area college education was still a relatively exceptional experience; in 1940 only 3.4 percent of the community's adult population (twenty-five years of age and over) had completed four years of college. *U.S. Census*, 1940.

3. Continuity and Undercurrents of Change

Note: the epigraphs are from interviews with David Graff, June 12, 1981, and Edgar Raines, September 22, 1980.

1. The quote is from the Baltimore *Evening Sun*, April 30, 1947; the center's opening also was cited in *Baltimore*, May 1947.
2. Advertisement, Baltimore *Sun*, February 24, 1946. The ad stressed the center's auto orientation: "An important feature of Edmondson Village is its parking facilities for about 800 automobiles—the principal portion of which will be in a specially designed Parking Plaza, surrounded by decorative walls, trees, and shrubbery, in keeping with the district in which the Village is located."
3. *Sunday Sun Magazine*, September 23, 1945. The article explained the reasons for the sale: "The present owner, Miss Mary Adelaide Jenkins, lives . . . in an atmosphere foreign to modern houses. . . . Meanwhile the city has moved steadily closer. More streets were cut through. Under present conditions Miss Jenkins finds it no longer possible to get help to keep things in condition, keeping grass cut, leaves raked. When the city condemned 10 feet along Edmondson Avenue and paved it, leaving her with 1,620 feet of Edmondson Avenue sidewalk to keep free of ice and snow, as well as 500 feet along Swann Avenue, she knew something had to be done. Vandals broke into outhouses, starting fires. She decided to sell."
4. *Evening Sun*, April 30, 1947; Baltimore *News American*, November 13, 1977; John F. Kelly, "'You Can't Take It With You'—Joe Myerhoff," *Sunday Sun Magazine*, September 12, 1982.
5. For an examination of the social and cultural politics of Rockefeller's involvement in Colonial Williamsburg, see Wallace, "Visiting the Past." Wallace cites a critic's view that during the 1950s suburban America was "Williamsburgered" (p. 64). Locally, the Depression decade passion for historic restoration found a smaller-scale echo in renovation of the nearby nineteenth-century mill village of Dickeyville.
6. *Urban Land Institute, Technical Bulletin No. 11* (1949), pp. 20-21; the review also noted that the style might make store rearrangement difficult.
7. *Evening Sun*, June 1, 1950 (full-page advertisement for the third anniversary). In its 1953 survey of shopping centers the Urban Land Institute underscored the value of architectural character in attracting people, citing one "astute developer" as insisting: "Give them something that makes the people want to proudly show off your center to the out-of-towners." *Urban Land Institute, Technical Bulletin No. 20* (1953), p. 12.
8. Advertisement, *Evening Sun*, September 6, 1951. References to provision for the auto appeared in *Urban Land Institute, Technical Bulletin No. 11*, p. 20; *Sun*, February 24, 1946; *Evening Sun*, April 30, 1947; *Baltimore*, May 1947.
9. Advertisement, *Evening Sun*, September 6, 1951.
10. Advertisements, *Evening Sun*, June 1, 1950; September 6, 1951. The latter described automobile as well as trolley and bus access: "It's easy to get to Edmondson Village from any place in Baltimore and the surrounding countryside. Edmondson Village is right on the doorstep of residents of Rognel Heights, Ten Hills, Nottingham, Lyndhurst, Hunting Ridge, Westgate, Edmondale, Catonsville, and the adjacent county areas. People in the southwestern section—Arbutus, Lansdowne, Halethorpe, etc., can reach Edmondson Village in a few minutes via Caton

Ave. and Hilton St. Northwest Baltimoreans, driving down Hilton Street, can be at Edmondson Village in a surprisingly short time. Folks in the Central and Eastern parts of the city can drive at express speeds straight out Franklin Street. Edmondson Village is served directly by the No. 9 and 14 streetcar lines, and by the No. 20 and 49 bus lines."

11. An interview with Marilyn Simkins, September 17, 1980, was typical of the response on the center's significance.

12. Brief discussion of the shopping center as part of the early Roland Park Company development is included in Waesche, *Crowning the Gravelly Hill*, p. 60.

13. Jackson, *Crabgrass Frontier*, pp. 258-59; *Urban Land Institute, Technical Bulletin No. 11*, (1949), pp. 26-27; *Urban Land Institute, Technical Bulletin No. 20*, (1953), pp. 7, 37. See also Gillette, "Evolution of the Planned Shopping Center." Gillette traces the role of the planned shopping center within the tradition of "environmental reform in which physical designs are used to advance social goals" (p. 449). The claim regarding precedence is a very difficult one to determine and hinges partly on definition. Rae, *The Road and the Car in American Life* (citing Homer Hoyt, "The Status of Shopping Centers in the United States," *Urban Land* 19, no. 9 [October 6, 1950]), includes three East Coast sites in his list of the eight shopping centers in the United States as of 1946 ("located outside central business districts, with ample parking space and easy access by automobile"): Upper Darby in West Philadelphia (1927); Suburban Square in Ardmore, Penn. (1928); and Shirlington in Arlington, Va. (1944), p. 230. However, several on Rae's list more closely resembled secondary business districts than suburban shopping centers of harmonious design.

14. Interview with Joe Slovensky, October 27, 1980.

15. Interview with Bertha Roberts, June 11, 1981.

16. Interview with Eunice Clemens, June 9, 1981.

17. *U.S. Census*, 1940, 1950, 1960.

18. "James Keelty" [obituary], *Evening Sun*, June 15, 1944. Keelty was at his office at 4200 Edmondson Avenue when he suffered the stroke that led to his death. In the late 1930s the Keelty family moved from west Baltimore just beyond Edmondson Village to Homeland, the prestigious Roland Park Company development in north Baltimore. Interview with Joseph Keelty, October 26, 1982.

19. Keelty Company ads from the late 1930s indicated a shift from English- to colonial-style housing, both in Wildwood and in Rodgers Forge (*Sun*, October 1, 1935; October 3, 1938). Dimensions and floor plans of the colonials also represented a retrenchment in size and scale from the earlier Wildwood models, evident, for example, in the contrast between the 600 and 700 blocks of Augusta Avenue or the 800 and 900 blocks of Woodington Road. (In the late 1930s Keelty also built scaled-down English-architecture houses in the 3800-4000 blocks of Cranston Avenue and Woodridge Road).

20. Examples of these early colonials can be found in such blocks as 700 through 900 Wildwood Parkway and 900 Woodington Road.

21. The earlier colonial-style houses had been approximately 22 by 37 feet; the later were 16 to 19 by 30 to 32. The mansard colonials with porches are

evident in the northeastern Wildwood section (800 block Mt. Holly St., 900 block Allendale Street) and in the 700 block of Augusta; mansard colonials without porches stretch along the northwestern Wildwood section (Kevin, Wicklow, Seminole, Flowerton, Rokeby, and Colborne).

22. *U.S. Census*, 1950; the comparable citywide rate was 50 percent. In *Crabgrass Frontier* Jackson examines the nature and impact of federal housing policy upon suburbanization (pp. 190-218).

23. The use of steel casement windows, a relatively new innovation no doubt employed because of its cost saving, rather glaringly compromised the colonial motif; examples are along Stokes Road.

24. *Sun*, April 3, 1949.

25. *Sun*, April 6, 1952.

26. *Sun*, April 3, 1954.

27. Colonial Gardens houses were advertised for $16,500. *Sun*, April 6, 1958.

28. Baltimore *News-Post*, March 8, 1946.

29. *U.S. Census*, 1940, 1950, 1960.

30. Frank Henry, "New Neighborhoods Are Keys to City's Pattern of Growth," *Sun*, September 10, 1950. In the same year the *Sun* noted that housing and population growth were changing the urban configuration: "This new city is not confined within the official limits of Baltimore, but the great majority of the new city's inhabitants will depend on Baltimore for their livelihood." *Sun*, April 16, 1950.

31. *Sun*, September 11, 1949.

32. *Sun*, October 2, 1950.

33. Interview with Stanley Greenberg, February 17, 1993.

34. *Sun*, September 11, 1949.

35. *Sun*, September 11, 1949; October 2, 1950. Unlike many of the apartment projects of the period, which offered a choice of either one or two bedrooms, Uplands consisted entirely of one-bedroom apartments, which filled rapidly despite skepticism about locating so many small units in one market area. The Uplands mansion house, on land not part of the development project, was renovated as a home for elderly church women according to the provisions of the Jacobs will. Today it serves as the site for the New Psalmist Christian School. *Evening Sun*, January 25, 1937; March 9, 1951; Baltimore *American*, March 30, 1952.

36. The quote is from the *Sun*, April 16, 1950; see also *Sun*, September 11, 1949.

37. *Sun*, September 11, 1949.

38. *Sun*, September 6, 1958.

39. *Evening Sun*, January 26, 1953; January 25, 1954; *Sun*, April 3, 1953; Baltimore *News-Post*, July 27, 1954.

40. *Sun*, July 1, 1962.

41. John Goodspeed, "Boom Around the Beltway," *Baltimore*, November, 1965.

42. *U.S. Census*, 1930, 1940, 1950. Between 1940 and 1950 three census tracts along the western edge of the westside ghetto had become more than 75 percent

African American; also, one on the northwest corner and one adjacent to the CBD had similar percentages.

43. Mimeographed copy of letter, J.D. Steele to Baltimore Mayor Theodore R. McKeldin, February 15, 1945, Enoch Pratt Free Library.

44. *Sun*, October 19, 1944.

45. Citizens Planning and Housing Association of Baltimore, "Memorandum on Negro Housing in Metropolitan Baltimore" (mimeographed report), August 1944, Enoch Pratt Free Library.

46. *Sun*, March 20, 1955; January 18, 1957.

47. Wartime and postwar changes in job opportunities for Baltimore's African Americans are discussed more fully in chapter 5.

48. Carroll Williams, "The Drive Behind Block-Busting," *Sun*, September 23, 1955; "Cure for Block-Busting," *Sun*, September 28, 1955; the quote is from the latter.

49. *Sun*, February 2, 1948.

50. Joynes, *Thirty-Two Years*, p. 27.

51. Interview with Samuel Brown, June 13, 1981.

52. The following discussion of the changing real estate racial boundary is based upon the author's survey of the *Sun* classified section in April of each year for real estate information relevant to the Edmondson area and its environs for the period 1910 to 1980. Specific references are from the *Sun*, April 3, 1950; April 1, 1951; April 6, 1952; April 5, 1953.

53. The following discussion is based upon K. Olson, "Old West Baltimore"; Calcott, *Maryland & America*, pp. 146-150; Hughes, *Fight for Freedom*, pp. 177-178; John C. Robinson, "Ma Jackson—Fighter from Way Back," *News-American*, January 24, 1971; Charles L. Wagandt, "Lillie May [Jackson] and Teddy [McKeldin]—They Led Baltimore Over and Around Prejudice," *Evening Sun*, November 15, 1979; and Goldberg, "Party Competition."

54. "Negroes Request School Control: Seek Full Charge of Colored Education in City," *Sun*, February 16, 1945; "Request Made for Negroes: NAACP Wants White School Open to Them," *Sun*, February 13, 1946. The Baltimore *Sun* noted in 1954 that since World War II African American public school enrollment in the city had increased by approximately twice the rate for white enrollment, with consequent overcrowding in segregated African American schools a major problem. "The Shifting Ratio," *Sun*, February 23, 1954.

55. *Minutes of the Board of School Commissioners* (Baltimore City), September 2, 1952; Furman L. Templeton, "Admission of Negro Boys." The closing statement prior to the vote was by Thurgood Marshall, who reviewed the nature of cases currently before Supreme Court, arguing that separate programs were by nature unequal. The coalition supporting the candidates' entry to Poly included the Baltimore Urban League, Americans for Democratic Action, the Council for Human Rights, the Citizens Committee on Education, and the Baltimore branch, NAACP. Governor Theodore McKeldin sent a letter to the board urging that its action be guided by the law, fairness, and good community relations, rather than an alternative that might lead to court litigation. Maryland Commission on Interracial Problems and

Relations [report by Elinor Pancoast], *Study on Desegregation in Baltimore Schools*, pp. 18-19. As one indication of the burden of continuing to maintain a segregated school system, the Pancoast report noted that in 1952-53 all-African American Frederick Douglass High School, built to accommodate 1,250, had an enrollment of 2,600. The report also observed that the school board president had indicated in February 1953 that if the Supreme Court ruled for desegregation, Baltimore might abandon segregation right away (pp. 22-23).

56. *Minutes of the Board of School Commissioners* [Baltimore City] (June 3, 1954). Baltimore had no mandatory school districts, so officials pointed out that the desegregation plan required no alteration in existing policies other than elimination of the racial distinction, though it was later clear that such open enrollment approaches produced very little racial integration. Edgar Jones, "How Desegregation Has Worked," *Sun*, June 26, 1955, and "City Limits," pp. 82-83; John H. Fischer, "Former School Chief Recalls 'Exemplary' City Reaction," *Evening Sun*, May 17, 1979. The Pancoast report noted that the matter had been handled by the board as normal business and that there had been little immediate public reaction. Pancoast report, pp. 30-31.

57. The following analysis is based upon tract data for 1608 and 2007 in the *U.S. Census* tract data report for the Baltimore Standard Metropolitan Statistical Area (SMSA) in 1940 and 1950 (for these two census years the tracts had the designations 16-8 and 20-7, but the numbers listed above are used throughout the study for consistency).

58. Sample block survey (see chapter 1 for the methodology of the sample block survey).

59. Sample block survey.

60. In Baltimore City as a whole, 35 percent of women were in the paid labor force; the figure for white women was 32 percent, for African American women 43 percent. (All figures are for women fourteen years of age and over.) *U.S. Census*, 1950.

61. Both calculations are for 1608; 2007 was slightly less.

62. The characterization was advanced by such contemporary social analysts as Riesman, *Lonely Crowd*, and Whyte, *Organization Man*. Whyte noted that the suburbanites he studied in Park Forest, Ill., had ambivalent feelings about privacy, since the 1950s suburban ethic placed so much emphasis on togetherness (pp. 389-90). Rowhouse suburbs of the Edmondson Village type afforded less space for privacy, with their small front yards close to the street, porches within easy view of neighbors, small backyards set apart by fencing but open to sight and sounds, and shared rear alleyways, physical features that gave rowhouse living a degree of contact with neighbors often associated with urban rather than suburban lifestyles. Wright discusses general trends in postwar suburban house construction and the evolution of a suburban lifestyle in *Building the Dream*, especially pp. 240-61.

63. May, *Homeward Bound*; for statement of her general argument, see pp. 5-10, 13-15.

64. *U.S. Census*, 1940, 1950.

65. Interview with Edith Romaine, October 27, 1980.
66. Interview with Alice Hughes, October 2, 1980. Agnes Malone noted, "until high school, everything we needed was right in our own neighborhood." Interview September 12, 1980.
67. Interview with Madge Cooper, November 4, 1982.
68. Alice Hughes said she knew only one woman who worked: "I had a friend whose father died when she was twelve, and when her mother went to work; my mother watched my friend, and the thought of taking money would have been an insult."
69. Joynes, *Christ Edmondson Methodist Church*, pp. 26-30.
70. Alice Hughes commented similarly: "St. Bernardine's was a very community-oriented church. It was the center for the Catholic people of the neighborhood, and I think for many of the non-Catholics also."
71. *Sun*, October 25, 1959.
72. Lynd and Lynd, *Middletown* and *Middletown in Transition*. In the latter the Lynds found considerable disillusionment among Muncie youth in the 1930s because they felt the adult world had failed dismally (p. 168); similarly, May discusses the economic pressure of Depression-era economics upon families as possibly contributing to the quest for economic security and the resurgence of traditional notions of gender among young adults in the 1950s (*Homeward Bound*, pp. 51-53).
73. The John Waters film, "Hairspray" (1988), set in Baltimore in 1962, is a satirical comment on these social trends.

4. A White Community Responds to Change

Note: Epigraph is from interview with David Graff, June 12, 1981.
1. *U.S. Census*, 1950, 1960, 1970.
2. See Appendix A for a discussion of the literature regarding neighborhood tipping, summarized in Goering, "Neighborhood Tipping," pp. 68-78.
3. Carroll Williams, "The Drive Behind Block-Busting," Baltimore *Sun*, September 23, 1955; "Cure for Block-Busting," *Sun*, September 28, 1955; the quote is from the latter.
4. Helper, *Racial Policies*, p. 201. On Baltimore area practices, Helper cites a 1950 Baltimore Urban League survey, *Civil Rights in Baltimore* (p. 233); a 1955 survey by the Maryland Commission on Interracial Problems and Relations (to which only 12 percent of the firms even responded) found only 17.8 percent willing to sell to African Americans in any [all?] section[s] of the city (*An American City in Transition* [1955], pp. 55-59).
5. Lief and Goering report that the FHA's own studies showed that through the later 1960s the agency made virtually no loans to racial minorities in most housing markets. "Implementation of the Federal Mandate for Fair Housing," p. 243.
6. U.S. Civil Rights Commission, *Hearing Before the U.S. Commission on Civil Rights, Baltimore, August 17-19, 1970*, p. 94. Sherman went on to testify that in 1963 when his firm announced a policy of selling to all individuals regardless of race,

creed, color, or national origin, brokers in the northwest Baltimore area "proceeded to tell the marketplace that they ought not to do business with us because we would sell to 'niggers' and they ought not to do business with our company because we would break blocks" (p. 95).

7. Interview with Stanley Greenberg, February 17, 1993.

8. "Acts to Bar Negro Homes," *Sun*, July 21, 1945. On the involvement of the Baltimore Jewish Council, see Vill, "Park Heights"; Vill cites the Minutes of the Baltimore Jewish Council, May 15, 1945.

9. "Block-Busters," *Sun*, August 18, 1955; "Not For Sale," *Sun*, August 26, 1955; "The Drive Behind Block-Busting," *Sun*, September 23, 1955; "Cure for Block-Busting," *Sun*, September 28, 1955; "'Block-Busting' Called Big Cause of Racial Tension," *Sun*, April 13, 1956; "'Block-Bust' Blame Is Put on Builders," *Sun*, April 25, 1956.

10. Maryland Commission on Interracial Problems and Relations, *Annual Report* (1957), p. 21 [report on the preceding year, 1956]. The commission concluded that the "only avenue of approach was to educate the white citizens as to the best means of protecting their property values and preserving their neighborhoods."

11. Martin Millspaugh, "'Block-Busting' Called Big Cause of Racial Tension," *Sun*, April 13, 1956. The commission called upon the Real Estate Board, the city government, and the neighborhood improvement associations to fight the speculators *in order to "save those parts of the city which may still be salvaged"* [emphasis added]. A 1955 *Sun* article discussing a "Not for Sale" campaign in the 700 block of Cold Spring Lane (in the northern section of the city) similarly tried to define the unacceptable elements in blockbusting: "the name that is given to the deliberate changeover of a neighborhood from white to Negro occupancy, by unscrupulous real estate operators and against the wishes of most affected property owners." "Not for Sale," *Sun*, August 26, 1955.

12. Josephine Novak quoted an early African American resident in a formerly all-white neighborhood who reported being the recipient of solicitation intended for her white neighbors: "So we would get circulars through the mail from real estate investors, and phone calls. How many Negro families have moved into your block? they would ask. They were trying to get us to sell our house; they didn't know we were Negro and had just moved in." "Negro Buyer Exploited as Neighborhoods [Change]" (unidentified newspaper article, c. 1969, in the files of the St. Ambrose Housing Aid Society, Baltimore).

13. "Anti-Blockbusting Bill Gets Mayor's Signature," *Evening Sun*, March 18, 1966. The following year the municipal law was ruled invalid because its provision regarding the mail usurped a federal prerogative ("'Blockbust' Law Voided," *Sun*, November 23, 1967). A new law, minus the mailing ban, was enacted in 1968 and upheld by the local criminal court in a test case ("Council to Vote on Bill to Ban Blockbusting," Baltimore *Evening Sun*, April 1, 1968; "Dorf Upholds Blockbusting Law of 1968," *Sun*, December 11, 1969). In that same year the federal Fair Housing Act outlawed discrimination in the sale of housing and specifically prohibited blockbusting.

14. "'Block-Busting' Called Big Cause of Racial Tension."
15. *Annual Report* (1957).
16. "Block-Busting," *Sun*, September 7, 1958.
17. The contention that some blockbusters introduced "lower class Negroes" into the first home "busted," often on a rental basis, sometimes even without rent, was contained in "'Block-Busting' Called Big Cause of Racial Tension" and "'Block-Bust' Blame is Put on Builders." In the latter, Samuel T. Daniels, executive director of the Maryland Commission on Interracial Problems and Relations, addressing the Baltimore City Council's Housing Committee in April 1956 asserted that "speculators buy homes in a stable neighborhood and then 'at little or no rent' put in tenants of the type who are truly undesirable."
18. "Revocation of Realty Permit Asked," *Sun*, September 6, 1958; "Block-busting Complaint Filed," *Evening Sun*, September 30, 1958; "New Real Estate Complaint Filed," *Sun*, October 1, 1958; "Real Estate Case Ends," *Sun*, March 25, 1959; "Board Acts Against 2 in Realty Firm," *Sun*, April 23, 1959; "3-Month Realty Suspension Is Linked to 'Blockbusting,'" *Sun*, July 21, 1960. The quote is from the last article; it noted that "the partners were not charged with blockbusting, which is not illegal, but it was implicit in much of the testimony."
19. Douglas Connah, Jr., "Blockbusting in Baltimore: Less Blatant and Rapacious, But Still the Subtle Cause of a Continued White Exodus," *Sun*, January 26, 1969.
20. William B. Dorsey, letter to the editor, *Sun*, August 30, 1955.
21. Simple excess markup was not the only way that speculators profited from blockbusting-induced sales. Ground rents, a standard mechanism under Maryland law, might be increased in the process of the transaction; speculators then would reap the benefit of the increase either by retaining the ground rent as an investment or by selling it off (whether to the new homeowner or to others as an investment).
22. In a 1960 study of Baltimore housing patterns, Favor found evidence to rebut the popular notion that property values declined when African American occupancy occurred. "The Effects of Racial Changes on Occupancy Patterns." In their review of studies of housing prices in instances of racial change, Kain and Quigley contend that most have shown that in the initial phases values rise rather than decline. *Housing Markets and Racial Discrimination*, pp. 75-82.
23. During the late 1960s and early 1970s fair housing advocates began to substantiate the extent of excessive markups by speculators in racially changing areas. Examples were reported in the local press, such as instances of markups amounting to 105 percent in Montebello and 81 percent in the Alameda section, both on the northeast side ("Montebello Negroes Held Overcharged," *Sun*, June 2, 1969; Connah, "Blockbusting in Baltimore"). James Dilts reported as a typical illustration from the Edmondson Village area a house bought by a speculator for $6,500 and sold for $13,000, a 100 percent markup ("Inflating Home Costs with the 'Black Tax'" [undated *Sun* newspaper clipping in the files of the St. Ambrose Housing Aid Society, Baltimore]); similar instances from the Edmondson Village area are in James Dilts, "2 Neighborhoods: Speculators Take a Cut," *Sun*, September 19,

1971. A number of these press accounts were based upon evidence compiled and published in reports by the Activists for Fair Housing, Inc., an organization originally founded by CORE; see, for instance, the Activists, "Communities Under Siege" (typescript report, September 1970). The Activists' charges are discussed more fully below and in chapter 5.

24. *An American City in Transition*, pp. 51, 54-55. The report cited the case of a Mr. X, who made arrangements to purchase a house on a land contract basis, making a downpayment of $260 toward a purchase price of $5,000 and agreeing to pay $12 weekly; of the $12, $6 was for interest, $3.50 for expense charges, and $2.50 applied toward the principal. However, when his complaints about needed repairs finally were addressed by the seller, he discovered that the charge for the work had been added to the total cost: "After two years, Mr. X does not know how much he has accumulated in real ownership of the property, for his present balance is almost the same as the amount after the original down payment" (p. 55). Similar problems regarding land contracts were noted in Odell M. Smith, "Slick Speculators: Few Home Buyers Know Rights Under 1951 Law," *Sun*, December 15, 1954. By Maryland law, sellers on installment contracts who declared a tenant in default on payments had to list the property for auction; in practice, they often were able to turn around and buy the property back themselves. Calvin Bradford provides an excellent discussion of land or installment contracts in "Financing Home Ownership," p. 319.

25. Janelle Keidel, "Orlinsky Files Three Bills On Real Estate Practices," *Sun*, August 10, 1969; Activists, "A Conspiracy to Defraud and Exploit Homebuyers: The Story of Jefferson Federal Savings and Loan" (typescript report; February, 1971); Novak, "Negro Buyer Exploited as Neighborhoods [Change]."

26. Dilts, "Housing Speculators Fill Void," *Sun*, September 25, 1971.

27. Vill, "Park Heights"; Vill mentions both "steering" and "pressure on local owners to sell" in Park Heights (pp. 23-26).

28. Ellsworth E. Rosen, "When a Negro Moves Next Door" ("A Baltimore resident tells how his neighborhood [Ashburton] welcomes Negro homeowners—and keeps white families from moving away"), *Saturday Evening Post* (April 14, 1959); at the time the article was published, the African American percentage in Ashburton was reported to be 5 percent. Alan Hillman in an interview discussed similar efforts in nearby Windsor Hills (June 16, 1981). These grassroots efforts eventually won support from the Greater Baltimore Committee, which was instrumental in the establishment of Baltimore Neighborhoods, Inc., in 1960. BNI supported initiatives to challenge blockbusting and stabilize city neighborhoods by promoting racial understanding. Cherrill Anson described some of these programs throughout the city in "Good Neighbor Pioneers," *Sun*, February 28, 1965.

29. West, "Urban Life and Spatial Distribution of Blacks in Baltimore"; Center for Urban Affairs, Johns Hopkins University and the Department of Planning, City of Baltimore, *Census Notes* (Baltimore, 1971) provides the census figures by race for sections of the city, 1960 to 1970.

30. For the methodology involved in the author's sample block survey, see chapter 1. The present analysis is based upon *Baltimore City Real Estate Tax Assess-*

ments volumes for the years 1955 to 1973 (published in odd years to report on current state-mandated property value assessments; the volume for 1971 was inadvertently missing). The names cited here are intended as a sample, not an exhaustive list. Addresses were checked in Baltimore city directories for 1961 and 1964. In only rare instances was ownership acquired by people already resident on the block (examples included Robert E. Lee and Vincent Mussachio on the 600-odd block of Augusta) or investors living elsewhere in Edmondson Village (for example, Thomas Creutzer on the 3300 block of Edmondson and elsewhere).

31. For example, on two blocks (the 3300 block of Edmondson Avenue and the 300 block of N. Hilton, both situated at the foot of the hill in the section with some of the oldest housing), a remarkable number of original settlers whose tenure dated to the 1920s persisted as resident owners as late as 1961. However, in that year some of the houses had been purchased by nonresident investors, and over the next several years many others showed outside ownership; this pattern continued to prevail in 1973, the last year examined.

32. The Activists' case regarding the Morris Goldseker Company was stated in "Communities Under Siege" (1970), which used the Lusk reports on real estate activity from 1960 to 1968 to identify 144 of 391 transactions in census tract 1608 as Goldseker Company-related. The Activists did not raise the specific charge of blockbusting, concentrating instead upon the issue of excessive profits. Their report calculated markups to have been 69 percent (additional data on Goldseker sales in Park Heights claimed approximately 80 percent). A follow-up study ("A Conspiracy to Defraud Homebuyers"), based on all real estate transactions in the city for the same period, contended that markups on 742 properties bought and sold by Goldseker (of 1,768 purchased) averaged 85 percent. The same study detailed charges on the relationship of financial institutions. On issues raised by the Activists' reports, James D. Dilts, "Housing Exploitation Charged," *Sun*, March 5, 1971, and a seven-part series by Dilts in the *Sun*, September 19-25, 1971. Bradford notes a 1963 report by the Chicago Human Relations Commission, which found markups averaging 73 percent in a racially changing area of that city where homes were bought through contract sales ("Financing Home Ownership," p. 325). On the matter of affiliate companies, it might be noted that none of those listed above showed up in Baltimore city directories for 1961 or 1964, although the Morris Goldseker Company advertised on its own, as in the 1964 directory, where its ad stated, "Modern Homes—Sold on Small Downpayment; Homes Purchased for Cash." The Goldseker Company ad included the seal of the National Association of Real Estate Brokers (Realtors).

33. In response to the Activists' charges and the suit the group filed against the Morris Goldseker Company, Sheldon Goldseker defended the policies and practices of his uncle's firm in "Comment from Sheldon Goldseker" (*Sun*, October 2, 1971); in his letter to the editor of the *Sun*, June 22, 1973; and in an article by James Dilts, "Landlord's Lament: 'Don't Blame Goldseker'" (*Sun*, March 9, 1971).

34. For example, the range of conflicting retrospective views is evident in such newspaper accounts as "Goldseker Foundation," *Sun*, July 14, 1973 (which

quoted his nephew, Sheldon Goldseker); Eric Siegel, "The Riddle of Morris Goldseker's Legacy," *Sun*, February 5, 1978; and Jesse Glasgow, "Goldseker Firm, Manager for Fund, to Close Its Doors," *Sun*, February 1, 1985.

35. The quote is from Sheldon Goldseker's letter to the editor, *Sun*, June 22, 1973. The Activists asserted that during the 1960s the Morris Goldseker Company and its affiliates bought 1,768 houses in the city ("A Conspiracy to Defraud," p. 1); Siegel ("The Riddle of Morris Goldseker's Legacy") claimed that in 1969 the Goldseker firm employed one hundred employees, with a payroll of a half million dollars.

36. In the legal suit brought by the Activists against the Morris Goldseker Company the group charged the firms' profit on these transactions had been 31 percent, while company representatives claimed a profit of 18 percent. The suit was withdrawn and, therefore, dismissed by federal judge Rozel C. Thomsen in March, 1972. The Activists insisted that the reason for not pressing the charges was their inability to afford the costs of an expert witness to conduct a full market study to verify their contentions regarding fair housing values; Goldseker representatives insisted that withdrawal of the suit constituted full vindication of the firm's position. James D. Dilts, "Plaintiffs Drop Goldseker Suit: Cite Lack of Funds," *Sun*, March 10, 1972; "Finally—The Truth About the M. Goldseker Suit" [Goldseker Company ad], *Catholic Review*, March 24, 1972; Reginald Bennett, "Version of Why Housing Suit Ceased," *Catholic Review*, May 19, 1972; Siegel, "The Riddle of Morris Goldseker's Legacy."

37. Interview with Agnes Malone, September 12, 1980.
38. Interview with Madge Cooper, November 4, 1982.
39. Interview with Ann Morgan, March 23, 1981.
40. Interview with Marilyn Simkins, September 17, 1980.
41. Interview with Alice Hughes, October 2, 1980.
42. Interview by Nancy Swartz with Vera Johnson, September, 1985.
43. Interview with Joe Slovensky, October 27, 1980.
44. Interview with Christine Wallace, March 23, 1981.
45. The following discussion is based upon 1955-56 newspaper accounts in "Not For Sale"; "The Drive Behind Block-Busting"; "'Block-Bust' Blame Is Put on Builders"; "Block-Busters"; "Cure for Block-Busting"; and "'Block-Busting' Called Big Cause of Racial Tension."
46. Interview by Nancy Swartz with Madge Morgenstern, September, 1985. Madge Cooper said that real estate agents would come after dark, especially approaching people they believed to be disaffected for one reason or another.
47. Interview with Eunice Clemens, June 9, 1981.
48. "Block-Busters."
49. Interview by Nancy Swartz with Nola Null, September, 1985.
50. Interview with Edith Romaine, October 27, 1980.
51. Interview with Father John Smith, February 15, 1983.
52. Joynes, *Thirty Years*, p. 27.
53. *Minutes of the Board of School Commissioners* (Baltimore) June 3, 1954. On the Baltimore Board's decision and the early desegregation process, Gertrude

Samuels, "School Desegregation: A Case History," New York *Times* (May 8, 1955); Edgar Jones, "How Desegregation Has Worked," *Sun* (June 26, 1955); Banks, "Descriptive Study of the Baltimore Board of School Commissioners."

54. Maryland Commission on Interracial Problems and Relations [report by Elinor Pancoast], *The Report of a Study on Desegregation in the Baltimore City Schools* (1956), pp. 33-67. Incidents occurred at eight elementary schools and several secondary schools, according to the report.

55. Pancoast report, pp. 68-78; the Clarence Mitchell incident is cited on p. 78 and discussed more fully in Mark Miller, "Gentlemanly Persuasion," *Baltimore Magazine* (September 1981), pp. 124-25.

56. Eric Siegel, "A Nonpolitical Mitchell, Who Is a Doctor and an Artist," *Sun*, February 5, 1984.

57. As part of its open enrollment plan, the school board insisted that there were no designated school districts, except in the case of overcrowded schools where districts were necessary to control total enrollment; in theory this meant that students might attend any school in the city, but the board clearly assumed that elementary school students would enroll in schools in their own neighborhoods.

58. Rock Glen opened in 1962 as a community school, with some elementary and junior high grades; in 1964 it became exclusively a junior high school under the new superintendent's open enrollment plan for the city, and the school's population soared (interview with Rock Glen teacher Dorothy Clark, October 24, 1988).

59. An article on the study surmised that resegregation had resulted from the removal of white children, changing housing patterns, and the higher density of African American children in neighborhoods. "De Facto Segregation," *Johns Hopkins Magazine* (October 6, 1963), p. 9.

60. A parents' group challenged the small amount of integration and raised a number of other concerns about the lack of educational opportunity for African American school children; see chapter 5 for further discussion of the issues raised. League of Women Voters [Baltimore], *Desegregation: Baltimore Public Schools: History, Problems, Solutions* (September 20, 1963), pp. 10-11. On the occasion of the twentieth-fifth anniversary of the adoption of the Baltimore school desegregation policy, former superintendent John Fischer, who provided leadership for the change, generally praised the smooth and orderly process but reflected that "freedom of choice has not entirely worked to assure equal educational opportunity." "Former School Chief Recalls 'Exemplary' City Reaction," *Evening Sun*, May 17, 1979.

61. Interview with Janice Watkins, May 24, 1983.

62. Case histories of racial conflict related to residential turf in Brooklyn (Canarsie) and Boston (Mattapan) demonstrate the impact of such incidents in escalating tensions and magnifying fears. Rieder, *Canarsie* (p. 71-78), and Levine and Harmon in their account of Mattapan, *Death of American Jewish Community* (pp. 215-18, 306-8), both cite actual (as well as rumored) incidents of increased crime and conflict in the schools as contributing to the hardening of white attitudes.

63. The following discussion is based upon the U.S. Census tract figures for tracts 1608 and 2007 (and subdivisions of those tracts), 1940 to 1960.

64. In dramatic contrast, the pioneer African American community in 2007 bore substantially higher percentages in the under fourteen and the twenty-five to forty-four age categories—young children and their parents—than had *ever* been the case in the white community's history.

65. Between 1950 and 1960 male percentages for white-collar participation changed only from 41 to 40 percent. Note that the white-collar figure was enlarged by the heavy concentration of female workers in sales and clerical categories.

66. In 1950, 52 percent of men in 1608 were in white-collar occupations; in 1960, 50 percent. Between 1950 and 1960 for men the greatest difference had been the decline in the craftsmen (skilled trades, foremen) category (from 17 to 12 percent); on the white-collar side, an increase in the professional category (from 8 to 13 percent) was offset by a similar decrease in managerial jobs (from 9 to 7 percent). For women, the greatest increases had come in sales and clerical positions. In 1960 nearly half of women workers were in these two categories, and they represented 21 percent of the total labor force.

67. In 1960 median housing values in tract 1608 were 19 percent above the Baltimore SMSA (metro area) median of $5,239, but values in tract 2007 closely approximated the metro figure.

68. See Appendix A for discussion of the literature on white avoidance and on filtering.

69. On northside sample blocks (Edmondson, Augusta, Wildwood, Walnut, and Flowerton) there were African American residents in seven of fifty-nine households in 1964. Sample block survey.

70. An earlier, expanded version of the following discussion originally appeared in Orser, "Racial Change in Retrospect." In this reconsideration of white perceptions, it is important to understand that interviewees not only sought to convey their own views but also tried to interpret the views of other members of the community, like those of their parents and neighbors.

71. Pioneer is defined broadly as a member of the first generation of African American settlers, generally those in the wave of settlement from 1955 to 1965. It is not always possible to isolate this group precisely for analytical purposes in the 1970 and 1980 census tract reports.

72. While home ownership rates dipped slightly from previous levels, they continued to exceed the metropolitan area median.

73. In 1960, African American pioneer households in 2007 had median incomes ($4,881) only minimally lower than white families who remained ($4,940 was the median for the tract as a whole), though whites in 1608, where racial change had not yet occurred, had higher levels ($6,239). In that same year, the citywide African American household median was $3,354, the metropolitan (SMSA) figure $5,329. In 1970 median incomes in the census tracts ranging from $8,162 to $8,312 compared with the city African American median of $5,590 and the SMSA median of $8,676. *U.S. Census*, 1960, 1970.

74. Lamphere demonstrates the usefulness of the concept of family strategies in her analysis of gender and ethnicity in a Rhode Island textile community, *From Working Daughters to Working Mothers*, pp. 27-31.

75. Note that the presence of women workers in the paid labor force helped to compensate for the lower percentage of African American males in job categories traditionally more closed to them; for instance, among white-collar occupations, African American women outnumbered men in professional and clerical jobs.

76. The discussion of discrepancy between the oral history recollections and the social profile from census and sample block data is not intended to imply the lack of credibility of the former. Rather, the oral testimony is extremely useful because it illuminates the perceptions individuals likely held at the time and therefore helps us understand the basis for the collective action that occurred. It might be argued that these perceptions represented the central social reality at the heart of the neighborhood experience, overriding other considerations of the type a retrospective examination of the demographic data permits. For further discussion of this point regarding oral history testimony, see Orser, "Racial Change in Retrospect," p. 51.

5. *African American Pioneers*

Note: This chapter is an expanded version of Orser, "Secondhand Suburbs." It examines the experience of the first generation of African American pioneers from 1955 to 1980. Epigraph is from interview with Elizabeth Jones, July 3, 1985.

1. In general, sociological studies of such indicators of socioeconomic status as education and income for African Americans who have initiated moves into predominantly white neighborhoods have found them to be comparable to those of whites residing in the area and in advance of blacks in the metropolitan region as a whole. See, for example, Long and Spain, "Racial Succession in Individual Housing Units"; Denowitz, "Racial Succession in New York City, 1960-1970"; Scott, "Blacks in Segregated and Desegregated Neighborhoods"; Edwards, "Family Composition as a Variable in Racial Succession"; Nelson, "Recent Suburbanization of Blacks"; Lake, *New Suburbanites*. For a general bibliographical review of the African American experience in succession communities, see Fairchild and Tucker, "Black Residential Mobility."

2. Rose raised a similar concern about the experience of African American settlers in new suburban settings when he observed, "given the fact of race and all its many implications, the question becomes whether such communities can survive without deteriorating into environments similar to those the initial mover wished to escape." *Black Suburbanization*, p. 11.

3. Leonard Downie, Jr., "Black Home Buyers' Protest Hits Baltimore," Washington *Post* (c. 1969, undated article in the files of the St. Ambrose Housing Aid Society, Baltimore); "6 Arrested in Goldseker Protest," Baltimore *Sun*, August 10, 1969; interview by the author with Samuel Brown, June 13, 1981. According to Sheldon Goldseker, nephew of Morris Goldseker and an associate in the business, the firm stopped selling houses and released its eight-man sales staff

in 1969, at least partly in response to the protests; as he told a reporter in 1971: "We haven't sold houses for two years, since the trouble. With the pickets, we can't close deals, we can't bring people into the office." James Dilts, "Landlord's Lament: 'Don't Blame Goldseker,'" *Sun*, March 9, 1971. Originally called the Activists for Fair Housing, the group took the name Activists, Inc., in 1967 because of the intention to extend its civil rights activities beyond housing; at that time the organization had two hundred dues-paying members, both African American and white. *Sun*, December 31, 1967. The campaign in Chicago to organize African American residents who had bought from speculators on a land contract basis had parallels to the Baltimore effort, and there is some indication that the two movements drew upon one another for concepts and strategy. The Chicago movement was chronicled in James Alan McPherson, "'In My Father's House There Are Many Mansions.'"

4. Activists, Inc., "Communities Under Siege" pp. 4-5. The comparison tract was 26-03, along Belair Road in northeast Baltimore. "Communities Under Siege" was based on a study undertaken by Charles Keeley of Western Michigan University on behalf of the Activists and completed in draft form in the summer of 1970; the term "Black Tax" was used in the early picketing campaign and was repeated in another draft document by the Activists, "From Ghetto to Ghetto: The Odyssey of the Working Class Black Family" (typescript, n.d., c. 1970), p. 11. One of the leaders of the Chicago Contract Buyers League used the term "a vile race tax" in describing the same concept. McPherson, p. 58.

5. "Communities Under Siege," pp. 5, 9 a-d. The contention that the variety of front names meant that clients did not know they were doing business with Goldseker was the basis for an Activists' complaint that the company had engaged in deceptive advertising practices. The report also documented patterns of excessive markups for Goldseker transactions in the Lower Park Heights area (alleged to be c. 82 percent for the cases examined), the third city district where the Activists focused their attention (p. 11).

6. Activists, Inc., "A Conspiracy to Defraud and Exploit Homebuyers," pp. 5-6. The report argued that the savings and loan firm had underwritten excessive sale prices and that it benefited from inflated interest rates on refinanced mortgages. It also noted that a Goldseker Company employee, Martin Weinberg, had been a member of Jefferson's board, implying a conflict of interest. The Jefferson Federal allegations were reported by James Dilts, "Housing Exploitation Charged," *Sun*, March 5, 1971. Later the same year the Activists published "Baltimore Under Siege," asserting that in 1968 twenty-four of Baltimore's state and federally chartered savings and loans institutions had made 78 percent of their housing loans to investors or those buying from investors (p. 11). It also contended that two major commercial banks, Equitable Trust Company and Maryland National Bank, provided major mortgage support for Goldseker companies and for Jefferson Federal during the 1960s (p. 25). James Dilts ran a seven-part series on the housing issues raised by the Activists in the *Sun*, September 19-25, 1971. The same article that contained the charges by the Activists against Jefferson Federal reported that the Home Loan Bank Board in 1969 had expressed concern to Jefferson about the vol-

ume of its loans to investors or speculators and that in March of that year Jefferson had ceased financing Goldseker Company customers. Dilts, "Housing Exploitation Charged."

7. Eric Siegel, "The Riddle of Morris Goldseker's Legacy," *Sun*, February 5, 1978.

8. The latter quote from Sheldon Goldseker is contained in Dilts, "Landlord's Lament." He defended the Morris Goldseker Company similarly in his response to the *Sun*'s series by James Dilts in September, 1971, and in "Comment from Sheldon Goldseker," *Sun*, October 2, 1971 (reprinted as an ad in *Catholic Review*, October 8, 1971). The Goldseker and Activists calculations regarding profit margin were cited in James D. Dilts, "Plaintiffs Drop Goldseker Suit: Cite Lack of Funds," *Sun*, March 10, 1972. In a 1973 letter to the editor Sheldon Goldseker took exception to repetition of the charges contained in the *Sun*'s obituary for his uncle (for the obituary, *Sun*, June 18, 1973; his letter, June 22, 1973).

9. The suit on behalf of forty-one individual homebuyers and the two community associations (Edmondson Village and Montebello), initially filed in 1969 and dismissed in March 1972, charged that Goldseker companies had conspired to fix housing prices and to monopolize the housing markets of the two neighborhoods; Goldseker lawyers denied both charges (Dilts, "Plaintiffs Drop Goldseker Suit"). *The Catholic Review* (published by the Archdiocese of Baltimore) contained a company ad claiming complete exoneration ("Finally—The Truth About the M. Goldseker Law Suit," March 24, 1972) and a letter to the editor that repeated the Activists' explanation for withdrawing the suit (Reginald Bennett, president of the Montebello Community Association, "Version of Why Housing Suit Ceased," May 19, 1971). The conflicting interpretation of the Goldseker record and legacy is discussed further in chapter 6.

10. "Communities Under Siege," p. 13.

11. "Testimony Presented by Congressman Parren J. Mitchell (D. 7th MD) [on a Senate bank reform bill]," May 6, 1975, pp. 1-2.

12. The following discussion of the politics of the civil rights movement in Maryland draws heavily upon Calcott, *Maryland & America*, especially pages 145-71; Goldberg, "Party Competition and Black Politics"; K. Olson, "Old West Baltimore"; and James D. Dilts, "The Warning Trumpet: CORE Is 'The Only Voice Black People Ever Had,'" *Sun*, December 1, 1968. Annual reports of the Maryland Commission on Interracial Problems and Relations (1952-1968) highlighted particular actions and accomplishments in the struggle against discrimination.

13. "393 Integrationists, Many Clerics, Arrested at Gwynn Oak Park," *Sun*, July 5, 1963. The demonstrations represented the first active participation of the National Council of Churches leadership in a civil rights demonstration as a group; together with demonstrators from Washington, Philadelphia, and New York, they joined local organizers—including CORE, clergy from the Interdenominational Ministerial Alliance, and other area civil rights activists—in the protests. After continued pressure and negotiation, the park's ownership agreed to desegregate; the victory proved short-lived, however, since the park was largely

destroyed by Hurricane Agnes in 1972 and subsequently closed. In John Waters's satirical film "Hairspray" (1988), set in Baltimore in the early 1960s, a similar amusement park protest occurs as a climactic scene.

14. The Truman administration's fair employment policies regarding federal agencies and the armed services are evaluated in McCoy and Reutten, *Quest and Response*, pp. 251-57, 281; and McCoy, *Presidency of Harry S. Truman*, pp. 108-9, 169-70. Reutter discusses employment practices regarding African Americans at Bethlehem Steel in *Sparrows Point*, pp. 252, 292-8, 347-352; see also Zeidman, "Sparrows Point, Dundalk, Highlandtown, Old West Baltimore," p. 190-91. On the CORE protests, Dilts, "The Warning Trumpet."

15. These developments are discussed in Calcott, *Maryland and America*, pp. 158-66. On the changing orientation of the Baltimore Chapter of CORE, Dilts, "The Warning Trumpet"; by 1969 membership in the Baltimore branch of the NAACP, once the nation's largest, had fallen to five thousand (William Stump, "NAACP Turns Face Inward," Baltimore *News American*, January 25, 1976).

16. "1,900 U.S. Troops Patrolling City; Officials Plan Curfew Again Today; 4 Dead, 300 Hurt, 1,350 Arrested," *Sun*, April 8, 1968; "West Baltimore Is an Ugly No-Man's Land," *Sun*, April 9, 1968; "1,900 More GI's Join Riot Forces as Snipers Peril Police, Firemen; Arrests in 3 Days Run to 3,450," *Sun*, April 9, 1968 (the report on Edmondson Village and Edmondson Avenue was contained in this article); "Backbone of Riot Reported Broken; Return to Normal Could Be Near," *Sun*, April 10, 1968. On the incident between the Governor and African American leaders, "Text of Governor Agnew's Statement to Civil Rights Leaders," *Sun*, April 12, 1968; Gene Oishi, "Negroes Quit Conference with Agnew," *Sun*, April 12, 1968. The casualty figures are from Jane Motz, "Report on Baltimore Civil Disorders, April, 1968" ([typescript] Baltimore: Middle Atlantic Region, American Friends Service Committee, September, 1968), pp. 5, 18.

17. Horace Davis, president of the Edmondson Village Community Association, was among those arrested in the protests at the Morris Goldseker Company in August 1969 ("6 Arrested in Goldseker Protest"); the membership figure is mentioned in Downie, "Black Home Buyers' Protest Hits Baltimore."

18. The following discussion is based upon analysis of the U.S. Census tract data for 1960, 1970, and 1980. The 1960 census provides the first opportunity to reconstruct a social portrait of African American pioneer residents south of Edmondson in tract 2007, where they outnumbered whites 5,714 to 3,528 by that date; in tract 1608, north of the avenue, only ninety-six African Americans had settled by that year. A decade later, after white flight and African American settlement had produced near total racial change in both census tracts, the 1970 census furnished a full-scale profile of the new African American community at a point when the effects of rapid in-migration were still very fresh. By 1980 it is no longer possible to isolate the pioneer group in the census tract data, though in that year they constituted a substantial 40 percent of the area's population. However, the 1980 census does provide an important benchmark for evaluating the community that resident pioneers continued to inhabit some fifteen to twenty-five years after the period of their first settlement.

19. White home ownership also declined during the decade in Baltimore, by 8 percent. Between 1960 and 1970 only 6,594 additional owner-occupied homes were secured by African Americans in all of Baltimore City; 2,744 (42 percent) of them were added in the Edmondson Village section alone. Center for Urban Affairs, Johns Hopkins University and the Department of Planning, City of Baltimore, "Changes in Housing by Race and Renter/Owner Status, Baltimore, Maryland, 1960-1970," *Census Notes* (February 15, 1972), p. 8.

20. Bianchi, Farley, and Spain used data from the 1960 census and the 1977 Annual Housing Survey to calculate the national home ownership rate for African Americans in the former year as 51 percent and in the latter as 60 percent ("Racial Inequalities in Housing," pp. 37-51). Comparable white figures nationally were 64 and 69 percent (p. 46). Scott's analysis of 1970 data found African Americans in "low-percentage" (i.e., "integrator") neighborhoods more likely to be home buyers than other African Americans. "Blacks in Segregated and Desegregated Neighborhoods."

21. In 1960, 80 percent of the African American population in census tract 2007 had moved in during the past five years, 88 percent of whom had come from Baltimore's central city.

22. The 1970 in-migration rate of 42 percent actually was less than the 50 percent rate of residence change for Baltimore City African Americans as a whole. For the SMSA population the figure was 45 percent. Eighty-six percent of Edmondson's new African American residents were from Baltimore's central city.

23. Comparable figures for the metropolitan (SMSA) region as a whole were 58 percent, for African Americans in Baltimore City, 59 percent. Goodman, and Streitwieser noted on the basis of 1974-76 national Annual Housing Survey data that African American city-to-suburb mobility continued to lag significantly behind white mobility, a factor they referred to as "black retention" and attributed to actual or expected racial discrimination. "Explaining Racial Differences."

24. The sample block survey was conducted for ten blocks at ten-year intervals (it also was compiled for 1964 to provide an additional reference point in the midst of the racial change period). See chapter 1 for a discussion of the sources and methodology employed in the study.

25. The housing cost figures are from "Communities Under Siege," p. 9b.

26. "Communities Under Siege," pp. 9, 9b.

27. Kain and Quigley's 1975 review of studies of housing prices in circumstances of rapid racial change found that most confirmed that housing prices rose rather than declined in the initial phases. *Housing Markets and Racial Discrimination*, pp. 75-82. Similarly, Lake noted that studies based on data from the 1950s and early 1960s found African Americans paid more than whites for comparable housing. However, his data from the mid-1970s on selected New Jersey suburbs found that as African American population in an area increased, African Americans paid less for comparable housing and that housing values declined over time, factors leading to an equity loss for early African American purchasers. *New Suburbanites*, pp. 180, 201-202. Schnare used 1970 housing data from Boston to argue that rapid expansion of available housing stock during the previous decade led to

an eventual decline in the relative housing price in the city's African American neighborhoods. "Racial and Ethnic Price Differentials," especially p. 114. On the "net penalty associated with being black" relative to housing opportunity and quality, see Bianchi, Farley, and Spain, "Racial Inequalities in Housing."

28. The metropolitan median for owner-occupied housing in 1980 was $51,400; Edmondson Village medians ranged from $21,500 to $28,100 in the four tracts.

29. African American population percentages in nearby suburban Baltimore County stood at 4 percent in 1960, 3.2 percent in 1970 and 8.2 percent in 1980, actual numbers rising from 17,054 in 1960 to 53,955 in 1980. Factors responsible for African American retention in areas like Edmondson Village no doubt include financial considerations, perceptions of a lack of receptivity in suburban areas beyond the city limits, and satisfaction with present housing and neighborhood. On these factors, see Goodman and Streitwieser, "Explaining Racial Differences"; Cottingham, "Black Income and Metropolitan Residential Dispersion," especially pp. 274, 280, and 287; and Farley and Colsanto, "Racial Residential Segregation."

30. The 1970 percentage is based upon median household income in the two tracts of c. $8,240, compared to $5,590 for African Americans citywide.

31. In 1980 Edmondson household income in the tracts averaged approximately $17,786, while the metropolitan median was $18,958, and the African American citywide median $11,158.

32. The list of employers is from the sample block survey, based on the 1964 city directory; unfortunately, the directories often did not provide a job designation for working wives. See the comment by Horace Green below on the significance of westside residence, even for those whose employment was on the east side.

33. In tract 2007 in 1960, 38 percent of white males were in operative or laborer positions, 53 percent of African American males; in tract 1608 in the same year, males (preponderantly white) in the two categories constituted only 14 percent, while in 1970, 58 percent of males (preponderantly African American) were in these two types of jobs (39 percent as operatives, 19 percent as laborers).

34. Note that in 1970 in tract 1608 the white-collar percentage for men was 20 percent, for women 46 percent (the greatest concentration of the latter being in clerical positions). In 1980 the occupational distribution for Edmondson workers continued to resemble closely the profile for Baltimore's African American population as a whole. Occupations classified as white-collar did increase by 8 percent during the decade to nearly 4 in 10 (38 percent), but blue-collar jobs still predominated.

35. The percentage of the Edmondson female labor force who were married (with husband present) stood at 52 percent in 1970 but dropped to 41 percent in 1980. Significantly, during the decade 1970-80 the percentage of Edmondson households headed by a female increased substantially. As an indication of household employment patterns, husband/wife combinations of occupations for pioneer residents interviewed by the author were as follows: skilled cabinetmaker/city

librarian; maintenance mechanic at Bendix/purchasing agent, Johns Hopkins Hospital; supervisor, U.S. Post Office/nurse, University Hospital; sod company worker/nurse, University Hospital; baker/Social Security staff.

36. In 1960 the median age for white residents had been approximatel forty. While half the African American populace was under twenty in 1970, by 1980 that percentage had shrunk to thirty-six.

37. In 1960 the African American citywide ratio of households with married couples to total households was close to five of eight; in 1970 and 1980, approximately five of ten.

38. The 1970 Edmondson figure of 18 percent compared to 25 percent for all African American city households. By 1980 the Edmondson figure was 32 percent and the African American city figure 46 percent, compared to an SMSA rate of 19 percent.

39. In 1980 median incomes in Edmondson households headed by a female ranged from $12,329 to $14,798 in the four tracts, approximately $4,000 to $6,000 below the median family income for the Edmondson area.

40. In tract 2007 in 1960 African American households were comprised of 4.24 residents; in the total tract, white and African American, the median was 3.67. By 1970 housing densities in the predominantly African American Edmondson tracts were 4.12-4.23 persons per household (compared to 3.6 for African American citywide). By 1980 density had declined to 3.17-3.73, a rate still higher than the SMSA (2.45) and African American citywide (2.74) medians.

41. Interview with Annie Green, December 13, 1982.

42. Similar opinions were expressed in a group interview at the Mary Rodman Center (senior citizens group), December 14, 1982.

43. Interview with Horace Green, December 13, 1982.

44. Interview with Margaret Dawkins, February 24, 1983.

45. In 1960, 88 percent of African American newcomers in census tract 2007 had come from Baltimore's central city, and in 1970 86 percent of newcomers in both tracks (during the preceding five years) had similar origins.

46. Interview with Mary Slade, March 14, 1983.

47. Interview with Janice Watkins, May 24, 1983.

48. The preceding quotes all are from the interviews at the Rodman Center, including the interview with Margaret Johnson on the same date.

49. Interview with Father John Smith, February 15, 1983.

50. Interview with Roberta Warren, January 5, 1983.

51. Interview with Eunice Clemens, June 9, 1981.

52. These concerns were expressed in interviews with Jones, Warren, and the Greens.

53. In 1963 controversy over desegregation policies surfaced when an interracial group of twenty-eight concerned parents charged that Baltimore's schools and classrooms remained largely segregated and challenged enrollment policies (including districting, transfer, and transportation), use of part-time instruction (alleging that 79 percent of students with part-time instructors were African American), and school construction. League of Women Voters [Baltimore], *Deseg-*

regation. The school board response in 1963 essentially reaffirmed open enrollment, though certain policies were revised, such as those governing districting.

54. On persistent concerns about the failure to achieve desegregation and the problems confronting the schools, see George Rodgers, "School Integration Woes Seen Worsening Here," Baltimore *Evening Sun*, February 2, 1967 [on the U.S. Commission on Civil Rights study, *Racial Isolation in the Public Schools*]; Mike Bowler, "City Magnet Schools, Open Enrollment Fail to Halt Segregation," *Sun*, November 25, 1972; John Crew, "Desegregating Baltimore City's Public Schools," *Baltimore Magazine*, 68 (September, 1975), pp. 18-19, 28. Noted earlier was former school superintendent John Fischer's observation that freedom of choice had not entirely worked to assure equal educational opportunity. "Former School Chief Recalls 'Exemplary' City Reaction," *Evening Sun*, May 17, 1979 [on the occasion of the 25th anniversary of the initial school board decision]. A 1968 study argued that the resegregation of Baltimore metro area schools was a problem related in part to the division of the metropolitan area into political jurisdictions that kept the city and suburban counties separate. Stinchcombe, McDill, and Walker, "Demography of Organizations."

55. Baltimore City Department of Planning, "Analysis of the Edmondson Village Shopping Center in 1979" (1979).

56. On concern about the shopping center and criticism of Weinberg's role, "Mayor Exhorts Merchants to Act at Edmondson," *Sun*, August 10, 1973; "Village Defects Found," *Sun*, November 7, 1973; "City Did Its Best in Edmondson, Mayor Says," *Sun*, November 8, 1973; "Boarded Up," *Sun*, January 8, 1974; "Boarded-Up Hochschild Building Called Edmondson Village Eyesore," *Sun*, November 3, 1975; "Failure to Renew Edmondson Mall Blamed on Powerful Absentee Landlord," *Sun*, June 14, 1979; "Coalition Works to Revitalize Edmondson Village," *Evening Sun*, December 30, 1977. On Weinberg's posture in resisting development proposals and the frustration of Baltimore municipal officials, Robert Douglas, "Honolulu Harry," *News American*, July 10, 1980; Alison Langley, "'Honolulu Harry' Holds Up the Works," *News American*, April 7, 1985; Michael Olesker, "Weinberg's Life Gave Few Clues to Final Kind Act," *Sun*, November 11, 1990.

6. The Legacy of Blockbusting

Note: Epigraphs from Walter Herman, "Edmondson Village: A Community of Townhouses in Various Styles," Baltimore *News-American*, March 31, 1984. interview with Marilyn Simkins, October 2, 1981; interview with Elizabeth Jones, July 3, 1985.

1. Robert D. Loevy, "Baltimore's Population Is Nearing Racial Stability," Baltimore *Evening Sun*, April 12, 1982. Loevy wrote that 73 percent of Baltimore residents lived in tracts that had experienced less than 10 percent racial change during the decade.

2. Eileen Canzian, "'70s Exodus from Baltimore Left It a Larger Share of Poor," Baltimore *Sun*, March 27, 1983. The article noted that during the decade

from 1960 to 1970 Baltimore City experienced a net migration loss of 120,791. The following decade the loss was an even larger 142,438; during that decade white net out-migration actually declined substantially (from 152,132 to 119,877), but the total figure was magnified by the net loss of 22,461 African Americans, a significant new development (in the 1960s, for instance, African American net gain in the city had been 31,341). Farley, et al., found strong evidence of the polarization of the Detroit metropolitan area between predominantly white suburbs and the predominantly African American city, in "'Chocolate City, Vanilla Suburbs.'"

3. *Hearing before the United States Commission on Civil Rights: Hearing Held in Baltimore, Maryland, August 17-19, 1970* (Washington, D.C.: U.S. G.P.O., [1970]), p. 486.

4. Szanton, in *Baltimore 2000*, warned of the trend toward a metropolitan configuration characterized as a "double-doughnut," with a revitalized central core, a poor and minority hub, and an outer ring of middle- and upper-income suburbs, largely white (p. 21). Note that the report was commissioned to commemorate the tenth anniversary of the Morris Goldseker Foundation, discussed in the next section.

5. M. William Salganik, "City Neighborhoods' Integration Increased in '70s, Study Says," *Sun*, July 18, 1981 (the article reported on a Johns Hopkins University study by Ralph B. Taylor and Rachel T. Taladay). The study found that during the decade the number of tracts that were mostly African American (i.e., 70 to 100 percent) increased from 84 to 95; those mostly white (70 to 100 percent) decreased from 136 to 107; and those mixed (30 to 70 percent white) increased from 17 to 35.

6. For example, along Liberty Road from the city/county line to the beltway, 4 of 6 census tracts lost more than 50 percent of their white population during the 1970s (percentage losses ranged from 52 to 69); by 1980 African American percentages in the four varied from 50 to 77. *U.S. Census*, 1970, 1980. In 1978 the Baltimore *Sun* ran a seven-part series on this "Corridor in Transition" (the series began on February 5, 1978).

7. The section between the city line and the beltway alone contained 25 percent of the county's African American population in 1980 and 30 percent in 1990. *U.S. Census*, 1980, 1990. In a study of the Washington, D.C., metropolitan area between 1970 and 1980 Gale, Grier, and Grier have observed similar concentration of African American suburbanization in a pattern they refer to as "black 'spillover.'" *Black and White Urban-to-Suburban-Outmigrants*, pp. 14-15. For other studies on recent patterns of African American suburbanization, see Appendix A.

8. Within the city limits, the two large census tracts west of Edmondson Village to the city line had African American percentages of 45 percent (in 2804.01, north of Route 40) and 30 percent (in 2804.03, south of Route 40) in 1980; these percentages had increased to 63 and 46 percent, respectively, in 1990. In 1980 Baltimore County the three census tracts along the north side of the Route 40 corridor west to the Beltway had African American percentages of 14, 3, and 12 percent; in 1990 these had become 21, 5, and 30. Along the same corridor

on the south side, no census tract in 1980 had more than 3 percent African American presence; in 1990 one registered 8 percent, but others remained at 3 percent or below. Except for these changes along the north side of Route 40, the preponderance of the African American population in the general Catonsville area of Baltimore County remained concentrated in the historically separate section of the community along Winters Lane. *U.S. Census*, 1980, 1990.

9. The 1990 U.S. Census figures reveal that African American presence in Baltimore City has reached 59.2 percent, in Baltimore County 12.4 percent (compared to 55 percent and 8.2 percent, respectively, in 1980). The evidence relative to residential segregation remains mixed. Areas of African American residency have increased throughout the metropolitan area, including the suburban counties, and exclusively white areas have decreased. *U.S. Census*, 1990. Nevertheless, in the words of *Sun* reporter James Bock, "the vast majority of blacks in Baltimore live in highly segregated areas while most whites in the metropolitan area's five suburban counties reside in neighborhoods where blacks are only a modest presence." "Race and Housing: Barriers Fall, But Patterns Endure," *Sun*, July 7, 1991.

10. Interview by Nancy Swartz with Nola Null, September, 1985.

11. Interview with Joe Slovensky, October 27, 1980. Note that twenty-five years earlier would have been 1954, apparently a symbolic year in a great many ways.

12. Interview with Edith Romaine, October 27, 1980.

13. Michael Olesker, "'For Sale' Can Be a Bad Sign, History Shows," *Sun*, February 10, 1983. Olesker was reflecting upon the decision by the Maryland State Real Estate Commission to lift a ban on "for sale" signs it had imposed ten years earlier in nineteen city neighborhoods designated as conservation areas under provisions of a 1973 state law. In 1974 the city council had banned signs in all city neighborhoods, an action ruled a violation of free speech by the U.S. Supreme Court in 1981. See below for current Maryland laws on discriminatory real estate practices, including blockbusting and steering.

14. Interview with Ann Morgan, March 23, 1981.

15. Interview with David Graff, June 12, 1981.

16. Rabin, for instance, concludes on the basis of his numerous studies across the United States: "While widespread hostility to blacks may be a major influence on the kinds of locational decisions made in private housing transactions, the actual spatial distributions that result are strongly influenced by public actions." "The Roots of Segregation in the Eighties," pp. 210-11. A similar judgment is found in Schlay, "Financing Community." On attitudinal and institutional factors, also see Goering, *Housing Desegregation and Federal Policies*.

17. Title VIII, Civil Rights Act of 1968 (Public Law 90-284). Lief and Goering summarize national fair housing legislation and review the role of federal agencies in their chapter, "The Implementation of the Federal Mandate for Fair Housing," pp. 227-67. They fault HUD during the early years of its responsibility for failing to "exercise what statutory and regulatory power it had with the aggression and determination necessary to change housing market patterns," while

during the 1980s the evidence of an affirmative federal role has been even less, in their view (p. 258).

18. Maryland Real Estate Brokers Act (Annotated Code of Maryland, Business Occupations and Professions, Article 16, Real Estate Brokers, 1982). Baltimore City passed an anti-blockbusting ordinance in 1966, which was subsequently found deficient by the courts; a revised law took effect in 1968 (*Evening Sun*, March 18, 1966; *Sun*, November 23, 1967; *Sun*, April 1, 1968; *Sun*, December 11, 1969). State and city restrictions on "for sale" signs in designated areas, originally enacted to curb blockbusting activities, were removed in the early 1980s. Ironically, the sign bans were successfully challenged by an African American real estate broker, James Crockett, who charged that they unfairly limited the freedom of African Americans seeking to buy homes and placed unnecessary restrictions on the business of African American real estate brokers (Laura Hammel, "Broker to Challenge Blockbusting Limits," *News-American*, April 18, 1979; "Crockett—Why He Fights the Law vs. For Sale Signs," *News-American* April 29, 1979).

19. A study based on interviews in the Woodmoor section of the Liberty Road corridor found respondents who contended that blockbusting occurred there as recently as the late 1960s and early 1970s and who feel strongly that steering continues to occur (April Lunn, "Black Suburbanization in Woodmoor," unpublished American Studies senior seminar paper, UMBC, 1988). In 1969 Douglas Connah, Jr., writing in the *Sun*, reported instances of intensive real estate activity that had the effect of blockbusting, if not all the usual components (less evidence of speculation and property devaluation, for instance) along Liberty Road ("Blockbusting in Baltimore: Less Blatant and Rapacious, But Still the Subtle Cause of A Continued White Exodus," *Sun*, January 26, 1969). In 1978 *Sun* reporters Mark Reutter and Antero Pietila quoted charges by the president of the Liberty Road Community Council that steering continued to be a problem there and noted that in 1972 the U.S. Justice Department reached an agreement with two of the largest Baltimore area real estate firms in which they did not admit past wrongdoing but agreed to refrain from steering in the future and to submit data regarding their sales activity to verify their practices. The authors observed that between 1972 and 1978 no specific charges of steering in the metro area were brought by the department. However, they cited allegations of practices that might have the effect of steering, such as selective advertising, preclusion of FHA and VA loans, and vest pocketing—holding multiple listings until a suitable buyer already had been found as a way of controlling clientele. ("Corridor in Transition: Charges of Illegal Steering Persist," *Sun*, February 6, 1978) When the U.S. Civil Rights Commission held hearings on suburban development in the Baltimore area in 1970, an African American real estate broker voiced similar charges regarding subtle forms of discrimination that excluded African American brokers and their clients. *Hearings Before the United States Commission on Civil Rights* (1970), pp. 132-33.

20. Interview with Samuel Brown, June 13, 1981.

21. Garland Thompson, "King's Housing Goals Still Unachieved," *Sun*, January 21, 1988. Thompson was reacting to several recently released studies by Anne B. Schlay, including "Maintaining the Divided City: Residential Lending

Patterns in the Baltimore SMSA" and "The Underwriting of Community: Evaluating Federally Regulated Depository Financial Institutions' Residential Lending Performance within the Baltimore Area from 1981-1984" (Baltimore: Institute for Policy Studies, Johns Hopkins University, March 1987). Also, see Schlay, "Financing Community."

22. James Dilts, "Franklin-Mulberry Highway's Cost Is Double 1972 Estimate," *Sun,* October 1, 1975.

23. Interview with Mary Slade, March 14, 1983.

24. "Morris Goldseker" [obituary], *Sun,* June 18, 1973; "Goldseker Foundation," *Sun,* July 13, 1973; Jesse Glasgow, "Goldseker Firm, Manager for Fund, to Close Its Doors," *Sun,* February 1, 1985; *Morris Goldseker Foundation of Maryland, Incorporated, 1989 Annual Report* (Baltimore, 1990).

25. At the time of his uncle's death, Sheldon Goldseker took issue with the obituary in the *Sun* (June 18, 1973), most of which was devoted to the controversy over the company's role in the housing controversy of the late 1960s; in a letter to the editor he defended his uncle's record, contending that the charges brought against his company were unjust, unfounded, and unproven in court (letter to the editor, *Sun,* June 22, 1973). A month later, when the Foundation was announced, Sheldon Goldseker insisted, "Mr. Goldseker was a pioneer in the selling of houses to low-income people" (*Sun,* July 13, 1973). For a very favorable weighing of the Goldseker legacy, see Eric Siegel, "The Riddle of Morris Goldseker's Legacy," *Sun,* February 5, 1978.

26. These statements, by Clarence Mitchell and Sampson Green respectively, were quoted in Siegel, "The Riddle of Morris Goldseker's Legacy."

27. David Simon, "Property Czar to Leave It All to 'Poor,' Not Kin," *Sun,* May 30, 1983; "Financier Weinberg Dies, Leaves $1 Billion to Poor," *Sun,* November 5, 1990; Michael Olesker, "Weinberg's Life Gave Few Clues to Final Kind Act," *Sun,* November 6, 1990; "Weinberg's Properties Put Under Group's Control," *Sun,* November 6, 1990; Edward Gunts, "Weinberg's Legacy," *Sun,* November 26, 1990; Frank Kuznik, "We Need More Angels," *Baltimore Magazine,* (December, 1990), pp. 40-45, 110-111, 116. The Weinberg Foundation legacy continues to be something of a riddle. In a report on a major grant to the Levindale Hebrew Geriatric Center and Hospital, the *Sun* noted that "the Weinberg foundation has been a low-profile organization that does not accept grant applications, has no published telephone number and only one full-time staff member." *Sun,* Jan. 13, 1992. Gradually, however, the profile of Weinberg Foundation-sponsored projects has risen, as has the volume of grants. Recipients in 1991 included Levindale, Meals-on-Wheels of Central Maryland, the American Red Cross of Maryland, Sheppard and Enoch Pratt Hospital, Israel Guide Dog Center for the Blind, and the Association for Retarded Citizens of Hawaii. Michael Ollove, "Don't Ask Them—and You Just May Receive," *Sun,* March 29, 1992.

28. *News-American,* March 31, 1984.

29. One of the best studies applying the classic concept of filtering in a metropolitan area where racial change has been a substantial factor is Little, Nourse, Read, and Leven, *Contemporary Neighborhood Succession Process.*

30. Gale, Grier, and Grier found in the Washington, D.C., metropolitan area that African American out-movers were more likely than whites to conform to the family type traditionally associated with the suburbs, though they had slightly lower socioeconomic status than white out-movers (*Black and White Urban-to-Suburban Outmigrants*, pp. 16, 20-31). There has been considerable discussion in recent years about the separation of a suburbanizing African American middle class from other segments of the African American community. This concern was articulated by Lemann, for instance, in "Origins of the Underclass," and amplified in his provocative interpretation of the impact of twentieth-century African American population changes, *Promised Land*. Wilson has argued that economic factors have become more important than racial discrimination in determining the class status of African Americans and has pointed to evidence of a growing split between the gains of those who might be considered members of the African American middle class and African Americans considered of lower socioeconomic status (*Declining Significance of Race*). Landry, in *The New Black Middle Class*, questions as overly optimistic Wilson's view of African American middle-class gains but agrees that entrenched economic and social structures continue to be serious stumbling blocks for the upward social mobility of an African American "underclass" (pp. 194-96; 224-33). A recent study of African Americans in Maryland confirms this view (James Bock, "Gulf Widens Between Black Middle Class, Those 'At Bottom,' College Park Study Says," *Sun*, April 28, 1990).

31. *U.S. Census*, 1980, 1990. During the 1980s the community's population continued to drop, declining by 11 percent to register at 15,821 in 1990.

32. Michael Ollove, "Crime vs. Community: Ever-Increasing Violence Threatens Neighborhood Bonds," *Sun*, January 3, 1993.

33. Ann LoLordo, "Communities Come Around," *Sun*, July 12, 1988; Brian Sullam, "Schmoke, Hailing Impact, Adds 18 'Drug Free' Zones," *Sun*, November 7, 1989.

34. Eileen Canzion, "'70s Exodus from Baltimore Left It a Larger Share of Poor."

35. These were the findings of Kelly O'Shea (with the assistance of Monica Murray) in interviews with a small sample of Edmondson Village young people, "Expectations of High School Students" (unpublished American Studies senior seminar paper, UMBC, 1990). She found the Edmondson Village teenagers to have more upwardly mobile career and residential aspirations than a working-class white sample from a nearby city neighborhood; moreover, they closely resembled a white middle-class suburban sample in career aspirations and in their reasons for rejection of the city.

36. Interviews with Claudette Newsome, February 18, 1983, and Amanda Franklin, May 8, 1983.

37. Interview with Alan Hillman, June 16, 1981. A 1989 survey conducted in twenty-five metropolitan areas nationwide using pairs to test for discrimination in the sale and rental of housing found instances of discrimination against African Americans in more than half of the cases and only slight variation by region. "Survey Finds Housing Bias Continues in U.S.," *Sun*, August 8, 1991 (the study

was published in 1991 and conducted by the Urban Institute of Syracuse University for HUD).

38. This critique is stated forcefully by Lake and Winslow, "Integration Management," and by two essays in Goering, *Housing Desegregation and Federal Policy*: Wilhemina A. Leigh and James D. McGhee, "A Minority Perspective on Residential Racial Integration," and Robert W. Lake, "Postscript: Unresolved Themes in the Evolution of Fair Housing." The Goering volume illustrates the divergence of views on this issue among fair housing advocates; see, for example, the essays by Gary Orfield, "The Movement for Housing Integration: Rationale and the Nature of the Challenge," and Alexander Polikoff, "Sustainable Integration or Inevitable Resegregation: The Troubling Question." Exploring this dilemma in Baltimore in 1991, *Sun* reporter James Bock quoted George N. Buntin, Jr., executive director of the Baltimore Branch of the NAACP: "I'm not sure integration is what we're looking for. What we're looking for is equal opportunity and open housing." "Blacks Less Eager for Housing Integration: Equal Opportunity is More Important," *Sun,* July 7, 1991.

Bibliography

Abrams, Charles. *Forbidden Neighbors*. New York: Harper, 1955.
Activists, Inc. "Baltimore Under Siege: The Impact of Financing on the Baltimore Home Buyer (1960-1970)." Typescript. Baltimore: Files of the St. Ambrose Housing Aid Society, September 1971.
———. "Communities Under Siege." Typescript. Baltimore: Files of the St. Ambrose Housing Society, September 1970.
———. "A Conspiracy to Defraud and Exploit Homebuyers: The Story of Jefferson Federal Savings and Loan." Typescript. Baltimore: Files of the St. Ambrose Housing Society, February 1971.
Aldrich, Howard. "Ecological Succession in Racially Changing Neighborhoods." *Urban Affairs Quarterly* 10 (March 1976): 327-48.
Argersinger, Jo Ann E. *Toward a New Deal in Baltimore: People and Government in the Great Depression*. Chapel Hill: Univ. of North Carolina Press, 1988.
Banks, Samuel Lee. "A Descriptive Study of the Baltimore Board of School Commissioners as an Agent in School Desegregation, 1952-1964." Unpublished Ed.D. diss., University of Maryland, 1976.
Bender, Thomas. *Community and Social Change in America*. New Brunswick, N.J.: Rutgers Univ. Press, 1978.
Bianchi, Suzanne M., Reynolds Farley, and Daphne Spain. "Racial Inequalities in Housing: An Examination of Recent Trends." *Demography* 19 (February 1982): 37-51.
Bradford, Calvin. "Financing Home Ownership: The Federal Role in Neighborhood Decline." *Urban Affairs Quarterly* 14, 3 (March 1979): 313-35.
Bromley, George W., and Walter S. Bromley. *Atlas of the City of Baltimore*. Philadelphia: Bromley, 1896 and 1906.
Calcott, George. *Maryland & America, 1940 to 1980*. Baltimore: Johns Hopkins Univ. Press, 1985.
Center for Urban Affairs, Johns Hopkins University and the Department of Planning, City of Baltimore. "Changes in Housing by Race and Renter/Owner Status, Baltimore, Maryland, 1960-1970." *Census Notes* (February 15, 1972).
Chudacoff, Howard. "Success and Security: The Meaning of Social Mobility in America." *Reviews in American History* 10 (December 1982): 101-12.
Clark, Thomas A. *Blacks in Suburbs: A National Perspective*. New Brunswick, N.J.: Rutgers Univ. Press, 1979.
Connolly, Harold X. *A Ghetto Grows in Brooklyn*. New York: New York Univ. Press, 1977.

Conzen, Kathleen Neils. "Community Studies, Urban History, and American Local History." In Michael Kammen, ed., *The Past Before Us: Contemporary Historical Writing in the United States.* Ithaca, N.Y.: Cornell Univ. Press, 1980.

Cost of Living in American Towns: Report of an Enquiry by the Board of Trade into Working Class Rents, Housing and Retail Prices, Together with the Rates of Wages in Certain Occupations in the Principal Industrial Towns of the United States of America. London: His Majesty's Stationery Office, 1911.

Cottingham, Phoebe H. "Black Income and Metropolitan Residential Dispersion." *Urban Affairs Quarterly* 10 (March 1975): 273-95.

Denowitz, Ronald M. "Racial Succession in New York City, 1960-1970." *Social Forces* 59 (December 1980): 440-55.

Di Leonardo, Micaela. "Oral History as Ethnographic Encounter." *Oral History Review* 15 (Spring 1987): 1-20.

Douglass, Harlan Paul. *The Suburban Trend.* New York: Arno, 1970; reprint of the 1925 edition.

Ebner, Michael. *Creating Chicago's North Shore: A Suburban History.* Chicago: Univ. of Chicago Press, 1988.

Edwards, Ozzie. "Family Composition as a Variable in Racial Succession." *American Journal of Sociology* 77 (January 1972): 731-41.

Erikson, Kai T. *Everything in Its Path: Destruction of Community in the Buffalo Creek Flood.* New York: Simon and Schuster, 1976.

Fairbanks, Robert B. *Making Better Citizens: Housing Reform and the Community Development Strategy in Cincinnati, 1890-1960.* Urbana: Univ. of Illinois Press, 1988.

Fairchild, Halford H. and Belinda Tucker. "Black Residential Mobility: Trends and Characteristics." *Journal of Social Issues* 38, 3 (1982): 51-74.

Farley, John. "Metropolitan Housing Segregation in 1980: The St. Louis Case." *Urban Affairs Quarterly* 18 (March 1983): 347-59.

Farley, Reynolds, and Walter R. Allen. *The Color Line and the Quality of Life in America.* New York: Russell Sage Foundation, 1987.

Farley, Reynolds and Diane Colsanto. "Racial Residential Segregation: Is It Caused by Misinformation about Housing Costs?" *Social Science Quarterly* 61 (December 1989): 623-37.

Farley, Reynolds, Howard Shuman, Suzanne Bianchi, Diane Colsanto, and Shirley Hatchett. "'Chocolate City, Vanilla Suburbs': Will the Trend Toward Racially Separate Communities Continue?" *Social Science Research* 7 (1978): 310-44.

Farrell, Michael R. *Who Made the Streetcars Go? The Story of Rail Transit in Baltimore.* Baltimore: Baltimore NRHS Publications, 1973.

Favor, Homer. "The Effects of Racial Changes on Occupancy Patterns." Unpublished Ph.D. diss., University of Pittsburgh, 1960.

Frey, W.H. "Central City White Flight: Racial and Nonracial Causes." *American Sociological Review* 44 (June 1979): 425-48.

Gale, Dennis, George Grier, and Eunice Grier. *Black and White Urban-to-Suburban Outmigrants: A Comparative Analysis.* Washington, D.C.: Center for Washington Area Studies (Occasional Paper No. 4), May 1986.

Galster, George C. "Black Suburbanization: Has It Changed the Relative Location of Races?" *Urban Affairs Quarterly* 26, 4 (June 1991): 621-28.

Gillette, Howard. "The Evolution of the Planned Shopping Center in Suburb and City." *APA Journal* (Autumn 1985): 449-60.
Goering, John, ed. *Housing Desegregation and Federal Policies.* Chapel Hill: Univ. of North Carolina Press, 1986.
———. "Neighborhood Tipping and Racial Transition: A Review of the Social Science Evidence." *American Institute of Planners Journal* 44 (January 1978): 68-78.
Goldberg, Robert Marc. "Party Competition and Black Politics in Baltimore and Philadelphia." Unpublished Ph.D. diss., Brandeis University, 1984.
Goldstein, Sidney. *Patterns of Mobility, 1910-1950: The Norristown Study.* Philadelphia: Univ. of Pennsylvania Press, 1958.
Goodman, John L., Jr., and Mary L. Streitwieser. "Explaining Racial Differences: A Study of City-to-Suburb Residential Mobility." *Urban Affairs Quarterly* 18 (March 1983): 301-25.
Goodwin, Carole. *The Oak Park Strategy: Community Control of Racial Change.* Chicago: Univ. of Chicago Press, 1979.
Green, Constance. *The Secret City: A History of Race Relations in the Nation's Capital.* Princeton, N.J.: Princeton Univ. Press, 1967.
Grier, George, and Eunice Grier. *Equality and Beyond: Housing Segregation and the Goals of the Great Society.* Chicago: Quadrangle, 1966.
Grodzins, Morton. *The Metropolitan Area as a Racial Problem.* Pittsburgh: Univ. of Pittsburgh Press, 1958.
Groves, Paul A., and Edward K. Muller, "The Evolution of Black Residential Areas in Late Nineteenth-Century Cities." *Journal of Historic Geography* 1, 2 (1975): 169-91.
Guest, Avery M., and James J. Zuiches. "Another Look at Residential Turnover in Urban Neighborhoods." *American Journal of Sociology* 77 (November 1971): 457-67.
Hall, Clayton Colman, ed. *Baltimore: Its History and People.* 3 vols. New York: Lewis Historical, 1912.
Harwood, Herbert H., Jr. *Baltimore and Its Streetcars.* New York: Quadrant, 1984.
Hayward, Mary Ellen. "Urban Vernacular Architecture in Nineteenth-Century Baltimore." *Winterthur Portfolio* 16 (1981): 33-63.
Helper, Rose. *Racial Policies and Practices of Real Estate Brokers.* Minneapolis: Univ. of Minnesota Press, 1969.
Henretta, James. "The Study of Social Mobility: Ideological Assumptions and Conceptual Bias." *Labor History* 10 (Spring 1977): 165-78.
Hillery, George A., Jr. "Definitions of Community: Areas of Agreement." *Rural Sociology* 20 (1955): 111-23.
Hirsch, Arnold R. *Making the Second Ghetto: Race and Housing in Chicago, 1940-1960.* Cambridge: Cambridge Univ. Press, 1983.
House, William A. "Street Car System and Rapid Transit." In Clayton Colman Hall, ed., *Baltimore: Its History and People,* 3 vols. New York: Lewis Historical, 1912.
Hughes, Langston. *Fight for Freedom: The Story of the NAACP.* New York: Norton, 1962.

Bibliography

Hunter, Albert. *Symbolic Communities: The Persistence and Change of Chicago's Local Communities.* Chicago: Univ. of Chicago Press, 1974.
Jackson, Kenneth T. *Crabgrass Frontier: The Suburbanization of the United States.* New York: Oxford Univ. Press, 1985.
———. "Race, Ethnicity, and Real Estate Appraisal: The Home Owners Loan Corporation and the Federal Housing Administration." *Journal of Urban History* 6 (August 1980): 419-52.
———. "The Spatial Dimensions of Social Control: Race, Ethnicity, and Government Policy in the United States." In Bruce M. Stave, ed., *Modern Industrial Cities: History, Policy, and Survival.* Beverly Hills, Calif.: Sage, 1981.
Jones, Edgar. "City Limits: Segregation-Desegregation in the Cities." In Don Shoemaker, ed., *With All Deliberate Speed: Segregation-Desegregation in Southern Schools.* New York: Harper, 1957.
Joynes, J. William. *Thirty-Two Years at Christ Edmondson Methodist Church.* Mimeographed typescript. Baltimore: Christ Edmondson Church, 1954.
Kain, John F., and John M. Quigley. *Housing Markets and Racial Discrimination: A Microeconomic Analysis.* New York: National Bureau of Economic Research, 1975.
Keeley, Charles. "From Ghetto to Ghetto: The Odyssey of the Working Class Black Family." Typescript. Baltimore: Files of the St. Ambrose Housing Society, n.d., c. 1970.
Kemp, Janet E. *Housing Conditions in Baltimore.* Baltimore: Baltimore Association for the Improvement of the Condition of the Poor, 1907.
Knights, Peter R. "Using City Directories in Ante-Bellum Urban Historical Research." *The Plain People of Boston, 1830-1860: A Study in City Growth.* New York: Oxford Univ. Press, 1971.
Lake, Robert W. *The New Suburbanites: Race and Housing in the Suburbs.* New Brunswick, N.J.: Rutgers Univ. Press, 1981.
Lake, Robert W., and Jessica Winslow. "Integration Management: Municipal Constraints on Residential Mobility." *Urban Geography* 2 (October-December 1981): 311-26.
Lamphere, Louise. *From Working Daughters to Working Mothers: Immigrant Women in a New England Industrial Community.* Ithaca, N.Y.: Cornell Univ. Press, 1987.
Landry, Bart. *The New Black Middle Class.* Berkeley: Univ. of California Press, 1987.
League of Women Voters [Baltimore]. *Desegregation: Baltimore Public Schools: History, Problems, Solutions* (September 20, 1963).
Lee, Barrett A. "Racially Mixed Neighborhoods During the 1970s: Change or Stability?" *Social Science Quarterly* 66 (June 1985): 346-64.
Lemann, Nicholas. "The Origins of the Underclass." *Atlantic Monthly* 257 (June 1986): 31-55.
———. *The Promised Land: The Great Migration and How It Changed America.* New York: Knopf, 1991.
Levine, Hillel, and Lawrence Harmon. *The Death of an American Jewish Community: A Tragedy of Good Intentions.* New York: Free Press, 1992.
Lief, Beth J., and Susan Goering. "The Implementation of the Federal Mandate

for Housing." In Gary A. Tobin, ed., *Divided Neighborhoods: Changing Patterns of Racial Segregation.* Newbury Park, Calif.: Sage, 1987.

Little, James T., Hugh O. Nourse, R.B. Read, and Charles L. Leven. *The Contemporary Neighborhood Succession Process: Lessons in the Dynamic of Decay from the St. Louis Experience.* St. Louis: Institute for Urban and Regional Studies, 1975.

Logan, John R., and Mark Schneider. "Racial Segregation and Racial Change in American Suburbs, 1970-1980." *American Journal of Sociology* 89 (January 1984): 874-88.

Long, Larry H., and Daphne Spain. "Racial Succession in Individual Housing Units." *Current Population Reports.* Washington, D.C.: U.S. Department of Commerce, September 1978; series P-23, No. 71.

Lynd, Robert, and Helen Lynd. *Middletown.* New York: Harcourt, Brace and World, 1929.

———. *Middletown in Transition.* New York: Harcourt Brace Jovanovich, 1937.

Marshall, Harvey. "White Movement to the Suburbs: A Comparison of Explanations." *American Sociological Review* 44 (December 1979): 975-94.

Maryland Commission on Interracial Problems and Relations. *Annual Reports,* 1952-1968.

———. *An American City in Transition.* 1955.

———. [report by Elinor Pancoast]. *The Report of a Study on Desegregation in the Baltimore City Schools.* 1956.

May, Elaine Tyler. *Homeward Bound: American Families in the Cold War Era.* New York: Basic, 1988.

McCoy, Donald R. *The Presidency of Harry S. Truman.* Lawrence: Univ. Press of Kansas, 1984.

McCoy, Donald R., and Richard T. Reutten, *Quest and Response: Minority Rights and the Truman Administration.* Lawrence: Univ. Press of Kansas, 1973.

McDougall, Harold A. *Black Baltimore: A New Theory of Community.* Philadelphia: Temple Univ. Press, 1993.

McPherson, James Alan. "'In My Father's House There Are Many Mansions—And I'm Going to Get Me Some of Them Too.'" *Atlantic Monthly* 229 (April 1972): 51-82.

Molotch, Harvey L. *Managed Integration: Dilemmas of Doing Good in the City.* Berkeley: Univ. of California Press, 1972.

Nelson, Kathryn P. "Recent Suburbanization of Blacks: How Much, Who, and Where." *American Planning Association Journal* 46 (July 1980): 287-300.

Neverdon-Morton, Cynthia. "Black Housing Patterns in Baltimore City, 1885-1953." *The Maryland Historian* 16 (Spring/Summer 1985): 25-39.

Olson, Karen. "Old West Baltimore: Segregation, African-American Culture, and the Struggle for Equality." In Elizabeth Fee, Linda Shopes, and Linda Zeidman, eds., *The Baltimore Book: New Perspectives on Local History.* Philadelphia: Temple Univ. Press, 1991, pp. 57-74.

Olson, Sherry. *Baltimore: The Building of an American City.* Baltimore: Johns Hopkins Univ. Press, 1980.

Orser, W. Edward. "Flight to the Suburbs: Suburbanization and Racial Change

on Baltimore's West Side." In Elizabeth Fee, Linda Shopes, and Linda Zeidman, eds., *The Baltimore Book: New Views on Local History*. Philadelphia: Temple Univ. Press, 1991, pp. 203-25.
———. "The Making of a Baltimore Rowhouse Community: The Edmondson Avenue Area, 1915-1945." *Maryland Historical Magazine* 80, 3 (Fall 1985): 203-27.
———. "Racial Change in Retrospect: White Perceptions of Stability and Mobility in Edmondson Village, 1910-1980." *International Journal of Oral History* 5 (February 1984): 36-58.
———. "Secondhand Suburbs: Black Pioneers in Baltimore's Edmondson Village, 1955-1980." *Journal of Urban History* 16 (May 1990): 227-62.
Osofsky, Gilbert. *Harlem: The Making of a Ghetto, 1890-1930*. New York: Harper and Row, 1966.
Perin, Constance. *Belonging in America: Reading between the Lines*. Madison: Univ. of Wisconsin Press, 1988.
Portelli, Alesandro. "The Peculiarities of History." *History Workshop Journal* 12 (Autumn 1981): 96-107.
Power, Garrett. "'Apartheid Baltimore Style': The Residential Segregation Ordinances of 1910-1913." *Maryland Law Review* 42, 2 (1983): 289-328.
———. "The Unwisdom of Allowing City Growth to Work Out Its Own Destiny." *Maryland Law Review* 47 (1988): 626-74.
Rabin, Yale. "The Roots of Segregation in the Eighties: The Role of Local Government Actions." In Gary A. Tobin, ed., *Divided Neighborhoods: Changing Patterns of Racial Segregation*. Vol. 32. *Urban Affairs Annual Reviews*. Newbury Park, Calif.: Sage, 1987.
Reutter, Mark. *Sparrows Point: Making Steel—The Rise and Ruin of American Industrial Might*. New York: Summit, 1988.
Rieder, Jonathan. *Canarsie: The Jews and Italians of Brooklyn against Liberalism*. Cambridge, Mass.: Harvard Univ. Press, 1985.
Riesman, David. *The Lonely Crowd: A Study of the Changing American Character*. New Haven: Yale Univ. Press, 1961; reprint of 1950 edition.
Rose, Harold. *Black Suburbanization: Access to Improved Quality of Life or Maintenance of the Status Quo?* Cambridge, Mass.: Ballinger, 1976.
———. "The Development of an Urban Subsystem: The Case of the Negro Ghetto." *Annals of the Association of American Geographers* 60 (March 1970): 1-17.
Rossi, Peter. *Why Families Move*. Beverly Hills, Calif.: Sage, 1980; reprint of 1955 edition.
Ryan, Mary. *Cradle of the Middle Class: The Family in Oneida County, New York, 1790-1865*. Cambridge, England: Cambridge Univ. Press, 1981.
St. Bernardine's Church Silver Anniversary, 1928-1953. No publication information.
Schlay, Anne B. "Financing Community: Methods for Assessing Residential Credit Disparities, Market Barriers, and Institutional Reinvestment Performance in the Metropolis." *Journal of Urban Affairs* 11, 3 (1989): 201-23.
Schnare Ann B. "Racial and Ethnic Price Differentials in an Urban Housing Market." *Urban Studies* 13 (June 1976): 107-20.

———. "Trends in Residential Segregation by Race, 1960-1970." *Journal of Urban Economics* 7 (May 1980): 293-301.
Schuyler, David. *The Redefinition of City Form in Nineteenth-Century America*. Baltimore: Johns Hopkins Univ. Press, 1986.
Scott, Richard R. "Blacks in Segregated and Desegregated Neighborhoods: An Exploratory Study." *Urban Affairs Quarterly* 18 (March 1983): 327-46.
Sennett, Richard. *Families Against the City: Middle Class Homes of Industrial Chicago, 1872-1890*. Cambridge, Mass.: Harvard Univ. Press, 1970.
Shivers, Natalie W. *Those Placid Rows: The Aesthetic and Development of the Baltimore Rowhouse*. Baltimore: Maclay, 1981.
Snow, David A., and Peter J. Leahy. "The Making of a Slum-Ghetto: A Case Study of Neighborhood Transition." *Journal of Applied Behavioral Science* 16 (1980): 472-74.
Sorensen, Annette, Karl Taeuber, and Leslie J. Hollingsworth, Jr. "Indexes of Racial Residential Segregation for 109 Cities in the United States, 1940 to 1970." *Sociological Focus* 8 (April 1975): 125-42.
Stilgoe, John R. *Borderland: Origins of the American Suburb, 1820-1939*. New Haven: Yale Univ. Press, 1988.
Stinchcombe, Arthur L., Mary Sexton McDill, and Dollie R. Walker. "Demography of Organizations." *American Journal of Sociology* 74, 3 (November 1968): 221-29.
Szanton, Peter L. *Baltimore 2000: A Choice of Futures*. Baltimore: Report to the Morris Goldseker Foundation, 1986.
Taeuber, Karl, and Alma Taeuber. *Negroes in Cities: Residential Segregation and Neighborhood Change*. Chicago: Aldine, 1965.
Taggart, Harriet Lee, and Kevin W. Smith. "Redlining: An Assessment of the Evidence of Disinvestment in Metropolitan Boston." *Urban Affairs Quarterly* 17 (September 1981): 91-107.
Templeton, Furman L. "The Admission of Negro Boys to the Polytechnic Institute 'A' Course." *Journal of Negro Education* 23 (Winter 1954): 22-29.
Thernstrom, Stephan. *The Other Bostonians: Poverty and Progress in the American Metropolis, 1880-1970*. Cambridge, Mass.: Harvard Univ. Press, 1973.
———. *Poverty and Progress: Social Mobility in a Nineteenth Century City*. Cambridge, Mass.: Harvard Univ. Press, 1964.
Tobin, Gary A., ed. *Divided Neighborhoods: Changing Patterns of Racial Segregation*. Urban Affairs Annual Reviews. Vol. 32. Newbury Park, Calif.: Sage, 1987.
Urban Land Institute, Technical Bulletin No. 11. 1949.
Urban Land Institute, Technical Bulletin No. 20. 1953.
U.S. Civil Rights Commission. *Hearing before the U.S. Commission on Civil Rights, Baltimore, August 17-19, 1970*. Washington, D.C.: U.S. G.P.O., 1970.
Van Valey, Thomas L., Wade Clark Roof, and Jerome E. Wilcox. "Trends in Residential Segregation: 1960-1970." *American Journal of Sociology* 82 (January 1977): 826-44.
Vill, Martha. "Park Heights: A Neighborhood Study." Unpublished ms. prepared for the Baltimore Neighborhood Heritage Project, Summer 1979.

Waesche, James F. *Crowning the Gravelly Hill: A History of the Roland Park-Guilford-Homeland District*. Baltimore: Maclay, 1987.
Wallace, Michael. "Visiting the Past: History Museums in the United States." *Radical History Review* 25 (1981): 63-96.
Warner, Sam Bass, Jr. *Streetcar Suburbs: The Process of Growth in Boston*. Cambridge, Mass.: Harvard Univ. Press, 1962; second edition, 1978.
Warner, W. Lloyd. *American Life: Dream and Reality*. Chicago: Univ. of Chicago Press, 1953; rev. ed., 1962.
West, Herbert Lee, Jr. "Urban Life and Spatial Distribution of Blacks in Baltimore, Maryland [1940-1970]." Unpublished Ph.D. diss.: Univ. of Minnesota, 1974.
Whyte, William H., Jr. *The Organization Man*. New York: Simon and Schuster, 1956.
Wiese, Andrew. "Driving a Thin Wedge of Suburban Opportunity: Black Suburbanization in the Northern Metropolis, 1940-1960." Richmond, Va.: paper presented to the Society for American City and Regional Planning History, November 9, 1991.
Williams, Raymond. *Key Words: A Vocabulary of Culture and Society*. New York: Oxford Univ. Press, 1976.
Wilson, William Julius. *The Declining Significance of Race: Blacks and Changing American Institutions*, second ed. Chicago: Univ. of Chicago Press, 1980.
Wise, David Owen, and Marguerite Dupree. "The Choice of the Automobile for Urban Passenger Transportation: Baltimore in the 1920s." *South Atlantic Urban Studies* 2 (1978): 153-79.
Wood, Peter B., and Barrett A. Lee. "Is Neighborhood Racial Succession Inevitable? Forty Years of Evidence." *Urban Affairs Quarterly* 26, 4 (June 1991): 610-20.
Wright, Gwendolyn. *Building the Dream: A Social History of Housing in America*. New York: Pantheon 1981.
Wurdock, Clarence J. "Neighborhood Racial Transition: A Study of the Role of White Flight." *Urban Affairs Quarterly* 17 (September 1981): 75-89.
Zeidman, Linda. "Sparrows Point, Dundalk, Highlandtown, Old West Baltimore: Home of Gold Dust and the Union Card." In Elizabeth Fee, et. al., eds., *The Baltimore Book: New Perspectives on Local History*. Philadelphia: Temple Univ. Press, 1991, pp. 175-201.
Zunz, Olivier. *The Changing Face of Inequality: Urbanization, Industrial Development, and Immigrants in Detroit, 1880-1920*. Chicago: Univ. of Chicago Press, 1982.
―――. *Making America Corporate, 1870-1920*. Chicago: Univ. of Chicago Press, 1990.

Index

Note: Unless otherwise stated, all buildings, neighborhoods, parks, and streets are located in the city of Baltimore.

Activists, Inc. (Activists for Fair Housing, Inc.), 96, 133-37, 140, 142, 169, 172, 206-7 n 23
age group norms, 43-46, 117-18, 145
Agnew, Spiro, 139, 140
Alameda neighborhood, The, 6, 93, 206-7 n 23
Allendale-Lyndhurst Association, 109
Allendale neighborhood, 42, 176
Allendale Street, 103, 105, 116
Americans for Democratic Action, 202-3 n 55
Anne Arundel County, 64
apartments, 60, 64
Arbor, Inc., 96
Archway family, 109
"areaway" rowhouses, *28*, 193 n 9
Arlington neighborhood, 94
Armed Forces, U.S., 144
Arundel soda fountain, 80, 81, 165
Ashburton neighborhood, 89, 94, 101, 129, 190 n 11, 207 n 28
Augusta Avenue, 121
Austin neighborhood (Chicago), 6
automobiles, 29, 52-53, 54, 55, 63, 74
Azrael, Louis, 63

baby boom, 72, 118
Baltimore: racial composition of, 2, 49, 66, 69, 93-94, 163; suburbanization in, 15, 33, 63-65, 85; segregation in, 18-19, 30, 49, 65-69; water and sewage services in, 28; home ownership in, 33, 141, 201 n 22; occupational profile of, 38-39, 144; urban renewal in, 67; city directories for, 95, 191-92 n 22; housing values in, 119; racial conflict in, 139-40; crime rate in, 177. *See also names of individual neighborhoods*
Baltimore 2000, 162
Baltimore *Afro-American*, 70
Baltimore Beltway, 48, 65
Baltimore Board of School Commissioners, 71, 111, 153
Baltimore City Public Schools, 144
Baltimore Commission on Human Relations, 88
Baltimore Community Foundation, 171
Baltimore County: beltway in, 48, 65; suburbanization in, 64, 73, 121, 162-63
Baltimore *Evening Sun*, 50
Baltimore Gas and Electric Company, 43, 144
Baltimore Jewish Council, 87
Baltimore Neighborhoods, Inc. (BNI), 190 n 11, 207 n 28
Baltimore *News-American*, 160, 173
Baltimore *News-Post*, 63
Baltimore Polytechnic Institute, 71, 111
Baltimore Real Estate Board, 86, 88
Baltimore *Sun*, 50, 64-68, 90, 103, 140, 161, 172
Baltimore Transit, 43, 144
Baltimore Urban League, 202-3 n 55
Baptist church, 152
Bedford-Stuyvesant neighborhood (Brooklyn), 6
Best Realty, 96

Index

Bethlehem Steel Sparrows Point complex, 138, 139, 144
"Black Tax," 134, 142, 159
blockbusting: social context for, x-xi, 85-94, 131; definition of, 4, 84, 87-88; ethics of, 5, 85-89, 108; in Jewish neighborhoods, 6-7; prohibitions on, 9, 168; and price victimization, 90-91, 103-4, 133, 134-36, 150; in Edmondson Village, 94-98; white perceptions of, 102-7, 122-29; white responses to, 107-17, 129-30, 163-67; demographics of communities susceptible to, 117-22; impact on African American pioneers, 133-37, 149-50
block reconstruction, 15
Boston (Massachusetts), 7, 21
Bouton, Edward, 15
Brooklyn (New York), 6
Brown, H. Rap, 139
Brown, Samuel, 68, 169
Brown vs. Board of Education, 70
Buffalo Creek (West Virginia), 12
bungalows, 65, 74
Buntin, George N., Jr., 225 n 38
Bureau of the Census, U.S., xii, 14-15
"buy-like-rent" contracts. *See* lease option contracts

Calvert Street, 25
Cambridge (Maryland), 139
Canarsie neighborhood (Brooklyn), 8, 210 n 62
Carpenter, John, 27, 30-31, 104, 109, 116, 117
Catholic Youth Organization (CYO), 78
Caton Avenue, 98
Catonsville (Baltimore County), 62, 163
census data, xii, 14-15
Cherry Hill neighborhood, 94
Chesapeake and Potomac Telephone, 443
Chiaro, Ralph, 64
Chicago (Illinois), 6
Chicago School of Sociology, 9-10
Christ Edmondson Methodist Church, 68, 78, 110

Christ Methodist Church, 68, 110
cities. *See* inner city neighborhoods; outer city neighborhoods
Citizens Committee on Education, 202-3 n 55
Citizens Planning and Housing Association of Baltimore, 67
city directories, 38, 95, 191-92 n 22
Civil Rights Act of 1964, 138
Civil Rights Commission, U.S., 86, 162
civil rights movement, 7, 49, 67, 69-72, 137-40
class. *See* socioeconomic status (class)
Clayton's Women's Shop, 55
Clemens, Eunice, 57, 103, 113, 153
Cleveland (Ohio), 7
college education, 76, 198 n 56
colonial-style daylight rowhouses, 58-59, 60
Colonial Gardens neighborhood, 62
Commission on the City Plan, 66
"Communities Under Siege" (report), 134, 135
community: definitions of, 12-15; institutional impacts on, 167-73
Community Conservation Areas (Baltimore), 177
concrete block construction, 59
Connah, Douglas, Jr., 89, 222 n 19
Contract Buyers League (Chicago), 133
Cooper, Madge, 35, 77, 98, 99-100, 105, 109, 111, 117
CORE (Congress of Racial Equality), 70, 133, 138, 139
Cost of Living in American Towns, The (report), 19
Council for Human Rights, 202-3 n 55
Country Club Plaza (Kansas City), 54
Creutzer, Thomas, 115, 207-8 n 30
Crockett, James, 222 n 18
Culver Street, 99

D'Alesandro, Thomas, Jr., 71
D & E Realty, 135
Daniels, Samuel T., 206 n 17
Davis, Horace, 215 n 17

Dawkins, Margaret, 148, 157
"daylight-style" rowhouses, 16, 25-27, *29, 31, 32*
Dean, Buddy, 80
Denison Street, 98-99, 122, 151
Department of Housing and Urban Development, U.S., 168
Department of Justice, U.S., 168
Detroit (Michigan), 192 n 30
Dickeyville, restoration of, 199 n 5
Dilts, James, 92, 213-14 n 6
discrimination: by custom, 6; prohibitions on, 9, 18-19, 168. *See also* segregation
double mortgages, 91, 92-93, 135
Douglass, Harlan, 18
"drapes," 80, 81, 82
Druid Hill Park, 94
dual housing market. *See* segregation, in housing
"duplex" rowhouses, 193 n 9

Eagle Corporation, 135
East Baltimore neighborhood, 33, 93
Eastern Shore (Maryland), 70, 139
Eastpoint Shopping Center, 52
East-West Expressway, 170-71
Edgewood Arsenal, 144
Edgewood neighborhood, 177
Edgewood Pharmacy, 80, 81
Edgewood Street, 98
Edgewood Theater, 56
Edmondale Apartments, 60, 64, 176
Edmondale Building Company, 60
Edmondale neighborhood, 58, 60
Edmondson Avenue, 6, 22, 42, 69, 95, 176
Edmondson Avenue Methodist Church, 68, 78, 110
Edmondson High School, 79
Edmondson Village: rowhouse development of, xi, 1-4, 15-17, *16, 17,* 21-47, *24,* 48; racial composition of, *3,* 35-36, 74, 83, 84-85, 99-100, 121-22; white flight from, 10-11, 20, 22, 68, 89, 94, 99, 128, 129; African American pioneers in, 11, 49, 84, 123, 128, 131-59; occupational profile of, 13, 36-41, 49, 73-74, 118-19, 121, 125-28, 143-45, 175-76; community identity and culture in, 22, 30-47, 49, 74-83, 125, 140-46; topography of, 22; home ownership in, 29-30, 33, 59, 74, 95-96, 106, 120, 124, 132, 141, 146, 158-59, 175, 186-89; population of, 30-31, 32, 72-74, 84, 124, 145; residential longevity and stability in, 31, 49, 72, 73, 95, 120-21, 123-24, 132, 141-43, 146, 158-59, 174, 175, 177-78; religious composition of, 35, 45, 78, 152-53; ethnic composition of, 35-36, 121; naming of, 42, 48, 57; boundaries of, 42-43; gender and age group distinctions in, 43-46, 76-78, 117-18, 144-45; second housing boom in, 48, 57-65, *58,* 85; blockbusting in, 94-98; white perceptions of African American settlement in, 98-102; housing values in, 119-20, 141-42, 176; reunions of former inhabitants, 164-65; crime rate in, 177
Edmondson Village Association, 140
Edmondson Village Shopping Center, 42, 48, 49-57, *50, 51, 56,* 140, 154-56, *155,* 173, 176-77
Edmondson Village Theater, 56
Edmunds, James, 52
education. *See* schools
Ellicott City streetcar line, 23, 28
Ellicott Driveway, 69, 98
"English-type" daylight rowhouses, 27, *36,* 59
Equitable Trust Company, 213-14 n 6
Erikson, Kai, 12
ethnicity, 35-36, 93, 121
Eutaw Place neighborhood, 94
Everything in Its Path (Erikson), 12

Fairbanks, Robert, 18
Fairfax Investment Corp., 96
Fairfield neighborhood, 94
Fair Housing Act of 1968, 9, 139, 161, 168, 205 n 13
FHA mortgages, 59, 64, 86, 169, 170, 222 n 19
filtering, 174
Fischer, John H., 71, 210 n 60
Flowerton Road, 121
Food Fair supermarket, 55, 56

Index

Forest Park neighborhood, 94
"for sale" signs, 221 n 13, 222 n 18
Franklin, Amanda, 178
Frederick Douglass High School, 71, 202-3 n 55
Frederick Heights neighborhood, 62
Fulton Avenue, 66, 68, 69, 87

garages and carports, 29, 59, 65, 75
garden apartments, 64
Gelston, Hugh, 22
Gelston Drive, 99
Gelston estate, 25, 27
gender norms, 43-46, 76-78, 144
George P. Murphy Homes housing project, 67
German immigrants, 35
G.I. Bill, 59
Goldseker, Morris, 96-97, 171, 172
Goldseker, Sheldon, 97, 136, 172, 208 n 33
Goldseker Foundation, 171-73
"good neighbor" policies, 94
Graff, David, 48, 84, 106, 107, 108, 167
Grantley Street, 122
"greasers," 81
Great Depression, 28, 33, 41, 59, 97
Greater Baltimore Committee, 207 n 28
Greek's soda fountain, 80, 81
Green, Annie, 147, 148, 149, 151, 157
Green, Horace, 148, 149, 157
Green, Sampson, 133, 135
Greenberg, Stanley, 88, 93
Greenmount Avenue, 25
ground rents, 30, 206 n 21
Guilford neighborhood, 15, 74, 94
Gwynn Avenue, 98
Gwynn Oak Amusement Park, 138
Gwynns Falls Park, 60, 101, 171
Gwynns Falls Park Junior High School, 111-12, 113, 153
Gwynns Falls valley, 22, 23, 29, 43, 94, 98

Harford Road, 6, 93
Harlem (New York), 5
Harlem Avenue (Baltimore), 69
Harmon, Lawrence, 7

Harry and Jeanette Weinberg Foundation, 173
Hecht Company Department Store, 53, 54, 56, 154
Henry, Frank, 64
Hesburgh, Theodore, 162
Hess Shoes (Hess's Shoe Store), 55, 57
Highland Park Shopping Village (Dallas), 54-55
Hillman, Alan, 179
Hilton Street, 35, 42, 98, 99, 122, 150, 176
Hochschild, Kohn department store, 50, 53, 55, 154
Homeland neighborhood, 94, 200 n 18
Home Loan Bank Board, 213-14 n 6
Honolulu Limited, 154
Hoover, Herbert, 18
Hough neighborhood (Cleveland), 7
House, William A., 21
Housing Authority of Baltimore, 67
Housing Conditions in Baltimore (Kemp), 30
Howard Street, 154, 173
Hughes, Alice, 44, 81-82, 98, 102-3, 105, 108, 114-15
Hunting Ridge estate, 48, 50-51
Hunting Ridge neighborhood, 43, 52

inner city neighborhoods, 7, 75
Inner Harbor, 178
integration. *See* segregation
Interdenominational Ministerial Alliance, 70, 214-15 n 13
Irish immigrants, 36
Irvington neighborhood, 43
Italian neighborhoods, 8

Jackson, Howard W., 29
Jackson, Lillie Carroll, 69-70
Jacobs, Mary Frick Garrett, 22
James Keelty Company, 48, 58-62, 85
Jameson, Mr., 109
James Rouse Company, 65
Jefferson Federal Savings and Loan, 135
Jenkins, Edward Austin, 23, 50
Jenkins, Mary Adelaide, 199 n 3

Jewish neighborhoods, 6-7, 8, 94, 162
Jewish real estate brokers, 87
JHP Realty, 156
Jim Crow system, 18, 71
Johnson, Margaret, 1, 151
Johnson, Vera, 99, 104, 108, 114, 116
Jones, Elizabeth, 131, 147, 150, 155, 157, 160, 180
Joynes, William, 110

Keelty, James, 15, 16, 25-30, 33, 42, 47, 52, 58, 105
Keelty, James, Jr., 58
Keelty, Joseph, 58, 59, 62
Keeper Hill neighborhood, 62
Kemp, Janet, 30
Kevin Company, 60-62
Kevin Road, 60-62
King, Martin Luther, Jr., 140, 155
Kreller, Frederick, 66

Lake Montebello, 6, 93. *See also* Montebello neighborhood
land installment contracts, 91-92, 135, 136, 170
Lanvalle Street, 69
Lawndale neighborhood (Chicago), 6
Leakin Park, 171
lease option contracts, 91, 92, 135, 136, 150, 170
Lee, Robert E., 207-8 n 30
Lee Realty, 96, 135
Levine, Hillel, 7
Lexington Terrace housing project, 67
Liberty Heights Avenue, 6, 94, 162
Liberty Road (Baltimore County), 162, 169, 177
Loevy, Robert D., 161
Los Angeles, shopping center development in, 55
Lower Park Heights neighborhood, 94, 213 n 5
Lutheran church, 35
lynchings, 70
Lynd, Robert and Helen, 79, 196 n 35, 198 nn 53, 56
Lyndhurst Elementary School, 78, 113
Lyndhurst estate, 25, 27

Lyndhurst Improvement Association, 42
Lyndhurst neighborhood, 42, 52

Mahoney, George, 139
Malone, Agnes, 77, 80-81, 98, 99, 100, 107, 108
Marshall, Thurgood, 70, 202-3 n 55
Martinez, John J., 133
Martin Marietta Corp., 144
Maryland Commission on Interracial Problems and Relations, 87, 88-89, 91, 204 n 4
Maryland Court of Appeals, 35, 70
Maryland National Bank, 213-14 n 6
Maryland National Guard, 140
Maryland property laws, 30, 91-92, 168-69
Maryland Real Estate Brokers Act, 168-69
Mattapan neighborhood (Boston), 210 n 62
May, Elaine Tyler, 76
McCormick's Spices, 443
McKeldin, Theodore, 70, 71, 138, 202-3 n 55
Medford neighborhood, 62
Mergenthaler Vocational and Technical School, 71
Methodist church, 35
Miller, Kenneth, 52
Mitchell, Clarence, Jr., 112
Mitchell, Kiefer, 112
Mitchell, Parren, 137
Monroe Street, 99
Montebello neighborhood, 6, 93-94, 133, 206-7 n 23
Morgan, Ann, 98, 167
Morgenstern, Madge, 103, 105, 108, 114, 116, 128-29
Morris Goldseker Company, 96-97, 102-3, 134-37, 140, 150, 171-72
"Mortgage Hill," 33
mortgages: and ground rents, 30, 206 n 21; through FHA and VA, 59, 64, 86, 169, 170, 222 n 19
Muncie (Indiana), 79, 198 nn 53, 56
municipal building codes, progressive, 27
Murphy, Carl, Jr., 70

Index

Mussachio, Vincent, 207-8 n 30
Myerhoff, Jacob, 50, 51-52
Myerhoff, Joseph, 50, 51-52, 54

NAACP (National Association for the Advancement of Colored People), 19, 69, 70, 71, 138, 139, 202-3 n 55
National Association of Real Estate Brokers, 35, 85
National Council of Churches, 214-15 n 13
natural succession, in urban neighborhoods, 10, 174
New Deal housing programs, 18, 33, 59
New Psalmist Christian School, 201 n 35
Newsome, Claudette, 178
Normandy Avenue, 27, *32*, 122
North Avenue, 94
North Rosedale Street, 109
Null, Nola, 108-9, 129, 164

Oak Park community (Chicago), 8
occupational profiles, 36-41, 67, 73-74, 118-19, 121, 125-28, 143-45, 175-76
Old West Baltimore neighborhood, 33, 69
Olesker, Michael, 166
Olmsted, Frederick Law, 15
Olson, Karen, 69
Olson, Sherry, 6, 27
oral history, xi-xii, 13-14
Orlinsky, Wally, 92
Osofsky, Gilbert, 5
outer city neighborhoods: racial homogeneity in, 5, 8, 75; housing deterioration in, 6, 63, 66-67

"panic peddling," x, 6, 88, 89, 102-4, 161
Park Forest (Illinois), 203 n 62
Park Heights Avenue, 94
Pechter, Jack, 156
Penrose, Mr., 109
philanthropy, 171-73
Pietila, Antero, 222 n 19
Pikesville (Baltimore County), 94, 96
Poplar Grove neighborhood, 25

Poplar Grove Street, 98, 99
Portelli, Alesandro, 14
Post Office, U.S., 43, 144
Power, Garrett, 4, 18
President's Conference on Home Building and Home Ownership (1931), 18
privacy, 75
Protestant church, 7, 35, 78, 110, 133, 178
public housing projects, 67
Pulaski Street, 66, 69

racial conflict, 114-17, 153
racial segregation. *See* segregation
Rainbow Realty, 96
Raines, Edgar, 48
ranch-style detached houses (ramblers), 48, 62, 63, 65, 74-75
Randallstown (Baltimore County), 94, 162
real estate brokers, African Americans as, 86
Reamer's Men's Store, 55-56
redlining, 86
Reformed Episcopal church, 35
Reisterstown Road, 6
religion and churches, 7, 35, 42, 45, 69, 78, 152-53
restrictive covenants, 6, 8, 35, 70, 100
Reuter, Mark, 222 n 19
Roberts, Bertha, 57
Rock Glen Junior High School, 113
Rodgers Forge neighborhood, 62, 200 n 19
Rodman Center, 155
Rognel Heights neighborhood, 23, 28, 43
Rokeby Road, 117
Roland Park Company, 15, 200 n 18
Roland Park neighborhood, 15, 54, 74, 94
Romaine, Edith, 76, 80, 109-10, 115, 117, 165
Roman Catholic church, 7, 35, 78, 110, 133
rowhouses: daylight-style, 16, 25-27, *29*, *31*, *32*; styles of, *26*, *37*, *61*; English-type daylight, 27, *36*, 59; areaway, *28*, 193 n 9; colonial-style

daylight, 58-59, 60; group home versions, 65; duplex, 193 n 9
rowhouse suburbanization, 15-20, 74

St. Bernardine's Roman Catholic Church, 29, *39*, 60, 78, 152
Schaefer, William Donald, 109
Schmoke, Kurt, 177
schools: availability of, 35, 45, 49, 76, 78-79; desegregation of, 49, 70-72, 83, 100, 111-13, 153
"secondhand suburbs," 7, 11, 132, 158-59
segregation: in housing, x-xi, 4-5, 18-19, 35, 49, 63, 66-69, 85-94, 161, 162, 168; and resistance to integration, 4-5, 8; ordinances enforcing, 28, 35; and desegregated schools, 49, 70-72, 83, 100, 111-13; and "good neighbor" policies, 94
Shaker Heights Center (near Cleveland), 54
Sherman, Mal, 86
Shirlington (Arlington, Va.), 200 n 13
Siegel, Eric, 112
Silver Spring (Maryland), 64
Simkins, Marilyn, 1, 35, 55, 77, 78, 81, 98, 99, 103, 104, 106, 109, 111-12, 113, 128, 160, 164, 165, 167
Slade, Mary, 148, 149, 150, 151, 157, 171
Slovensky, David, 165
Slovensky, Joe, 56, 76, 80, 81, 99, 100, 104, 164-66
slums, 9, 66
Smith, Father John, 110, 152
Social Security Administration, U.S., 138, 139, 144
socioeconomic status (class): and community identity, 13, 101, 122-23, 156-58, 175-76; and race, 13; and occupation, 36-41, 67, 73-74, 118-19, 121, 125-28, 143-45, 175-76
Sondheim, Walter, 71
South Baltimore neighborhood, 33
"squares," 80, 81, 82
Stallman, Leonard, 60
Standard Metropolitan Statistical Area (SMSA) data, 63, 191 n 21

status, socioeconomic. *See* socioeconomic status (class)
Steele, J.D., 66
streetcar suburbs, 21, 28-29, 30, 41-42
Suburban Square (Ardmore, Penn.), 200 n 13
Suburban Trend, The (Douglass), 18
suburbia: postwar development of, 7, 62-65, 74, 85; population of African Americans in, 9, 161, 162-63; and community identity, 12-13; idealized, 15, 17, 23-30, 48-49, 62, 74, 148, 179-81; decentralized, 18
Supreme Court, U.S.: and restrictive covenants, 7-8, 35, 70, 100; and school desegregation, 70, 71-72, 100, 111, 153
SWOC (Steel Workers Organizing Committee), 138
Sykes, Raymond, 177-78
Sykes, Vivian, 177

teenage culture, 45, 56, 72, 79-83
Ten Hills neighborhood, 43
Thompson, Garland, 170
Thomsen, Rozel C., 209 n 36
Truman, Harry S., 138

United Railways and Electric Company, 28
University of Maryland, 70
Uplands Estate, 64, 201 n 35
Uplands neighborhood, 58, 64, 176
Upper Darby (West Philadelphia), 200 n 13
Urban Land Institute, 52, 53
urban neighborhoods. *See* inner city neighborhoods; outer city neighborhoods
urban renewal, 67
Utica (New York), 198 nn 53, 56

Vaeth, Monsignor, 110
VA mortgages, 59, 64, 86, 169, 170, 222 n 19
Voshell's, 81
voter registration, 70
Voting Rights Act of 1965, 138

Index

Walbrook neighborhood, 69, 94
Wallace, Christine, 101
Warner, Sam Bass, Jr., 21
Warren, Roberta, 152, 154, 156
Washington, D.C., 6, 55
Washington *Post*, 133
Watkins, Janice, 151
Weinberg, Harry, 154, 156, 173
Weinberg, Martin, 213-14 n 6
West Baltimore Street, 25
West Baltimore Street concrete bridge, 29
Western High School, 71
West Fayette Street, 25, 68, 69
Westinghouse, 144
Westland Gardens neighborhood (Baltimore County), 64
West Lanvale Street, 69
West Saratoga Street, 69
Westview Shopping Center, 52, 54, 154
Whalen's Drug Store, 80, 81
white avoidance, 121

"white blackmailers," 5
white flight (out-migration), 4, 10, 19-20, 22, 68, 89, 94, 99, 128, 129; African American reaction to, 147, 150-52
white resistance, 68, 109-10, 113-14, 128
Wildwood neighborhood, 16, 27-29, 42, 52, 59
Wildwood Parkway, 121, 147
Williams, Carroll, 64, 65, 67, 85
Williamsburg, colonial, 52
Windsor Hills neighborhood, 94, 101, 129, 190 n 11, 207 n 28
women, in workforce, 38, 44-45, 73-74, 77, 126-27, 144-45, 146, 149
Woodhaven Investment Corp., 96, 135
Woodlawn neighborhood (Baltimore County), 138

youth culture, 45, 56, 72, 79-83

www.ingramcontent.com/pod-product-compliance
Lightning Source LLC
Chambersburg PA
CBHW020646230426
43665CB00008B/340